War in the Philippines

1941-1945

Ray Merriam
Editor

MILITARY MONOGRAPH 91
BENNINGTON, VERMONT
2013

First Edition published in 2000 by the Merriam Press

Fourth Edition (2013)

Copyright © 2013 by Ray Merriam
Book design by Ray Merriam
Additional material copyright of named contributors.

ISBN 978-1481197366
Merriam Press #MM91-P

This work was designed, produced, and published in
the United States of America by the

Merriam Press
133 Elm Street Suite 3R
Bennington VT 05201

E-mail: ray@merriam-press.com
Web site: merriam-press.com

The Merriam Press publishes new manuscripts on historical subjects, especially military history and with an emphasis on World War II, as well as reprinting previously published works, including reports, documents, manuals, articles and other materials on historical topics.

ON THE REAR COVER

Japanese war art depicting Japanese raid on Clark Field.

Contents

out ships, 18,000 civilians evacuated from other areas, and some 6,000 civilian laborers.

On the island of Mindanao, Brigadier General William F. Sharp commanded a small group of American soldiers, but they had insufficient small arms to supply the 30,000 Filipinos who could have been called into service. On the island of Cebu only 1,500 obsolete rifles were available for the native troops and for the few Americans assigned to lead them. During the first two months of the war every effort was made to run ammunition and supplies through the Japanese blockade to the troops in the Philippines, but two ships were lost for every one getting through.

There were, besides the above, four small regiments of harbor defense troops on the four fortified islands (Fort Drum, Fort Hughes, Fort Frank, and Corregidor) at the entrance to Manila Bay; and there was the 26th Cavalry, which was later to make a record on Bataan never surpassed by a cavalry unit, forced finally to shoot their own horses for food to sustain life in those Americans that survived that terrific ordeal.

Major General George Gruener was Commander of the Philippine Department and stationed in Manila. In late July 1941 General Gruener called all senior officers to Department Headquarters and communicated to them as follows: "Major General Douglas MacArthur, retired, is placed upon active duty in the grade of lieutenant general and is assigned command of all United States forces in the Far East. The induction of the Philippine Army into the services of the United States is authorized."

General Gruener was returned to the U.S. in September 1941, and General MacArthur designated General Wainwright as senior field commander and placed him in command of the North Luzon force, with headquarters at Stotsenburg, and with General Edward P. King as chief of staff. On 25 November, Wainwright closed his Fort McKinley office. MacArthur directed Wainwright to continue with the organization and training of the Philippine Army units, and said: "Jonathan, you'll probably have until about April 1942 to train those troops." From this we can infer that General MacArthur felt at that time, twelve days before Pearl Harbor, that war was imminent, but that the Japanese would not begin the attack for four or five months.

On arriving at Fort Stotsenburg on the evening of 25 November 1941, General Wainwright noted the poverty of the situation. All he had with which to organize a field army was General King, the chief of staff; a post adjutant who must also serve as adjutant general of the new field forces; a supply officer; and a surgeon. Little ammunition was on hand: hand grenades, .50 caliber machine gun, infantry mortar ammunition, and a few shells for 295 mm howitzers, which model was already obsolete.

This new field army, which was destined in two short weeks to receive the blow of almost a quarter million Japanese, had practically no transportation—only a few trucks and a very few automobiles. The only means of communication with the various divisions composing this new field army was by public telephone lines, and the great majority of the soldiers were untrained, undisciplined, and were led by inexperienced Filipino officers. Of this situation General Wainwright later said: "The Philippine Army units with the North Luzon force were doomed before they started to fight. That they lasted as long as they did is a stirring and touching tribute to their gallantry and fortitude. They never had a chance to win."

The four divisions of this force were scattered, but an inspection was ordered to begin on 6 December 1941, and on that day General Wainwright inspected the 26th Cavalry, a battery of the 23rd Field Artillery, and a pack train, which units were stationed at Fort Stotsenburg. This was Saturday, and the inspection of the other units of the field army was set to begin on the following Monday.

Such was the situation when the Japanese struck at Pearl Harbor on the morning of 7 December 1941 (8 December, Manila time). General MacArthur's assistant chief of staff, Colonel Irvin, phoned General Wainwright about 4:35 a.m. on that morning that "Admiral Hart [whose Asiatic Fleet lay in Manila Bay] has just received a radio dispatch from Admiral Kimmel, commander of the Pacific Fleet at Pearl Harbor, informing him that Japan has initiated hostilities."

INITIAL JAPANESE ATTACKS ON THE PHILIPPINES

Just before 9 a.m., 8 December 1941, Wainwright was notified by MacArthur's headquarters that the Japanese had bombed Baguio, the Philippine's summer capital, some ninety-five miles north of Stotsenburg, and directed General Wainwright to protect Clark Field, which lies close to Stotsenburg. The 26th Cavalry under command of Colonel Clinton Pierce was deployed to the east of the field, and a battery of pack artillery was placed at the western end. No infantry units were available. Not long after midday, about eighty Japanese planes, mostly bombers with some dive bombers and fighters, swept over Stotsenburg and dropped their heaviest bombs on Clark Field, most of whose bombers were on the ground in plain sight. The raid lasted only about fourteen minutes, but left Clark Field in a shambles. Most of the B-17s that had just come in were totally destroyed. Barracks and quarters, machine shops and hangars were leveled to the ground. In this attack, ninety-three were killed outright and seven died that night, leaving ninety-three wounded.

On that day our fighting planes were not at Clark Field but at a new field at Iba, about forty miles north of Olongapo, but they did not escape. The Japanese destroyed them at the same time they were raiding Clark Field. The enemy lost only two planes at Clark Field, these being shot down by the 200th Coast Artillery's anti-aircraft battery.

Wainwright had only the public telephone and telegraph system for communications, and none were available from General Aiken, MacArthur's chief signal officer. He had little transportation except for a few borrowed buses and trucks. He had no navy and no air force, except reconnaissance P-40s, and besides, all five of his divisions were still in process of mobilization.

The beach defenses of the Lingayen Gulf were manned by the 11th and 21st Divisions. On 10 December the Japanese bombers wrecked most of the installations at Fort Stotsenburg and destroyed a large part of the men and horses of the 26th Cavalry.

RECESSION OF THE U.S. ASIATIC FLEET

In addition to these land and air forces, the small Asiatic Fleet of the U.S. Navy had Manila as its home base, and was under the command of Admiral Thomas C. Hart. The Asiatic Fleet consisted of two cruisers (the heavy cruiser Houston and the light cruiser Marblehead), twelve overage destroyers, the tender Langley, twenty-three Catalina patrol planes comprising Patrol Wing 10 (Patwing 10), about twenty-nine submarines, and a few gunboats and auxiliaries, which could not be counted on for combat. The cruiser Boise happened to be in Asiatic waters at the time. With these ships we attempted to hold the Japanese in check until we could muster sufficient strength to make a real resistance.

Late in November 1941, when the Japanese "creeping advance" down the coast of China indicated an approaching crisis, Admiral Hart sent the Marblehead and eight destroyers to Borneo. The *Houston, Boise*, and the destroyer tender *Blackhawk* were also dispatched to operate in southern waters. This left only a skeleton organization in Manila Bay when the Japanese struck Pearl Harbor on 7 December 1941, and the larger ships still remaining in Manila Harbor left at once for southern waters, in compliance with standing orders to depart as soon as hostilities began.

The part played by our Navy in the defense of the Philippines must be accorded recognition. While the Navy's part may not have been as spectacular as that of the Army, its work was effective and was characterized by many instances of heroic daring and wise judgment.

On 8 December 1941, the Japanese struck first at the island of Mindanao and attempted to destroy our naval defenses in that area. Early in the morning of 8 December, Japanese bombers attacked our two seaplanes (our others being out on patrol) and the seaplane tender *Preston* on location in the Gulf of Davao. The planes were destroyed but the Preston escaped after shooting down one enemy plane. Four Japanese destroyers entered the Gulf of Davao at once.

On 10 December, the third day of the war, the Japanese planes came to Cavite in Manila Bay and practically wiped it out. Some of our ships escaped to improvised places along the Manila waterfront, the supplementary naval base facilities at Mariveles Bay being still under construction and of no present value, but the submarine Sealion was damaged, as was the destroyer *Peary*. We had to sink the Sealion to prevent its capture by the enemy.

Since our Navy could not operate in or near Manila Bay without danger from enemy aircraft, Admiral Hart ordered the remaining vessels to move south to safer waters. On 11 December, Admiral Hart also advised all merchant shipping to leave the Manila area; thus 200,000 tons of merchant shipping, some of it very valuable, cleared to the southward, and all but one of the ships escaped via the Sulu Sea and Makassar Strait. After the major portion of our fleet had gone south, and the cargo ships had retreated, only a few submarines and motor boats were left to render what aid they could to our forces as well as to harass the enemy as much as possible.

While Cavite was undergoing attack, enemy troops landed at several places on Luzon, from shallow draft vessels of the Japanese fishing fleet. These shallow craft were difficult for our submarines to hit. But December 1941 marked the beginning of a continuous, extensive, and effective submarine campaign in all Japanese and nearby waters—a gallant fight that continued throughout the war.

Admiral Hart moved his headquarters from Manila to the Netherlands East Indies about 21 December, and Admiral F. W. Rockwell, in command of our naval defense forces in Manila Harbor, moved to Corregidor on 26 December. Manila Bay by this time was under constant bombing attacks. By 31 December, all our submarines had, under orders, retired to the Malay Barrier in the south. Rear Admiral Rockwell as senior naval officer remained on Corregidor. By the end of December 1941 our Asiatic Fleet had been pushed out of the Philippines and had taken refuge in the waters of the Netherlands East Indies. The Japanese already were preparing bases at Davao on Mindanao and at Jolo in the Sulu Archipelago.

The Navy proceeded to reorganize in the south. It was realized that even the Malay Barrier might not be able to withstand enemy assault, and it was decided to develop a major naval base at Port Darwin on the north coast of Australia. But its facilities were not adequate and the distance was too great to be of much service for some time to come. So it was that operational command was set up at Surabaya on the north coast of Java.

The Japanese objective was to capture and occupy and exploit all the rich area of the Malay Barrier and the South China Sea. By January the Japanese had overrun the Philippine Islands, and the greater part of our naval strength was in the Netherlands East Indies, toward which the Japanese were headed. Our submarines and motor torpedo boats were engaged in slowing down as much as possible the advance of the enemy, so as to give us time to get organized for the surface action that was in prospect.

JAPANESE LANDINGS IN THE PHILIPPINES

The Japanese Army began to land at several places in the Philippines on 10-12 December, first at Aparri and Vigan on the northern tip of the island of Luzon, and on the far southeastern coast off the Bicol Peninsula at Legaspi. The Japanese landing at Aparri proved to be a feint, some 3,000 men trying without success to pull General Wainwright's forces away from the Lingayen Gulf.

The enemy struck in full force at Vigan, just up from Lingayen Gulf, with a task force of warships and some eighty-four jammed-to-the-rails transports landing troops. The only air protection Wainwright's army had was one P-40 reconnaissance plane, and the Navy's motor torpedo boats were far away to the south. In the face of such a wave of enemy troops, Wainwright maneuvered for position in order to delay the Japanese as much as possible, hoping he soon would have reinforcements sufficient for a counterattack.

The first land skirmish which really started the long, tedious days and almost endless nights of killing, being killed, and withdrawing, began on 16 December. General MacArthur ordered Wainwright to hold a line running across, east to west, the narrow coastal plain fifty miles below Vigan at San Fernando La Union. The Japanese came down the coastal plain on 21 December, where they were met by one battalion of the 13th Infantry Regiment, and one battalion of the 12th Regiment, near San Juan, five miles north of San Fernando. Being out-flanked by the enemy, our forces scattered into the mountains and were filtering back to our command for a period of two weeks.

THE FALL OF MANILA

By this time enemy landings had been made at Davao on Mindanao Island, some 600 miles south of Manila. The Japanese also landed in Lamon Bay below Manila and closed in on that city from the north and south. Before the end of December 1941, due to the recession of the fleet, the Arm' position in Manila had become precarious. Manila Bay by this time was under constant air bombardment. Seeing the impending danger of being encircled, General MacArthur began evacuating Manila and declared it an "open city" withdrawing all his forces into the mountainous peninsula of Bataan and to the island fortress of Corregidor. Manila, however, was bombed by the Japanese in violation of international law and was finally occupied by them on 2 January 1942.

A first-hand account of the fall of Manila comes from war correspondents Carl and Shelley Mydans, who wrote in Time Magazine:

> January 2nd, 1942, nearly 3,500 Americans were hauled to the campus of the University of Santo Tomas in Manila. This was to serve as one of the Japanese prison camps for the duration. We were housed in two large buildings, with no provision for food, water, sewage, garbage disposal, or medical care. For a week the only food came from Filipino friends who were allowed to throw it over the fence to us. It was six months before the Japanese began to feed us. On 12 September 1942, 125 of us were removed from Santo Tomas to Shanghai.

The withdrawal of our troops from Manila and the consolidation of the defense forces on the peninsula of Bataan on a very much shortened front constituted a most important and dramatic phase of the Philippine Campaign. On 3 January 1942, the siege of Bataan began.

On the Bataan Peninsula our defensive operations resolved themselves into delaying of the Japanese advance toward inner Bataan and nearby Corregidor, and making that advance as costly as possible. Successively retreating lines of defense were carefully drawn, and heroically defended as long as possible.

In General Wainwright's North Luzon army, Lieutenant Colonels Moses and Noble commanded the 13th Infantry Regiment, and Major Ganahl commanded the 12th Regiment, all of whom disappeared from the picture.

Our forces suffered a setback, but they held on as best they could. On the night of 21 December, sixteen more enemy transports landed troops just south of Bauang and along the shores of Lingayen Gulf, as far down as Agoo. Here they met our 11th Division, which was not able to stand the onslaught of superior numbers. Neither was the 71st Infantry and the battalion of field artillery under Colonel David Bonnett. Bonnett was ordered to retire to a better position. The 26th Cavalry also had to withdraw from the death trap at Damortis. The reason was the enemy had planes, we did not. A company of sixteen tanks from the command of Brigadier General R. N. Weaver was requested, but only five were sent, and they were not adequate to hold the enemy in check. Many incidents of valor marked the withdrawal of our soldiers to Bataan before the avalanche of Japanese troops.

Wainwright's new field headquarters were established at Alcala on the Agno River. The 26th Cavalry had lost about 150 men killed and wounded in the fighting from Damortis to Bued. On 23 December, Wainwright withdrew behind the Agno River. When General MacArthur ordered General Wainwright to withdraw his troops to Bataan, Wainwright's still scattered forces numbered about 28,000, of whom 25,000 were still only partly trained for warfare. Before he could withdraw the 150 miles necessary, he had to round up and consolidate his forces as much as possible, so that his rear guard could delay the Japanese advance as he retreated. He ordered that the line of the Rio Grande de Pampanga be held fast, so as to enable General Jones's command of the South Luzon forces to withdraw north from the Japanese attacking in the south, and to swing around Manila Bay and come into Bataan about the same time that Wainwright's North Luzon forces arrived there.

The Filipino and American forces on Bataan at first made an effort to defend our secondary naval base at Subic Bay. An increasingly large number of enemy troops being thrown into the line, our forces were compelled to fall back to the main line of defense running across the peninsula. In fox holes, trenches and dugouts, our forces fought on from the middle of January to early April, waging a fight so gallant that it inspired the American people to unceasing endeavors to achieve a successful outcome of the war.

After Malaya, Singapore, Burma, and the Netherlands East Indies had fallen to the Japanese, more troops were released to reinforce the Japanese armies in the Philippines. General Yamashita, who had commanded the Malaya offensive, was put in command for a final and overwhelming drive against our troops in the Philippines.

Our men were worn out by exposure, weakened by short rations, and many of them were ill from malaria and other tropical diseases; yet they fought on. In their desperation they at times were compelled to eat carabao, monkeys, and even horses and mules. It is estimated that 20,000 of them were disabled by malaria of a malignant type, and no quinine was available with which to combat the disease. The only air protection they had was a few Curtiss P-40s flying from emergency air strips carved out of the jungle. Tanks and heavy guns—they had none. Under these conditions even the most valiant soldiers could not hold out indefinitely.

Brigadier General Clyde A. Settick commanded the 71st Division at the time. It was a difficult task to round up thousands of inexperienced and bewildered men and organize them for withdrawing before the enemy. On 24 December some elements of the enemy got behind our forces and between them and Bataan. The 26th Cavalry, under Colonel Pierce, was busy trying to protect the retreat of the 71st to Agno. Checking up on 24 December, the 26th had been reduced by casualties to about 450 men. At Binalonan the 26th held off the Japanese in overwhelming numbers.

According to a report from General MacArthur, American air defense was almost impotent: on Luzon we had thirty-five B-17s, thirty medium and eight light bombers, 220 fighters, and twenty-three other planes. At the end of the first day of fighting, we had left only seventeen heavy bombers and about seventy fighters. Fourteen of the B-17s reached Australia after a short time, but all our fighters were destroyed.

Wainwright's withdrawal toward Bataan was in five phases: D1, D2, D3, D4, and D5. Wainwright's forces were to delay the Japanese advance as long as possible to permit General Jones's South Luzon force to clear around Manila Bay and get into Bataan; also to enable Major General George M. Parker to prepare the Bataan defenses.

The withdrawal into Bataan was not exactly a retreat, for we fought delaying actions all the way. It was hard for an American, even at that. The withdrawal toward Bataan began on 23 December and ended 31 December 1941. At Cabanatuan on 27 and 28 December, the 91st Division had to fight the Japanese tanks, cavalry, and infantry. Late on 29 December, the 91st was attacked again and routed with heavy losses and was forced to retire toward the south. About a thousand troops of the 12th and 13th Infantry Regiments that had been trapped two weeks before, broke through and joined the 11th Division at D5. The 91st Division reformed its broken forces and started on its retreat toward Bataan.

The South Luzon forces under General Jones, withdrawing north to reach the only road leading to Bataan, had to cross the Pampanga River by means of the Calumpit bridge. The bridge was known to the Japanese and to us as a bottleneck. The 500 men left of the 91st Division plus a regiment of the 71st Division and a battalion of field artillery took position along the Pampanga at 11:00 p.m. on 30 December to protect the crossing of the South Luzon forces. During the night a company of the 192nd Tank Battalion was added to the defense.

The Japanese struck at 10:30 a.m. on 31 December, while General Jones's Southern Luzon forces were crossing the bridge under heavy fire, being protected by the 11th and 21st Divisions. Most of them were across on the road to Bataan by midnight. New Yea' Day, 1942, the last elements of the 91st Division had crossed, just as the advance Japanese guard rushed the bridge. At 6:15 a.m. our forces blew up the bridge. The Japanese now had before them the wide, deep, and unfordable Pampanga River.

Wainwright's and Jones's North and South Luzon forces reached Bataan on 6 January—Bataan that was to be the scene of unspeakable suffering and humiliation. During the withdrawal to Bataan, Wainwright's North Luzon forces had been cut down from 28,000 to about 16,000, and they were in poor shape to undertake the defense of Bataan. The march into Bataan was costly and depressing, but at that it was only a suggestion of the march out of Bataan, the "Death March" some three months later.

Our men walked into Bataan, many of them shoeless, stumbling, feeling that Bataan was or might be a death trap awaiting them.

About 7 January, General Wainwright was designated by MacArthur as commander of the I Philippine Corps, to defend the western side of the Bataan Peninsula, while Major General George M. Parker was to command the II Corps of Philippine troops to protect the east side of the Bataan Peninsula.

Between these two corps, the Silanganan Mountains, running north and south, divided Wainwright from Parker, and steep jungle walls of the mountains made it difficult for them to maintain contact and liaison with each other. Besides, this situation favored Japanese penetration between the forces of the two American commanders.

On arriving and taking up position on Bataan, it was necessary to put all men on half rations, and these were Filipino rations, not sufficient for the Americans. To supplement the shortened rations, soldiers were sent out to shoot and bring in every carabao they could find, and veterinary supervision was given when these animals were killed and issued for meat. Even young carabao is not any too palatable, and the old carabao had to be soaked in salt water overnight, and then beaten to a pulp before it could be eaten.

On 19 January, General MacArthur came to Bataan and inspected the I and II Corps. Just after MacArthur had returned to Corregidor the Japanese penetrated down Mount Silangayan, hugging the slopes on both sides, and this threatened to separate the I Corps from the II Corps. So Wainwright's 31st was assigned to Parker's II Corps, to attempt to hold the enemy.

By 16 January, fresh Japanese troops had landed from the sea at Port Binanga on the northwestern coast of Bataan, then marched through the jungle and attacked the 1st Philippine Division. The 26th Cavalry, aided by units of the 1st Division, drove the Japanese back across the Moron River. Meanwhile, Parker's II Corps was deteriorating rapidly, and Wainwright's I Corps was threatened on three sides, west, north and east. This situation made it necessary for the American line to be so extended that they were in great peril.

By 21 January the Japanese had infiltrated through our lines and had taken possession of the Moron-Bagac Road. The 1st Philippine Division was in a trap and had to fight its way south along the narrow beaches of the China Sea on the west and the Moron-Bagac Road on their east, which was controlled by the Japanese. In this escape all heavy guns had to be destroyed, and all transportation equipment also. Carrying their wounded by hand, the survivors worked their way back. On orders from General MacArthur, all forces withdrew to the reserve battle position at the waistline of Bataan Peninsula.

The withdrawal was completed by 26 January, and gave the I and II Corps the advantage of less rugged terrain in which to fight. This put the Americans and Filipinos in possession of the lower end of Bataan Peninsula, including the Bay of Mariveles. Our troops had now fallen back to their last position on Bataan, and it was do or die. No food, and little hope of getting any. No letup of the steaming jungle heat by day or night. No quinine to stop the malaria that was killing our men. No cessation of the moans of the wounded. Altogether it was a soul-racking thing to go through. Our men had to shoot the horses of the 26th Cavalry and eat them to keep themselves alive.

And now the Japanese landed at four points along the southern and western extremity of Bataan. At Longaskaway they were met by the 45th Infantry of Philippine Scouts and by about 450 sailors, under command of Commander Bridgett of the U.S. Navy. They also landed at Quinaun Point, where they were met by a group of Air Corps engineers, and the 3rd Battalion of the 45th Infantry under command of Major Dudley H. Strickler.

The Japanese also landed at Agloloma Point. In their landing operations they were shelled and machine-gunned by our few P-40s and ground troops, and those not exterminated were scattered. They also landed at a small peninsula between the Anyasan and Salaiian Rivers, and this landing proved most dangerous, for if the enemy succeeded in landing, he might cut the road south to Mariveles, the take-off point from which our forces might escape to Corregidor. The miscellaneous troops guarding this point were thrown back by superior numbers and fierceness of the attack.

The battle at Quinaun Point lasted twelve days, the 3rd Battalion of Major Strickler doing heroic fighting. As no troops could be spared to aid them, the battalion fought alone. When it went into action, the battalion had a major, four captains, eight or ten lieutenants, and 600 men. Twelve days later, after having driven the Japanese into the China Sea, the battalion was commanded by a second lieutenant, with only 212 men, the rest of the battalion having been killed or wounded.

Many of the Japanese troops took cover in caves along the shores of the China Sea. They would not surrender. A small American gunboat was called into action to shell the caves, while our engineers crept in from the land side and lowered electric mines into the mouths of the caves and blew the cliffs to pieces.

A strong Japanese force attacked our forces on the center of the 11th Division, and penetrated a mile in depth and a mile in width, while a smaller Japanese force infiltrated down the gorge of the Cotar River, attempting to link up with the first-mentioned force, which coordinated action resulted in cutting off a large number of our men. But the tables were turned when, after a week of fighting, the 1st Philippine Division encircled the smaller enemy force.

The 11th Division, plus a battalion of the 2nd Philippine Constabulary, two battalions of the 91st Division, and a battalion of the 45th Infantry Scouts under Lieutenant Colonel Lathrop, encircled the other Japanese force. Both Japanese forces dug in, in fox holes and tunnels, and it required twelve days to exterminate them. It was a fierce fight, much of it being underground. By 17 February our forces held every foot of ground they had occupied on their arrival at the reserve battle position.

In this intense fighting our losses were heavy. The land was dotted with crosses of our dead, and our improvised hospitals near Mariveles were crowded with the wounded. Two of the best native generals, Brigadier General Segundo and Brigadier General Vinconte Lim, of the 41st Division, suffered at the hands of the Japanese. General Lim was murdered in the most horrible way the Japanese General Yamashita could devise. Segundo, as well as many other Filipino officers, were also murdered by Yamashita.

The Japanese were now preparing for an all-out attack. Their forces outnumbered ours six, to eight, to ten to one. Many of our patrols were composed of loyal Filipino Igorots, whose ability to move Indian-like through mountains and jungles proved that they were our best and often our only means of reconnaissance.

MacArthur Ordered to Australia

On 10 March 1942, General Wainwright was summoned to headquarters on Corregidor, where he was informed that twice in recent weeks the President had strongly suggested that General MacArthur retire to Australia to command the newly-created Southwest Pacific Area, preparatory to a counterattack. MacArthur had just as strongly protested leaving the Philippines. But now, explicit orders had come from Washington and MacArthur was to go at once.

Wainwright was placed in command of all American troops in the Philippines. On Luzon he had the I Corps under command of General Jones, the II Corps under command of General Parker, all service troops, and the troops scattered in the Cagayan Valley and the mountain provinces in the north. General Moore was to command the Manila Harbor defenses, General Chenowith to command the troops on the Visayan Islands, and General Sharp to command the troops on

Mindanao. These subcommands were to be under the supreme command of General MacArthur from Australia.

On that day, 10 March 1942, MacArthur is reported to have said: "If I get through to Australia... I'll come back as soon as I can."

General Wainwright now had under his command only about 70,000 men, a small proportion of them being combat troops. Meanwhile, a new Japanese landing under General Homma had brought the enemy total to around a quarter of a million men.

At 7 p.m. on 11 March, four MTBs under command of Lieutenant Bulkeley started south with General and Mrs. MacArthur, their son Arthur, a nurse, and the personnel of the general's staff. It was a hazardous journey through the enemy mine fields at the entrance to Manila Bay, ever in danger of being spotted by enemy surface ships or aircraft.

By dawn on the 12th the party reached the Cuyo Islands, where they hid from sight for the day. By now one of the four MTBs was out of fuel and had to remain at Cuyo. Clearing the Cuyos at 6:30 p.m., running in sight of enemy ships and through a rough sea, the party reached Cagayan in the Mindanao Sea early on the 13th. Four Flying Fortresses had been ordered from Australia to carry the party on the last lap of their journey to Australia, but these airplanes had been delayed and would not be available for five days.

While waiting at Cagayan, two of the MTBs went to Negros Island and brought over President Manuel Quezon of the Philippine Commonwealth, who would accompany the party to Australia. General MacArthur arrived at Melbourne, Australia, on 17 March and assumed command of all American Army forces in the Southwest Pacific area.

General MacArthur's official entourage on his trip to Australia consisted of the following members of his staff: Major General Sutherland, chief of staff; Brigadier General Richard J. Marshall, deputy chief of staff; Colonel Charles P. Stivers, assistant chief of staff, G-1; Colonel Charles A. Willoughby, assistant chief of staff, G-2; Captain Joseph MacMicking, Air Corps, assistant chief of staff, G-2; Brigadier General Spencer B. Aiken, signal officer; Lieutenant Colonel Joe R. Scherr, assistant signal officer; Brigadier General William S. Marquat, antiaircraft officer; Brigadier General Harold H. George, air officer; Brigadier General Hugh J. Casey, engineer; Lieutenant Colonel Sidney L. Huff, aide-de-camp; Lieutenant Colonel Francis H. Wilson, aide-de-camp; Lieutenant Colonel Legrande A. Dillar, aide-de-camp; Major Charles H. Morehouse, Medical Corps; Master Sergeant Paul P. Rogers, secretary.

Back on Bataan, the enemy contemplated a continuous assault regardless of losses, thinking that by numerical superiority he could crush the defenders, but every bit of ground was fiercely contested by our troops, with heavy losses on both sides. Bataan became a hell of bombs and fox holes and destruction, with enemy infiltrations along the beaches on the west coast, savage hand-to-hand fighting in the underbrush, infantry skirmishes, sharp artillery duels, aggressive patrol duty on both sides, relentless air raids, bloody attacks, and fierce counterattacks.

The Japanese resorted to propaganda leaflets, urging Filipino soldiers to give up their arms and go home. The fighting Filipinos paid no attention; they fought on. Enemy attempts to land troops were broken by deadly artillery fire. Those who reached the shore were quickly mopped up. But fresh enemy reinforcements kept coming in, and the enemy was able, through the prodigious use of aircraft, tanks, and artillery fire, to keep the weary defenders under constant harassment day and night. With each man subsisting on only fifteen ounces of food a day for several weeks, exhausted by the ceaseless fighting, outnumbered in both men and materiel, the defenders were pushed back and back.

The months of fighting on Bataan were heart-breaking ones. Ever since the surprise air attack on the first day of the war, which destroyed most of their planes on the ground, the Americans had fought valiantly against impossible odds. They had retreated foot by foot through Luzon and Bataan until their backs were to the sea. There, with a small trickle of supplies, makeshift defenses, and magnificent bravery, they withstood the Imperial Army of Japan. Day after day they held their ground, at times even attacking the enemy and forcing him to retreat. So tenaciously did they hold that one Japanese general was reported to have killed himself in humiliation.

The I Corps under General Jones had about 25,000 men; the II Corps, under General Parker, about 35,000 men. Among these troops were about 10,000 service corpsmen, some quartermaster troops, and about one hundred American nurses. Two guerrilla bands of about 2,000 men were operating in the far north of the island. On Corregidor and the three smaller islands in the bay, Fort Drum, Fort Frank, and Fort Hughes, were about 10,000 men. Most of these were commanded by Major General George F. Moore. All the navy that was available to us at the time was four motor torpedo boats, commanded by Lieutenant John Bulkeley, a few small minesweepers, and a few miscellaneous craft. The air force was now reduced to one P-40, and it was in poor condition. Our other three P-40s had cracked up after a raid on a concentration of Japanese ships in Subic Bay.

General Wainwright moved his headquarters twenty miles south, just east of Mariveles Bay, where General MacArthur had had his advance headquarters. General Beebe on Corregidor was in charge of supply, and on 15 March he announced that a lack of supplies made it necessary to further reduce the ration from one-half Filipino rations by another one-third, if our men were to be able to keep alive another month.

On 20-21 March General Wainwright was notified that he had been advanced to the rank of lieutenant general, and that all the forces in the Philippines were to be called the U.S. Forces in the Philippines, with him as commander in chief, as of 21 March. General Wainwright thereupon took up his headquarters at Corregidor.

On 22 March the Japanese served their first demand for surrender, dropping it from a plane over Bataan: "If you do not reply to this by special messenger within three days we will feel free to act in any way at all." This demand for surrender was signed by "the Commanders in Chief, Imperial Japanese Army and Navy Forces in the Philippines."

General Wainwright made no reply.

Food was rapidly playing out, and the men on Bataan were famished, sick, war-weary, hollow-eyed, yet they fought on. The Japanese, having established long-range 105 mm guns six miles away at Cavite, began to bomb Forts Drum, Hughes, Frank, and Corregidor, wreaking great havoc.

The Japanese commander, General Yamashita, issued a demand for the surrender of the American troops, a demand which General Wainwright rejected. Then during the first two weeks of April the enemy, with superior numbers of troops, was able to penetrate our lines and turn back our flanks, until we became powerless to sustain the delaying action on Bataan much longer. From the air the enemy dropped bombs in ever increasing number. On 22 March, our Bataan forces were confronted with the main Japanese Army, aided by more and more warships that had come into Manila Bay.

By 24 March the intensity of the bombing of Corregidor made it necessary for our personnel to take to the tunnels, especially Malinta Tunnel. On 25 March and again on 28 and 29 March the Japanese made furious assaults on Bataan.

THE FALL OF BATAAN

On 29 March 1942, the Japanese bombers hit a plainly marked base hospital on south Bataan, killing men on stretchers and nurses and doctors, who were standing by their patients. Bataan was now receiving in mounting fury the Japanese assault from warships, from the air, and from land troops. On 4 and 5 April the Japanese had mounted 75 mm guns on the barges and had struck General Parker's line from his rear.

Late on 7 April 1942, General Parker sent word to General Wainwright that he might have to surrender because of Japanese pressure on his malaria-ridden, half-starved forces. General Wainwright's orders were for General Parker's II Corps to hold out, and for both him and General Jones's I Corps to attack again. But it was futile, as man after man dropped in his tracks utterly exhausted, as he attempted to move forward.

On 8 April the Bataan nurses, what remained of them, were put on a barge and taken to Corregidor. They were disheveled, many of them were wounded, they were fatigued, but they were a gallant lot. After weeks of waiting, two submarines brought food on 9 April for the men on Bataan, but few of them lived to receive any of it, many dying of starvation.

On 9 April General King was compelled to surrender. After noon on that day of 9 April 1942 there was silence on Bataan, but it was the silence of death. For it was on 9 April 1942 on Bataan that a small open car displaying a white flag could be seen rolling along the highway toward the Japanese lines in the vicinity of Limay, thus signaling the surrender of the American-Filipino forces on the Bataan Peninsula. In addition to the soldiers surrendering, there were also many civilians. Our stand was gallant but hopeless. Our men had the courage but not enough food. At last, weakened by malaria and dysentery, with the enemy bombing them day and night and pushing forward by the overwhelming weight of numbers, they surrendered because of sheer exhaustion.

Bataan had fallen. But the noble defenders, both American and Filipino, had written an imperishable page on the scroll of fame.

THE DEATH MARCH FROM BATAAN

The humiliation of defeat was bad enough, but worse was yet in store for our heroic defenders of the Philippines: the Death March of Bataan and the unspeakable atrocities of Japanese prison camps. Many of these men were to die of starvation and malnutrition, all of them to bear in their bodies for life the scars of one of the most inhuman experiences that men were ever called upon to suffer.

By 15 April the Death March from Bataan had begun, up the peninsula toward Camp O'Donnell. From reports since available, we find that the Japanese rounded up our defeated men and put them in groups of about 1,000 each. The first stage of the march was about sixty miles, to San Fernando Pampanga, a continuous march of a day and night. Then they were herded into railway boxcars and shipped to Capan in the province of Tarlac. They were then taken out of the boxcars and marched seven miles more to Camp O'Donnell. Their only food en route was a small amount of rice, and scarcely any water.

Camp O'Donnell was the home cantonment of the 71st Philippine Army Division before the war started, and water and sanitary systems had not been installed, except for a few pumps. The only water available was three miles away, the muddy Bampan River. No transportation was available, and the Japanese having taken all of the prisoners' canteens away, there were no containers with which to get water. These thousands of starving and thirst-crazed prisoners were in torment.

According to Captain Reeder, American medical officer in Camp O'Donnell, from about 20 April to the end of July, at least 20,000 of the 45,000 Filipino and 1,400 American troops there died of starvation, disease, and torture. Men who were craving water and stopping to lap a little from muddy creeks were shot or bayoneted while drinking. The principal diseases were malaria and dysentery, and no medicine was allowed the men.

Sergeant Carl A. Carlsson: From his own memories of the Death March of Bataan, Sergeant Carl A. Carlsson relates: "I'll never forget it. What hell! No words ever could describe it—cold, brutal, and all unnecessary. They'll shove a man in a hole and bury him alive if he was too weak to walk. Some of the men would fall back out of line, and we'd hear a shot or a scream and the next thing we knew, a Nip would come up the road wiping off his bayonet, and you knew there was one less."

Among these wearied, hunger-stricken marchers, were two American chaplains, Colonel John K. Borneman and Colonel Alfred C. Oliver. Both of these chaplains managed to survive the horrors of the prison camps. Colonel Borneman says that he witnessed twelve murders of U.S. Army officers at Cabanatuan, murders following sadistic beatings for twenty-four hours. Colonel Borneman also tells what happened to Colonel Oliver, who was beaten pitilessly for days, and then suffered a broken neck. He in some way survived the ordeal, but he must go the rest of his life with his head in a high leather collar. Colonel Oliver lived to tell the story of his experience, but never once mentioned his own sufferings as he portrays for us in a later section of this article the sufferings of his comrades in the Japanese prison camps.

LAST DAYS ON CORREGIDOR

Bataan having fallen, the Japanese now concentrated their attacks on Corregidor, using surface ships, air bombs, and long-range artillery. We had at Corregidor about 11,000 men, opposed to about 250,000 enemy troops, advancing on us like a mighty torrent. Some 2,000 men and women were able to cross the two-mile wide water from Bataan and found refuge for the time being on Corregidor, on the night of 8 and 9 April. About 300 survivors of the 31st Infantry (American) and a number of Filipino troops, some Navy men from Mariveles, about four survivors of the 26th Cavalry, and the nurses—these also escaped Bataan.

By this time all hospital facilities on Corregidor were crowded, with hundreds more waiting to be hospitalized. The sick and wounded were laid out on the beaches.

In order to defend Corregidor every available man was used, including some 1,500 Marines recently from China, commanded by Colonel Sam Howard, and the 300 survivors of the 31st Infantry.

The enemy began to bomb Corregidor from the shores of Bataan, two miles away, with 240 mm howitzers. This, added to the incessant bombing by 105 mm guns from Cavite and with continuous air bombardment, made Corregidor a living hell. On top of the 4,700-foot Mariveles Mountains, the Japanese observation posts gave their gunners correction of fire. The shelling of Corregidor did not entirely cease at any moment during the twenty-seven days our troops were under attack. There was no escape from the enemy fire except in the deep recesses of the Malinta Tunnel, and it could hold only a small part of our forces.

On 9 April about a dozen planes commanded by Brigadier General Ralph Royce raided the enemy installations at Nichols Field, and then returned to Mindanao. On 13-14 April, a squadron of American bombers from somewhere in the south successfully attacked Japanese installations and shipping in the Philippine area. Then came two weeks of even more intensive enemy bombardment by planes, ships, and artillery. On 5 May the Japanese avalanche buried many of our shore batteries under a landslide, and under cover of darkness the enemy crossing the narrow channel from Bataan, were able to make a landing on the North Point of Corregidor. The shattered defenses were unable to check the enemy tide; our depleted and exhausted troops were in danger of being overwhelmed.

Late on 9 April, General Wainwright received from President Roosevelt an assurance of confidence, giving him freedom of action to do as he thought best, and hoping that he would still be able to hold Corregidor. General Wainwright replied: "The American flag still flies on this beleaguered island fortress."

On 16 April, a week after the fall of Bataan, the enemy landed in force at Iloilo on North Panay Island, and prepared for a mass attack on Mindanao.

On 18 April, General Marshall sent the following message to General Wainwright: "The continuing demonstration that you and the members of your command are giving to the world of courage and devotion is worthy of the finest traditions of American and Filipino soldiers. We are immeasurably proud of every man serving in the fortifications of Manila Bay. Please convey the special commendation and gratitude of the War Department to the nurses on Corregidor, whose service is an inspiration to all of us."

FIRST BOMBS ON JAPAN

On 18 April 1942, the world was electrified at the news that a squadron of American planes under command of General James H. Doolittle, accompanied by seventy-nine other aviators, had raided the Japanese mainland, striking Tokyo, Yokohama, Kobe, Nagoya, and Osaka, flying at low altitude in broad daylight.

By 25 April the Malinta Tunnel hospital was treating 1,000 wounded men each twenty-four hours and blood-stained doctors and nurses worked day and night, most of the 150 nurses being veterans of Bataan. On 28 April, the Japanese barrage increased in fury. A 240 mm shell exploded near General Wainwright, bursting his left eardrum.

On the night of 29 April, two U.S. Navy rescue planes succeeded in landing at Corregidor. Fifty men and women, thirty of them nurses, were put on board, and started south. One plane reached Australia; the other was marooned on Mindanao, and the occupants were captured and made prisoners of war by the Japanese. The rest of our people on Corregidor remained to fight off as long as possible the hour of doom.

Because of damages to the water and electric system, damages caused by the enemy guns, those facilities began to play out. For a few weeks only, an occasional two-seater plane would reach Corregidor with medicine, and took away about a dozen more of our people.

On 3 May they managed to evacuate from Corregidor by submarine a fairly good number of nurses, and officers that were key men or who were in desperate physical condition. Some of the nurses, from a sense of duty to the wounded, refused to leave on that last submarine; among them was Captain Mieler, chief nurse of the Malinta Tunnel hospital.

On 4 May the Japanese bombing reached an all-time high from 7:00 a.m. until 12:00 noon. It is estimated that a 500 pound bomb hit Corregidor every five seconds during that five-hour period, twelve every minute, or 3,600 shells in five hours, enough to fill six hundred trucks, and all this in addition to thirteen air raids on that same day.

CODES AND TREASURES

As the war in the Philippines waxed ever more furious, more and more American and Filipino treasure was moved to Corregidor for safekeeping. Just before Corregidor fell, $140,000,000 in Philippine currency and $15,000,000 in silver were locked in Corregidor. The gold reserve of the Philippines had in the early days of the war been sent to the U.S. for safekeeping. Following MacArthur's instructions, Wainwright put down the serial numbers of the bank notes and radioed them to the Treasury Department at Washington. Then he cut up and burned the money and destroyed the lists. The $15,000,000 in silver was sealed in wooden boxes, towed into Manila Bay, and sunk at locations that were radioed to Washington, and all records and codes were destroyed.

By 5 May it was evident the enemy was ready to invade Corregidor, and surrender would be inevitable. At 8 p.m. on 5 May, the Japanese began a furious bombardment preparatory to landing, and at 11:15 on the night of 5 May, the landing began.

The night of 5 May and the following day was to be their last stand. The first wave of Japanese came in landing boats and motor boats. Our beach forces gave them the strongest fight that was in them, but the enemy, by sheer weight of numbers, broke through our defenses and advanced toward the Rock. At 4 a.m. on 6 May General Wainwright received the following message by radio from President Roosevelt: "In spite of all the handicaps of complete isolation, lack of food and ammunition, you have given the world a shining example of patriotic fortitude and self-sacrifice. You and your devoted followers have become the living symbols of our war aim and the guarantee of victory."

Our men continued to fight the Japanese at every step. About 10 a.m. on 6 May the Japanese landed more men and tanks and headed for the tunnel. At this moment our troops on Corregidor faced these appalling facts: All beach defenses had been blown to dust; all barriers had been wrecked; machine gun emplacements had been pulverized; seacoast guns and fire control instruments, destroyed; forty-six out of forty-eight of our 75 mm guns had been knocked out; communications had been severed. The landing of the enemy could not be stopped by what we had.

At 10:15 a.m. on 6 May 1942, General Wainwright announced his momentous decision, that in order to save the sick and wounded and starving men and women, he would cease firing at 12 o'clock noon. At 10:30 General Beebe went on the radio: "Message for General Homma: For reasons which General Wainwright considers sufficient, and to put a stop to further sacrifice of human life, the Commanding General will surrender to Your Excellency today the four fortified islands at the entrance to Manila Bay, together with all military and naval personnel. At 12:00 noon, 6 May 1942, all firing will cease, unless a landing by Japanese troops in force is attempted without flag of truce."

But the Japanese continued the attack; at 11:00 a.m. General Beebe repeated the message, and at 11:45 a.m. the fighting had not stopped.

Between 10 a.m. and 12 noon, 6 May 1942, General Wainwright sent a radio message to President Roosevelt saying: "With broken heart and head bowed in sadness, but not in shame, I report to Your Excellency that today I must ask for terms of surrender of the fortified islands of Manila Bay. There is a limit of human endurance, and that limit has long since been passed. Without prospect of relief, I feel it is my duty to my country and to my gallant troops to end this useless effusion of blood and human sacrifice."

Promptly at noon the white flag went up and all firing by the Corregidor defenders came to an end, but the Japanese continued to maul us without let up. At 12:30 p.m. General Beebe went on the radio again, and a Marine officer with a white flag went to the enemy forward positions, now within a few hundred feet of the entrance to Malinta Tunnel, to request the senior Japanese officer to come into the tunnel and meet with General Wainwright. For nearly an hour the Japanese guns were firing on our troops continuously. When the Marine officer returned, he reported that the Japanese senior officer would not come to see Wainwright, but insisted that Wainwright come to see him.

General Wainwright, Major General George F. Moore and his aide Major Bob Brown, Wainwright's aide Colonel Johnny Pugh, and Major Tom Dooley started for the enemy lines. Japanese planes swooped low and sprayed machine gun bullets upon them as they approached the Japanese lines. More than two hours after our white flag had been raised, the enemy bombers were still attacking our troops, and continued to bombard Corregidor until late in the afternoon.

The Japanese officer was a dudhead, so General Wainwright insisted upon seeing General Homma. After long delay, Wainwright and his staff were ferried to Bataan, where finally they met General Homma. After vain attempts by Wainwright for justice and fair play for his troops on Corregidor, Homma refused, and announced that fighting would go on until Corregidor's personnel had been destroyed and all of the Philippines had been surrendered. Being taken back to Corregidor, Wainwright found that large parties of Japanese had landed and now were overrunning everything. It was close to midnight before the surrender papers were completed. General Wainwright and all personnel were made prisoners of war. But any further continuation of resistance would have meant utter annihilation to all on Corregidor.

The next day, 7 May, Wainwright was taken to Manila, where at 1 a.m., 8 May, he was required to go on the radio and broadcast that he had surrendered and give the terms which he had been compelled to sign. General Wainwright, against his will, was forced to surrender all troops in the Philippines wherever stationed. This was almost impossible to effect, owing to lack of communications, however, orders were sent out in the expectation they might be received. On 11 May Wainwright was informed that Major General William F. Sharp had surrendered in Mindanao, the Japanese having completely overrun the island. Our troops on Palawan and at Legaspi also had surrendered. Other groups, mostly natives in scattered positions, chose to become guerrillas rather than surrender. And of these guerrillas, representing the masses of the people of the Philippines, it can be said: "The Philippines never surrendered."

While our campaign of Bataan and Corregidor resulted in an inglorious defeat, yet as a delaying action, to further the interests of the Allies in the Southwest Pacific, it has been pronounced a success, a triumph of American and Filipino courage that gave a promise that would inspire their brother Americans to transform defeat into victory before the war should end.

And after Corregidor fell, General MacArthur spoke as follows: "Corregidor needs no comment from me. It has sounded its own story at the mouth of its guns. It has scrolled its own epitaph on enemy tablets. But through the bloody haze of its last reverberating shot, I shall always seem to see the vision of its grim, gaunt, and ghostly men still unafraid."

The only three-star general in the war to suffer the bitterest experience in a soldier's life, Jonathan M. Wainwright stood up and surrendered in the Philippines after directing some of the fanciest holding tactics of that desperate, drawn-out struggle. Already holding the Distinguished Service Medal for staff work against the Germans in World War I, he received the Distinguished Service Cross "for extraordinary heroism in action" against the Japanese, awarded after his capture and imprisonment.

In defending the Philippine Islands, our troops had fought a gallant delaying action designed to slow down the Japanese advance into the South Pacific. It was well understood in Washington that the islands, almost surrounded as they were by Japanese-controlled areas, could not hold out for long against a strong and determined enemy attack. But a delaying action would facilitate our plans, already considered, for building up supply lines to Australia so as to have in the Southwest Pacific a base for developing a counterattack.

Wainwright and his staff were kept under guard at the University Club in Manila. In one of the last days they had the heartbreaking experience of seeing a long column of ragged Americans and Filipinos trudging down the street. They were the men of Corregidor being marched through the streets of Manila to let the thousands of native Filipinos know that the Japanese were a superior people. At Bilibid prison the Americans were separated from the Filipinos, the Americans to be sent to Cabanatuan, while the Filipinos were to be sent to Camp O'Donnell.

One of General Wainwright's last acts before being carried away to Tarlac prison camp was to write a letter to General Homma of the Japanese Army, requesting him to radio President Roosevelt asking that a ship be dispatched to the Philippines with food, clothing, and medical supplies for the American and Filipino prisoners of war, who were dying at the rate of three hundred a day. This request was ignored by the Japanese officer.

General Wainwright and his staff arrived at Tarlac prison camp on 9 June 1942, where about 180 other American officers were already imprisoned. They were crowded, all 180 of them, into a building designed to hold just eighty. Thus began the years of torture and suffering, as these valiant Americans were shuttled back and forth from prison camp to prison camp—Tarlac, Formosa, Japan, Manchuria—covering a period of more than three years. Heroes, all of them.

Indicating the valiant spirit of General Wainwright and the troops under his command, the general wrote in a letter just before Corregidor fell the following words: "As I write this we are subjected to terrific air and artillery bombardment, and it is unreasonable to expect that we can hold out for long. We have done our best, both here and on Bataan, and although beaten, we are still unashamed."

Losses in American and Filipino personnel at Bataan and Corregidor have officially been set as follows: On Bataan, 36,853; and on Corregidor, 11,574; making a total of 48,427 killed or taken prisoner by the Japanese.

The defense of Corregidor lasted from 9 April to 6 May 1942. In the other islands of the Philippine Archipelago approximately all our troops surrendered and were made prisoners of war. On 8 April, 15,000 Japanese troops captured the island of Cebu and the capital by the same name. The enemy hurriedly occupied every city and port.

Quite a number of American officers and men escaped to the mountains of the various islands where they were hidden and protected from the enemy by the native Filipinos, and then organized and conducted an underground and guerrilla movement to harass the enemy and prepare the way for the return of General MacArthur and his liberating American forces; for General MacArthur, in leaving the Philippines for Australia, had said: "I shall return."

PHILIPPINE INCIDENTS

Before bringing this article to a close, we wish to invite the reader's attention to certain personal experiences and observations that have found a lasting place in history. No one's pen is capable of portraying all the incidents of bravery connected with our defeat in the Philippines. The story of many a hero is buried with him in the silent halls of death, and innumerable instances of the highest valor may never be revealed. However, the picture of this epic battle would be too incomplete without a reference to certain known incidents and personalities.

EXPERIENCES AT JAPANESE PRISON CAMPS
O'DONNELL AND CABANATUAN

From the report of Colonel Alfred C. Oliver, Chaplain Emeritus of the National Sojourners, and formerly Chief of Chaplains of the U.S. Army.

Colonel Oliver was on duty in the Philippines at the outbreak of the war and was taken prisoner by the Japanese. The statements given below, taken from the National Sojourners Magazine for August 1945, give his observations and experiences in Japanese prison camps. This is perhaps one of the most scathing indictments of the inhumanity of the Japanese soldiers ever written.

According to Colonel Oliver, the Japanese do not react like normal civilized human beings; whenever they are stripped of the veneer of their present-day civilization, they always act as savages. These opinions are based on years of experience, of association with and observation of the Japanese.

The general attitude of the Japanese soldier toward all Filipinos was cruel and domineering, and toward all Americans, one of deepest hatred. The Filipino people have always shown friendship for the Americans and often risked their lives to supply them with water or some dainty like sugar or rice. Because of these acts of mercy, Colonel Oliver saw young girls and old women beaten cruelly by the Japanese guards with the butts of their rifles. One woman, large with child, was bayoneted through the abdomen and left along the road writhing in horrible death agony.

When the Japanese guards wished to severely punish one of the American prisoners of war, they would strip him to only a "G string" and then tie him up by his wrists outside one of their guard houses which was located at the main prison camp gate alongside the public road. Here, as the Filipino country women came walking by on their way to market, balancing baskets of garden stuff on their heads, the Japanese guards would require them to stop, remove their baskets, bow, and then compel them to beat the American prisoners hanging there. For this purpose they provided a four-foot long, two-inch thick, green bamboo cudgel. And if a woman refused to beat the American severely, she was herself severely beaten.

There is one other phase of Japanese barbarism which Colonel Oliver feels should be presented: namely, their treatment of helpless, sick prisoners of war. He ran into this at Camp O'Donnell where the survivors of the Bataan Death March were imprisoned. When these thousands of American soldiers arrived, there was only one faucet available to them for water. Desperately dehydrated men got in line and stood there sometimes twenty-four hours to obtain a drink. Later, the strongest carried water a mile and a half from a polluted river. During the first six weeks, when 1,700 men died, there was never sufficient water except for cooking and drinking.

The American Army doctors had no medicines or surgical equipment. Fifty percent of the prisoners had malaria, ninety percent had beri beri, and at least ninety-five percent had dysentery. Practically everyone in camp was burning up with fever from one or the other of these diseases. Prisoners in rags, without blankets, lay on the bare hospital floors, on bamboo slats in the barracks, or on the ground. Hundreds were too weak to go to the latrines, and the stench from fecal matter was sickening. Clouds of big blue flies arose from around the feces and bodies of those to whom Chaplain Oliver tried to give a drink. Desperately sick men crawled down by the latrine and under the buildings to die, sometimes remaining there for days before they were found and buried.

Soon after arriving in Camp O'Donnell, the senior American Army doctor and the chaplain wrote a joint letter to the Japanese camp commander pointing out the above conditions and requesting help under the Articles of the Geneva Convention. These two officers were called before the Japanese commander who categorically refused each and every request made. These officers then begged the privilege of sending out those Americans who needed emergency operations to either Japanese or Filipino hospitals. This was also denied. The Japanese commander became more and more furious as other requests were made, until finally he said: "Japan did not sign the Geneva Convention. I hate you Americans and will always hate you. The only thing I am interested in is, when one of you dies, then I'll see you bury him." This closed the interview.

During the period described above by Chaplain Oliver, the Red Cross tried to deliver two truckloads of medicines and other needed supplies, but this same Japanese commander would not permit them to be unloaded. Colonel Oliver believes that the Japanese have great possibilities for development; but we in America must ever keep in mind that it will take not only years but generations for the Japanese people to acquire the ingrained characteristics of gentleness which are now the passion of civilized people and acquired after centuries of trial and error.

For months after the Bataan and Corregidor survivors were assembled at Camp No. 1 near Cabanatuan, the treatment by the Japanese of the sick American prisoners of war was as criminally culpable as at Camp O'Donnell. Some 2,700 American prisoners of war lie buried at Camp No. 1. During July 1942, over 750 died here. Practically every death was the result of Japanese starvation and failure to provide the sick with the medicine needed. The most pitiful incident of this period was the death of 135 Americans of diphtheria. American doctors had to stand impotently by and watch these helpless men choke to death. They died in horrible agony because the Japanese refused to supply the necessary anti-toxin, although it was in a storehouse about one hundred yards away. This was equally true in the hundreds of malaria deaths due to the lack of quinine, which the Japanese had on hand and refused to supply to our doctors.

Colonel Oliver closed his report with a call to Americans to be on their guard, because the Japanese do not react like civilized human beings. And the world is in danger until they do.

NEW MEXICO'S 200TH COAST ARTILLERY

Among the National Guard units on Bataan were two tank battalions coming from many states of the west and south. There was a whole regiment of anti-aircraft from New Mexico: Deming, Carlsbad, Clovis, Silver City, Gallup, Taos, Roswell, Hobbs, Santa Fe, Albuquerque, and the A and M College at Masilla Park. They belonged to the 200th Coast Artillery whose fantastic marksmanship made news day after day as they shot down enemy planes by the score and prevented others from flying low enough to deliver accurate fire. Of them Helena Huntington Smith, writing in Collier's for 29 August 1942, said:

> They stood up without complaint under constant furious fire for more than three months. They were besieged by land, blockaded by sea, cut off from all sources of help in the Philippines and America, and they knew it. But they only fought the harder.

Again:

> The men of Bataan have done all that human beings could do to the limits of endurance. They were sustained every day of their fight by something more than physical strength. I knew the men out in Bataan, and I knew they were thinking of their people and their country and of freedom and dignity and pride.

It was no ordinary fight.

Early in 1940 this regiment, originally cavalry, was converted into anti-aircraft, and was inducted into the Federal service in January 1941. Being trained at Fort Bliss, this regiment was chosen for Philippine service because it was efficient, and for the further reason that a large percentage of its members had knowledge of the Spanish language. At the end of August 1941 the regiment was headed west, destination unknown to its members. And when the Japanese struck at Pearl Harbor, these eighteen- to twenty-two-year-old boys were on Bataan. They fought on through February, March, and into April, giving devastating blows to the enemy planes and ships. They pushed back wave after wave of enemy troops, who outnumbered them by many times, and on 5 April frustrated a landing attempt, with heavy losses to themselves. Weary, hungry, sick, they came to their limit on 6 April, and on the 9th from "complete physical exhaustion" they were compelled to surrender: "In such a fight as this, the flesh must yield at last, endurance must melt away, and the end of the battle must come. Bataan has fallen but its spirit stands, a beacon to the liberty-loving peoples of the world."

Three officers and 104 enlisted men of the 200th escaped to Corregidor, and there fought on until the surrender of that island fortress.

The First U.S. Tank Action in World War II

by Colonel Thomas Dooley, U.S. Army (Retired)

IN direct contrast to the lightning-like thrusts of U.S. armored divisions across France and Germany during the last year of the war, the first U.S. tank action was a slow, difficult, retrograde movement on the opposite side of the world in the Philippines.

In July 1940, there was only one Reserve tank battalion, the 70th General Headquarters (GHQ) Reserve Tank Battalion (Medium) stationed at Fort George G. Meade, Maryland. It was sadly lacking in personnel.

When news came to Major General Adna R. Chaffee that the War Department planned to use many similar units as special task forces, although they had made no provision for their organization, the "Father of the Armored Force" could foresee that without authorization for these reserve units, his armored divisions would be chopped to pieces to supply them and he dispatched a letter of protest to Chief of Staff Marshall. "So, already they are contemplating breaking up our divisions to fritter them away for small purposes," he wrote indignantly. "G-3 has set up no additional GHQ Reserve tank battalions so far. At least four more should be set up at once. We will have material."[1]

---

[1] Mildred Hanson Gillie, *Forging the Thunderbolt*, Military Service Publishing Co., Harrisburg, Pennsylvania, 1947, page 195.

In October 1940, General Chaffee wrote to Major General William Bryden, Deputy Chief of Staff, repeating his plea for "prompt formation of efficient GHQ Reserve Tank Battalions."[2] It was his proposal to use eighteen scattered National Guard tank companies to provide personnel for the immediate formation of four tank battalions, with training of cadres for ten more battalions to begin soon.

General Chaffee's work resulted in the first of these additional battalions being formed about one month later when, on 25 November 1940, the 192nd GHQ Tank Battalion was inducted into Federal service at Fort Knox, Kentucky. Three more battalions were soon organized: the 193rd at Fort Benning, Georgia, on 6 January 1941; the 194th at Fort Lewis, Washington, on 22 January 1941; and the 191st at Fort Meade, Maryland, on 3 February 1941.

Inasmuch as these battalions were only expected to be in Federal service for one year, no attempt was made to standardize them or to made them conform with any established tables of organization or equipment.[3] Two of these units, the 192nd GHQ Tank Battalion (Light), and the 194th GHQ Tank Battalion (Light), along with the 17th Ordnance Company (Armored), would soon become the Provisional Tank Group, U.S. Army Forces in the Far East (USAFFE).

After the formation of USAFFE in August 1941, General Douglas MacArthur, then commanding, had asked for an armored division. However, the Provisional Tank Group was to be the only armor in USAFFE and its nucleus was never augmented; although a medium GHQ tank battalion had been completely equipped and was on forty-eight-hour standby for departure for the Philippines when its orders were canceled on 10 December 1941. Furthermore, the group would have little time for training before embarking for the Philippines. The 192nd GHQ Tank Battalion from General Sylvester's 1st Tank Group at Fort Benning, Georgia, had carried out a defensive role in the 1941 Louisiana maneuvers. The 194th GHQ Tank Battalion had come from the West Coast where it had been taking part in minor maneuvers with, what was at that time, Fourth Army. Both battalions had worked during this maneuver period with early models of the M1 light tank.

The first of the units to arrive in the Far East, the 194th Tank Battalion and 17th Ordnance Company (Armored), reached Manila on 26 September 1941. One tank company of this battalion and a part of the

---

[2] Ibid.
[3] Ibid., pages 194-96.

battalion headquarters company had been detached to Alaska. Upon movement to Port of Embarkation, this battalion (as was the 192nd later) was re-equipped with the new M3 light tanks and half-tracks. The armament of these new tanks was strange to the personnel. The M3 had for its main battery the 37 mm gun with a .30-caliber machine gun co-axially mounted in the turret. The two fixed sponson guns (fired by remote control by the driver) and the anti-aircraft machine gun were all new to the crews. This light tank was heavier and longer, had better flotation, and was equipped with radio facilities that were different from those of the M1. So little time and direction had been possible before departure that the unit had thought it necessary in installing the new radios, to remove the right sponson gun to make space, and to spot weld armor over the gun port.

The 194th was assigned to Fort Stotsenberg adjacent to Clark Field, in Pampanga Province. Before the group commander arrived, this unit undertook limited reconnaissance in North Luzon. It did not accomplish any firing problems nor cross-country driving as no ranges, fuel, or ammunition were released for these purposes.

The group commander, Colonel James R. N. Weaver, with Headquarters and Group Headquarters Detachment and the 192nd GHQ Tank Battalion (Light) arrived in Manila on 20 November 1941. The headquarters detachment consisted of ten enlisted men, no tanks, two half-tracks, two two-way radios, two $1/4$-ton command and reconnaissance cars, one sedan, and no trucks.[4] These units were also stationed at Fort Stotsenberg and were housed in tents pending completion of semi-permanent housing to be built of sawali, a siding for houses and buildings made by the natives who wove two-inch reeds onto a bamboo frame. The only training at this time was limited reconnaissance work as far north as Lingayen and Baguio, the Philippine summer capital.

The Provisional Tank Group, USAFFE, was organized on 21 November 1941. Eight days later on 29 November, the 17th Ordnance Company (Armored) was assigned to the group at Fort Stotsenberg.

On 27 November, a general alert had been sounded for all forces in the Philippines, but for some reason or through the oversight of someone, the tank units were not included in the warnings. However, the commanding officer of Clark Field had been ordered by Far East Air Force (FEAF) to execute two alerts, one by day, one by night, before 2

---

[4]   *Operations of the Provisional Tank Group, U.S. Army Forces in Far East, 1941-1942.*

December, and the tank group had been asked to participate, and on 1 December moved into battle positions for the defense of Clark Field.

The general change in commands which became effective about 22 November, may have contributed to the disrupted communication channels: FEAF, North Luzon Force, South Luzon Force, and the Philippine Division, all had new commanders. On 28 November, when General Jonathan Wainwright arrived at Fort Stotsenberg to take command of North Luzon Force, his staff consisted of a chief of staff, two officers in the G-3 section and one in the G-2 section.

In the chain of command, the Provisional Tank Group was a separate tactical command under the commanding general, USAFFE, and was associated with the General Reserve only for administrative reports. The major unit of this reserve was the Philippine Division.

CLARK FIELD ATTACKED

On 8 December (7 December in the U.S.), when the news of the Pearl Harbor attack was received, the crews were at their tanks, and at 0830 the word was passed that Japanese planes were forty minutes away. Final checks were made as the men stood by, but no attack came. However, at 1230, while the noon meal was being served, a surprise attack was made on Clark Field. Bombers at about 20,000 feet accurately blasted Air Force installations throughout the Stotsenberg area. The tank weapons were of no use until the strafers came in low immediately after the bombing. In this action, Technical Sergeant Zenon "Bud" Bardowski, Company B, 192nd, is credited with the first enemy plane brought down by a U.S. armored unit in World War II. During the attack, he drove his M3 half-track out into the open to gain a better field of fire and put a seventy-five-round belt of .50-caliber into a Zero. The Air Corps commander, Colonel Maitland, submitted his actions for a Medal of Honor, but evacuated the islands before the paperwork was returned. (The first armored soldier to die in combat in World War II was Private Brooks of Company D, 194th. Brooks Field, the main parade ground at Fort Knox, Kentucky, is named in his honor.)

After the attack, the tanks were re-deployed, with the 194th moving about three kilometers northeast and the 192nd spreading out to more fully protect the relatively unbroken terrain to the south of the airfield.

There were two more air attacks, on 10 and 13 December, but the group losses amounted to only one half-track destroyed and two men wounded. During this time, tankers brought in the first prisoners of war, who were apparently Japanese naval aviators.

With landings imminent in southern Luzon, the group headquarters moved to Manila and the 194th moved to an area north of Manila after having sent reconnaissance and liaison groups to the areas of Muntinlupa, Nasugbu Bay, Balayan Bay, Battaangas Bay and east and north around Lake Taal.

After the tank group commander arrived, General Wainwright entered Rosario. Movement of any kind was hampered due to unopposed enemy air activity, for after the air strikes on 8 December, FEAF, on Luzon, consisted of only a few P-40s, useful only for sneak reconnaissance missions, and a few Philippine Army BT-1s, which were good only for courier service. The general situation was not clear, but reports indicated that two companies of the 11th Philippine Army Division were engaged north of Damortis. Elements of the 26th Cavalry were en route from Rosario to the point of contact but, as witnessed by the writer, the horse troops were at the mercy of enemy fighter-bombers.

An enemy motorized unit was reported approaching Damortis and General Wainwright asked the tank commander, "What can you do?" Re-supply gas had not yet arrived, but the company fuel resources were pooled and a single platoon was gassed up and sent to contact the enemy reportedly moving on Damortis. This platoon was commanded by Lieutenant Morin.

FIRST TANK-VERSUS-TANK ACTION

The platoon did not encounter opposition as they moved north out of Damortis and they continued on to Agoo. There they met an enemy tank unit on the road and the first U.S. tank-versus-tank action occurred in World War II. The enemy tanks were of low silhouette, had no turrets, and with sloped sides so that penetration was difficult to achieve. On the other hand, their 47 mm gun was quite effective against our tanks with their perpendicular sides and high profiles—points that had caused their rejection by our allies before the war. Lieutenant Morin's tank, which had left the road in an attempt to maneuver, was hit and caught fire. This was the first U.S. tank lost in tank-versus-tank action in World War II. It was later determined that the crew survived and was captured, making them the first armored force POWs in World War II. The other four tanks were all hit but were able to pull out, one under tow. However, they were all lost later in the day to bombings and mechanical mishaps. The assistant driver of the platoon sergeant's tank, Private Henry Deckert, Company B, 192nd, had been decapitated when a direct hit penetrated the forward deck at the ball and socket joint of the bow gun mounting. This man was the first armored soldier killed in tank-versus-tank action in World War II. Hits on enemy tanks with our 37 mm guns had been observed during the fight, but many of the shots were seen to ricochet off the sloping armor.

Later, the situation around Damortis decayed to such a degree that it was imperative that tanks be used to cover the withdrawal of the 26th Cavalry. The company at Rosario (gas had finally arrived by truck) was sent in with instructions to cover the withdrawal with a series of leap-frog actions.

Later that day the tanks were deployed to the north and west of Rosario but the rapidly developing situation caused the commanding general of the 71st Philippine Army Division to order all elements south of the Bued River bridge, which was burned in the face of advancing Japanese tanks and cyclists.

The 192nd at this time was deployed to the east of Highway 3, and on 24 December, because of the dire straits of the North Luzon Force, the 194th Battalion (less Company C) was sent from the south of Manila to the west flank of the arterial highway.

About this time a British ship, which had been unable to reach Singapore, put in to Manila and from its holds came potential augmentation for the tank group. Some forty Bren gun carriers were made available and the initial plan called for organization of two companies. Bren machine guns were not available, but ordnance was to arm the carriers with either .50-caliber or .30-caliber Browning machine guns. Had this organization been completed, the tanks would have been strengthened by a much-needed economy force capable of carrying out both reconnaissance and security roles. Notice of the impending enemy landings in the Lingayen Gulf area, and subsequent moves of the tanks, halted this augmentation. Eventually all carriers were armed—those operating with tank units, with salvaged guns from tank casualties. About twenty of the carriers were kept with the tank group and the remainder were sent to the Philippine Army divisions and to the 26th Cavalry. The latter group of Bren carriers, commanded by a Veterinary officer, did noble work throughout the Bataan campaign. Those carriers that were retained by the tank units did good work in emergency supply runs and on cross-country reconnaissance patrols over doubtful terrain before committing tanks to action. It was soon found that the heat-baked ground that gave the appearance of good driving conditions was only a crust that would not support the 4-ton Bren carriers.

TANKERS MOVE TO LINGAYEN GULF

At a staff conference at USAFFE Headquarters on the evening of 21 December, orders were received to dispatch one company from the 192nd by midnight and by re-supplying with gas at Gerona and at Bauang, to get to the Lingayen Gulf area by daylight, where, according to reports, it was anticipated the enemy would land a sizable force at first light. The 192nd was ordered to move up Highway 3 for such supporting moves as the battalion commander might direct after his contact with the commanding general, North Luzon Force (Wainwright).

When the group commander arrived in the Lingayen Gulf area, he found the company which had been dispatched before midnight, stranded at Rosario, out of gas. The tank company commander reported that contradictory orders had prevented his refueling at Gerona and that his mission had been changed to that of providing cover for the rear elements of the 11th Philippine Army Division. This instance of changed orders was to be the case on several occasions in the next few weeks due to the confusion and lack of coordination between units of untrained troops and staffs.

It is only fair to explain that all Philippine Army divisions were comparatively untrained and under strength. Many of the troops had gone through five months of Philippine military training but some had not even had this background. Also, some of the units that were now moving to contact with well-trained Japanese divisions, had not been mobilized until after the declaration of war.

No steel helmets or individual entrenching tools were available to Philippine Army troops. The uniforms habitually worn by these units were light tropical hats, fatigue clothes, and canvas-topped shoes. All men were equipped with bolt-action Enfield rifles, but very few spare parts were available. This point was of concern to unit commanders due to the many malfunctions caused by broken ejectors.[5]

Since the Orange Plan (the pre-World War II operational plan covering the Philippines) was in effect, the mission assigned the Provisional Tank Group was to cover the withdrawal of the Filipino-American

---

[5]   *Report of Operations of North Luzon Force and I Philippine Corps in the Defense of North Luzon and Bataan from 8 December 1941 to 9 April 1942.*

forces into the Bataan peninsula. There, the troops were to make a stand and await reinforcements from the States. But the Philippines had already been written off and the reinforcements never came.

TANKERS PREVENT A ROUT

The withdrawal plan called for a retrograde movement to delaying positions on four successive phase lines (see map). The tanks carried out this mission amid much confusion. Because of the tropical nature of the terrain, all units were instructed to plan each delay position to occupy all north-south roads and at the same time they were to reconnoiter for exit routes that would tie in with Highways 3 and 5 (the two north-south axil roads). Tanks occupying positions on the main routes were ordered to pay particular attention to enemy mechanized units, and were given detailed instructions on how to cover turns in the highway and to coordinate their efforts with the self-propelled 75 mm guns mounted on half-tracks.

A number of tank actions now took place, one of the most notable of which was the action at Baliuag, Pampanga, where two platoons of Company C, 192nd, in a back-and-forth fight through the town, bagged eight Japanese medium tanks and prevented a complete rout of American and Filipino troops in the area.

Another, more tragic incident occurred north of the Agno River when, due to lack of coordination between units, ten tanks had to be abandoned due to blown bridges and a hard-pressing enemy.

The first phase of the final action before the withdrawal into the Bataan peninsula came in covering the Calumpit bridge position. At this junction, the last troops of the South Luzon Force joined the route of the North Luzon Force. The Calumpit bridge was blown during the night of 31 December-1 January. After the destruction of the bridge, the 192nd was passed through the 194th, now reduced to about thirty tanks. Because of this reduction, Company A of the 192nd was attached to the 194th and this force was to cover the retirement from the Calumpit junction to the Lavac junction position.

The attached company, in one instance, attempted a makeshift counterattack in the vicinity of Guagua with elements of the 11th Philippine Army Division. The infantry elements at one time mistook our tanks for the enemy and laid down very accurate mortar fire. They repeated this tactic on the group commander's jeep as he attempted to establish some sort of coordination. The tank company, by trail and cross-country travel, and with the eventual loss of three tanks, rejoined the 194th on Highway 7 at a point west of Guagua.

On the afternoon of 5 January, C Company of the 194th, supported by four self-propelled 75s, ambushed an enemy unit of about seven or eight hundred infantry, and caused losses of about fifty percent. This group worked continuously during the withdrawal at retrieving tank gas cached along the route.

One other fire fight marked the covering action just before entry into Bataan. This engagement, with few casualties, lasted from 1430 to about 1700 when the enemy withdrew. It is of particular interest only because it marked he first use of smoke by Japanese units.

The period from 6-26 January was marked by further covering actions in the east coast road and one attempted foray in the west (I Corps sector). The covering action on the east was to aid II Corps in pulling back after a main effort was made by the Japanese in the Abucay Hacienda area.

The new and last main line of resistance was along the Pilar-Bagac road.

The action in the I Corps sector was an attempt to open up a road to extricate the 1st Philippine Army Division that had been cut off north of Bagac by a sizable infiltration of Japanese units. In this attempt, the lack of close-in infantry protection and the cleverly concealed Japanese road mines caused the loss of two tanks and the eventual withdrawal of the foot troops, without their heavy equipment, over a circuitous beach trail.

Also, during this period, the bulk of the tank units gained their first respite since 8 December, in a bivouac area south of Pilar. The tank units were reorganized, companies of the 194th being reduced from seventeen to ten tanks; platoons from five tanks to three. This same reduction was shortly to be imposed upon the 192nd. Tank overhaul and maintenance was done by the 17th Ordnance Company (Armored) that carried out third- and fourth-echelon maintenance using ordnance stocks on south Bataan that had not been released before 8 December. For the first time since hostilities began, crews were fed from their own kitchens, but this luxury was dampened due to the forced reduction in supplies on 6 January, which placed all troops on half rations.

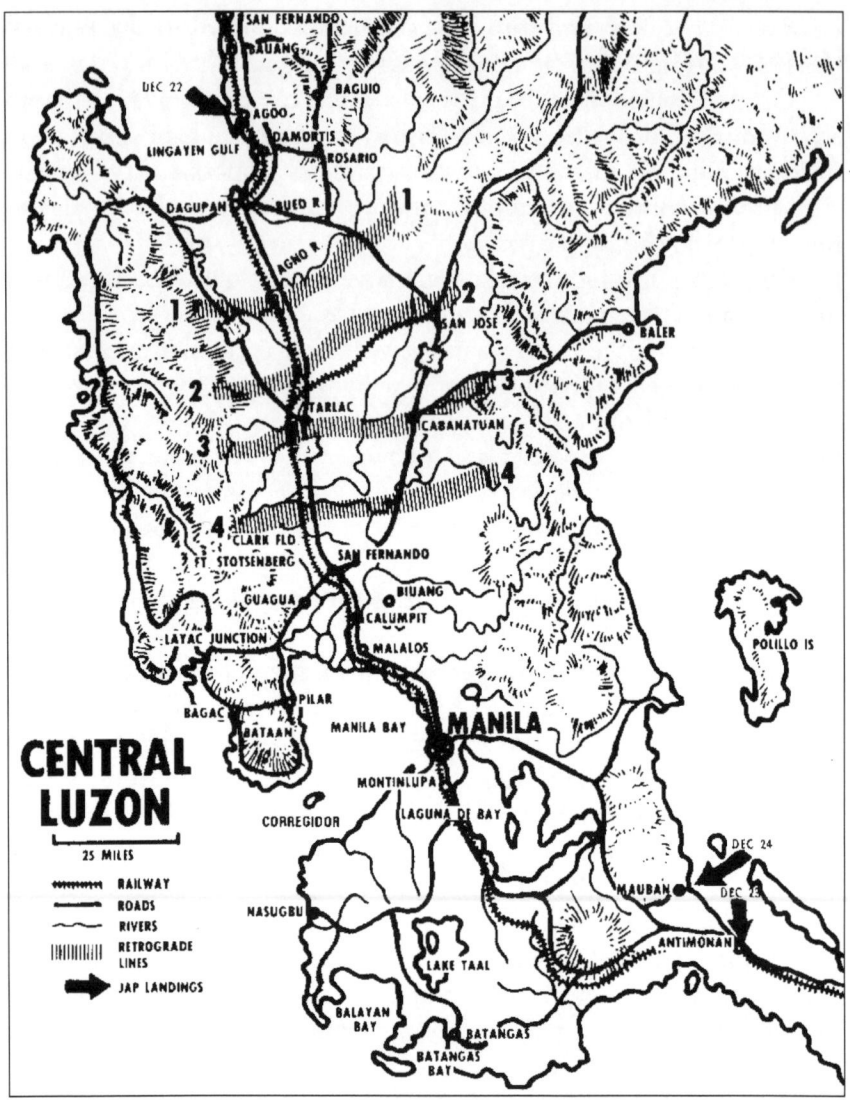

TANKS NOT USED PROPERLY

During this period, the lack of knowledge among the infantry commanders of the characteristics, capabilities, and limitations of tanks was noted when requests were made for tanks to seek out and destroy snipers, flush Japanese troops from sugar cane fields, and to make sorties in front of the main line of resistance into areas that had been extensively mined by our own troops.

The beach defense of the east coast was assumed on 28 January, and with it came contingency missions for the tank units: the 192nd over-watched the north half of the east coast and was on call to support the western half of the II Corps front; the 194th was assigned the southern half of the beaches and was to provide secondary support to the western half of II Corps. The difficulty in supporting any front line unit was accentuated by the narrowness of new trails. The old trails leading off the coast road were dead-end avenues, originally having been cut for timber operations.

On 1 February, composite platoons of tanks and half-tracks were assigned to each of three airfields that had been built on the peninsula in anticipation of the reconstitution of local air force units that were to have assisted the beleaguered troops.

Upon the request of the I Corps commander, the 192nd (less one company) was dispatched to the western sector to support foot troops in erasing three enemy pockets: the Tuol pocket formed by the infiltration of Japanese units on the I Corps front before the main line of resistance had been cleared and definitely established; and the Aglaloma and Anyasen pockets formed through the uncoordinated Japanese landings in their attempt to cut the main supply route (the west coast road).

The difficulties typical of these actions can best be described by quoting from the citation awarded Lieutenant John Hay of the 192nd:

> During this period and in the terrain involved, a rugged, dense jungle wherein tank movement had to be limited to the space cumulatively cleared by repeated charges of a few yards each, Lieutenant Hay's gallantry, persistence, and complete disregard of personal danger, in an entirely new phase of tank warfare, pre-eminently contributed to the ultimate success of the tanks and troops which they supported.[6]

In the Tuol pocket, the tank-infantry combination worked very effectively against the Japanese dug in around banyan trees, and Lieutenant Bianchi of the infantry company was awarded the Medal of Honor. Also in this action, one U.S. tank commanded by the platoon leader Lieutenant Edgar Winger, was lost when its crew was blinded by a Japanese flame thrower (the first used in the campaign; it was destroyed by Sergeant Bardowski). After running blind off the trail,

---

[6] *Operations of the Provisional Tank Group, USAFFE, 1941-1942.*

Winger became disoriented. When he opened his hatch to gain his bearings, a nervous member of the Philippine Army fatally wounded him with a burst from a BAR.

After the clearance of the pockets in the I Corps sector, the tank group instituted a plan for a comprehensive instruction in tank-infantry tactics among Philippine Army troops, but this was limited, due to gas rationing and lack of personnel. Although movement was at a minimum due to lack of gasoline, ammunition was adequate and ordnance personnel contributed to the effectiveness of the tanks by converting considerable armor-piercing (AP) 37 mm to high explosive (HE) and canister. These shells were much more useful in the absence of enemy armor. After the entry into Bataan, enemy tanks were never observed in strength—never more than three at a time—usually less, and these only in April during the last days of Bataan when U.S. artillery and anti-tank weapons had been virtually reduced to inaction.

On 3 April, the Japanese started their all-out offensive and as enemy activity increased on the II Corps front, the 194th took on its contingency mission as its primary mission and moved its companies to support the front line units to the west of the east coast road. The 194th was later supported by one company of the 192nd. The activities of the tank units in the next five days, with the resulting confusion of untrained, half-fed, malaria-ridden troops attacked by a superiorly-equipped, better-trained, better-organized enemy, can hardly be given in detail. Suffice it to say that the tank units supported the infantry at every opportunity and on every trail that was not completely blocked by the supply vehicles of the retreating troops. At about 1830 on 8 April 1942, the tank battalion commanders were given the following order: "You will make plans, to be communicated to company commanders only, and be prepared to destroy within one hour after receipt by radio, or other means, of the word 'CRASH,' all tanks and combat vehicles, arms, ammunition, gas, and radios, reserving sufficient trucks to close to rear echelons as soon as accomplished."[7]

DECISION TO SURRENDER IS MADE

At about 2230, 8 April, Major General E. P. King, commanding Luzon Forces, announced that further resistance would result in the massacre of the 6,000 sick and wounded in the area and of the 40,000 civilian refugees now congested closely about; that he was not in touch with

---

[7] Ibid.

any troops that were still resisting behind the closely drawn lines; that there were less than twenty-five percent effective of those in being; that at most he could not expect to hold more than one more day; that upon his, and his only, responsibility, he would send a staff officer with a flag of surrender across the lines the next morning. When asked by the tank group commander if any help was in prospect, General King could answer only "No." The destruction of the main ordnance dump was to commence at 2340. Troops were to destroy all arms and ammunition and cease resistance at 0700, 9 April 1942.

After the surrender, the tank group commander and his staff were questioned several times by the Japanese and from these investigations it was learned that the:

- Japanese had feared most the artillery and the tanks.
- Tanks, by their cordon coastal guard, had caused the Japanese to cancel an invasion from Manila Bay.
- Japanese had overestimated our tank strength by from 33 to 900% (158 to 1,080).

The Japanese had about two hundred tanks, inferior to ours in armor, but better adapted to tropical terrain and better armed with a very effective 47 mm gun. (Report and recommendations on armored equipment was radioed to the War Department, by direction, sometime after the withdrawal to Bataan.)

These were the actions and circumstances that brought the members of the Provisional Tank Group, USAFFE, to that state, which is so ably described by Winston Churchill as:

Prisoner of War! It is a melancholy state. You are in the power of your enemy. You owe your life to his humanity, your daily bread to his compassion. You must obey his orders, await his pleasure, possess your souls in patience. The days are very long. Hours crawl by like paralytic centipedes.

Moreover, the whole atmosphere of prison, even the most easy and best-regulated prison, is odious. Companions quarrel about trifles, and get the least possible pleasure from each other's society. You feel a constant humility in being fenced in by railings and wire, watched by armed men and webbed about with a tangle of regulations and restrictions.[8]

THE AUTHOR

Colonel Thomas Dooley, U.S. Army (Retired), was commissioned from Texas A&M in 1935. Prior to World War II he served with the 1st Cavalry Division. During the Philippine campaign he was aide-de-camp to General Jonathan Wainwright and was a POW from 1942 to 1945. He attended the Armor Officer Advance Course in 1948 and later was Chief of Staff, U.S. Army Armor Center, Fort Knox, Kentucky, until his retirement in March 1969.

---

[8] Winston S. Churchill, "A Roving Commission," *The Reader's Digest,* July 1940.

200th and 515th Coast Artillery (Anti-Aircraft) Regiments in the Philippines

26 September 1941–9 April 1942

by Charles H. Bogart

THE year 1940 saw the U.S. taking a new look at its defense force. A quick survey soon proved that the U.S. Army, and especially its Reserve and the National Guard components, were totally unprepared for modern war. Steps were therefore taken to reorganize a number of these units.

Among the National Guard units reorganized was the 111th Cavalry of the New Mexico Guard which, in the spring of 1941, was converted to the 200th Coast Artillery (Anti-Aircraft) Regiment. (All anti-aircraft units of the U.S. Army from World War I to the Korean War were part of the Coast Artillery Corps.)

The 200th Coast Artillery (Anti-Aircraft), along with many other National Guard outfits, was called into Federal service in 1941. Receiving its orders on 6 January 1941, the 200th Coast Artillery (Anti-Aircraft) moved to Fort Bliss, Texas, for training. Here it remained until 31 August 1941 when, under sealed orders, the 200th moved out for San Francisco. There they and the 194th Tank Battalion boarded Army transports for what was to prove to be a voyage to the Philippines.

Sailing in two separate detachments the 1,809 officers and men of the 200th arrived in the Philippines during September 1941. By 26 September the regiment had taken up their assigned defensive positions around Fort Stotsenberg and Clark Field. The regiment's total armament consisted of twelve 3-inch and twenty-four 37-mm guns plus a number of .50 and .30 caliber machine guns. The only other anti-aircraft unit in the Philippines was the 60th Coast Artillery (Anti-Aircraft), a Regular Army unit, assigned to the forts in Manila Bay.

The next few weeks saw the 200th digging their guns into place and setting up ammo dumps. Plans were also laid out for the troops to conduct gunnery shoots. Though the 200th had been in Federal service for eight months before sailing for the Philippines, it had never conducted a gunnery exercise against towed targets.

Time, however, was to never allow the 200th a chance to shoot at a towed target. Full of theory, but having no experience, the 200th awoke to find themselves at war with Japan on 8 December (7 December Pearl Harbor time).

The 200th fired its first shot in anger when at 1230 on 8 December 1941 a force of three hundred Japanese planes attacked the Fort Stotsenberg–Clark Field area. In a savage attack using high-level bombing and strafing the Japanese destroyed American air power in the Philippines. While the 200th claimed five planes shot down, they found their weapons far from perfect.

Only one out of six of the 3-inch shells exploded at the correct altitude and even those which exploded at the correct altitude were two to four thousand feet under the bombers. This poor performance was due to the fact that the shell's fuses had become badly corroded. A check showed that the newest shells in the regiment's ammo dumps had been manufactured in 1932. As a result of their long storage in the humid Philippines the shells had deteriorated and the metal had started to corrode. In one incident sixteen shells were fired and only two exploded.

The day after the attack saw the 200th lose thirty officers and 596 men through transfers; ninety-six men along with their trucks were assigned to the Provisional Group Self-Propelled Artillery created from forty-eight excess 75-mm self-propelled guns. The personnel assigned to these guns were still staging through Pearl Harbor on 8 December. In addition, another thirty officers and five hundred men from the 200th were assigned to man, in the defense of Manila, a number of spare 3-inch anti-aircraft guns taken from the Philippine Ordnance Depot.

The 200th detachment at Manila was, on 19 December, redesignated as the 515th Coast Artillery (Anti-Aircraft) and placed under the command of Colonel Harry M. Peck, Executive Officer of the 200th. Shortages in personnel for both the 200th and the 515th were later made good through the use of excess Air Corps personnel who no longer had aircraft to service.

The 515th fired its first shots on 10 December when Manila was attacked for the first time. Once again the Japanese flew above the range of the 3-inch guns. The 200th in the meantime had had to disperse their weapons to cover other potential targets; two of their guns were sent to protect the Calumpit railroad and highway bridges on the Pampauge River over which the Northern Luzon Forces had to retreat to reach Bataan.

With the declaration of Manila being an open city by MacArthur and the destruction of Clark Field, the two anti-aircraft regiments found themselves assuming the role of anti-air defense for the ground troops. The 515th was placed under the command of the Southern Luzon Force, while the 200th was assigned to the Northern Luzon Force. The job of both regiments was to protect the bridges and bottlenecks through which the troops retreating to Bataan had to pass. In the performance of this duty they succeeded mainly due to the failure of the Japanese to launch any sustained air attack on the American-Filipino forces line of retreat.

Upon successfully completing the retreat to Bataan, the 200th and 515th were assigned to protecting the Cabcaben and Bataan airfields. For the next two months the two regiments carried out their assignments so well that no U.S. plane was lost on the ground.

Once on Bataan, both regiments began to function as a brigade, rather than as two separate regiments. In recognition of this, on 7 April, the 200th and 515th were formed into a provisional Coastal Artillery Brigade (Anti-Aircraft) by General King, commanding the troops on Bataan.

The existence of the brigade was short-lived, for the next day Japanese ground forces broke through the American last line of resistance on Bataan. The 200th and 515th on that day were the only organized reserves on Bataan. General King, therefore, ordered them to destroy all their equipment which was only of use against aircraft and to form a last line of resistance south of Cabcaben Airfield, the 515th forming to the left of the 200th.

The men of the 200th and 515th, however, were spared from acting as a last ditch defense force, for on 9 April, before they were attacked, General King surrendered the American-Filipino Forces on Bataan to the Japanese 14th Army. The last act of the 200th and 515th Regiments was to take part in the Bataan Death March.

The 200th Coast Artillery (Anti-Aircraft) and the 515th Coast Artillery (Anti-Aircraft) had, during their short existence, earned themselves a footnote in history. Fighting on half rations from 6 January to 9 April 1942, the two regiments had not lost heart. Fighting at half strength and less, Battery B of the 515th, for example, had only nineteen officers and men fit for duty out of its authorized strength of one hundred.

At the end, the two regiments had returned a shot for each bomb dropped on them. In all, the two regiments claimed eighty-six Japanese planes shot down between 8 December 1941 and 8 April 1942. The honors were fifty-one aircraft to the 200th and thirty-five to the 515th. Of the eighteen hundred officers and men who sailed to the Philippines in September 1941, approximately one thousand returned to the U.S. four years later in 1945. For their service in the Philippines both regiments received the Distinguished Unit Citation.

Target: Corregidor

by Kemp Tolley, Rear Admiral, U.S. Navy (Retired)

ON 10 December 1941 the little 3,500-ton China coaster S.S. *Anhui* lay in Manila harbor taking refuge from the new war, diverted from her Shanghai-Singapore run. The nine enemy planes that worked over the anchored merchant ships that day, before hitting Cavite Navy Yard, near-missed and badly shook *Anhui* and her 400 civilian Shanghai evacuees, who next morning were put ashore in Manila. Following the advice of Commander-in-Chief, Asiatic Fleet, Adm. Thomas C. Hart, *Anhui* was underway that same day, arriving in Australia 24 December. But she would be back.

Some of the most courageous and ingenious people of this whole era were the blockade runners. In mid-January 1942, $10,000 was made available to be spent in whatever manner would get the goods through. The American and Filipino troops on Bataan were already down to half rations, and soon would be lucky to have a bit of monkey meat, carabao or boa constrictor to eke out the dwindling food supplies. Drugs were desperately short. It was essential to get cracking.

General George Marshall ordered how the job was to be done: "Organize groups of bold and resourceful men. Dispatch them with funds by air to the Netherlands East Indies, there to buy food and charter vessels. Rewards for actual delivery to Bataan or Corregidor must be fixed at a level to insure utmost energy and daring ..."

All this was inspiring rhetoric. But the operation was Russian roulette in reverse; in place of five empty chambers and one loaded, all the chambers but one were charged. Would the hammer fall luckily on that empty one?

In early March 1942, S.S. *Anhui* at her all-out ten knots, was headed north, once more into the dragon's mouth, destination Cebu in the central Philippines. Her officers, the usual assortment of British and Chinese, had accepted the dangerous assignment reluctantly, their decision helped by the terms offered: four months pay for accepting the voyage, and a nine months salary bonus for successful delivery of the cargo. Six months pay would go to the dependents of those ending up dead or disabled as a result of enemy action. Success would mean $8,450 in the skipper's pocket, $1,300 for a seaman.

In the hold were 2,000,000 rounds of .30-caliber, 6,000 81-mm mortar shells, medical, signal and engineering supplies, about 450 tons of food and a shipment of propaganda leaflets especially requested by MacArthur. Six .50-caliber machine guns, manned by eight U.S. Army soldiers had better keep the bombs away, or all hands were in for a big sneeze; she also carried one ton of pepper to make more palatable what rotting stores of meat still remained to the Americans.

After a suspense-packed voyage north, outside the island chain, *Anhui* was feeling her way through blacked out Surigao Strait when she came to with a shudder. She had run aground. A small outboard motor boat was put over the side and soon two officers and two Chinese crewmen were high-tailing it for Cebu, 50 miles away.

At Cebu it had been a busy day. Another valiant blockade runner from Australia, the 5,500-ton *Dona Nati*, just unloaded, had by a hair's breadth managed to steam out before the arrival of a Japanese destroyer that shelled the port, damaging or sinking several small inter-island ships. Consequently, when *Anhui*'s outboard arrived, its occupants were soon congratulating themselves on *Anhui*'s good luck in running aground. Had she not, and continued on to Cebu, the Japanese tin can would surely have potted her.

That night a tug and lighter set out for *Anhui*'s reef to bring off part of the cargo. On Friday the 13th, certainly no day of ill omen here, two small inter-island craft arrived to help. The lightened ship wrenched free at sundown and by noon next day was alongside a Cebu dock.

Mixed up in the port's affairs or watching from a hilltop snuggery such diverting fireworks as the port bombardment was Ensign George Pollak, USNR. He had come out to Manila in August 1941 to duty in the Cavite Navy Yard, evacuated to Mariveles on Bataan's tip when Cavite was destroyed 10 December, then served in a polyglot battalion of Marines, grounded aviators, sailors and casuals that had fought Japanese infiltrators until relieved by a Philippine Scout regiment. He had then hopped a Cebu-bound blockade runner, the S.S. *Legaspi* loaded with Philippine troops, there being no further useful employment for him on Bataan.

On a hillside back of Cebu, Pollak and another ensign had set up housekeeping in a bungalow equipped with a case of orange soda and one of "square face" gin. In the evening, when port duties were over, they could watch the magnificent view of the straits from their verandah. An Army car was at their disposal by virtue of double wages paid its driver, a secret not shared with the motor pool commander. It had been Pollak in charge of that tug going to ground *Anhui*'s rescue.

The ship's unloading at Cebu had been an around-the-clock affair; the enemy destroyer was still reported in those general parts. Things had got off to a bad start when an Army Transportation Corps officer whacked a Chinese sailor over the head with an automatic pistol, in a way perhaps he had seen in some early cinema thriller on how to handle the "heathen Chinee." Pollak was substituted to mollify the half-mutinous, resentful crewmen. He found the skipper a wonderful, red-bearded Welshman, the mate a prim Britisher, and the chief engineer, naturally enough, a Scotsman. All wore whites to dinner and as young Pollak appreciatively noted, had a bountiful supply of Scotch. On his periodic visits to the cabin to report progress, the skipper would clap his hands and there instantly, like magic, *again* appeared that bottle of Scotch and two glasses.

Next morning the chilling news arrived that the Japanese destroyer was approaching. *Anhui*'s ship's company made a lightning departure for the heights back of town to watch. Then a wholly incredulous thing happened. The destroyer, moving fast, slid up through the south channel and toured the outer harbor with guns trained on the waterfront. But not a shot was fired! The enemy could have sunk or even boarded and captured *Anhui* with ease; the Americans' biggest weapon was a .50-caliber machine gun. Perhaps they felt she could be taken intact later, at their leisure, or sunk at their leisure. Who could fathom the Japanese mind?

Anhui's Capt. Evans had ideas of his own, which did not include hanging around Cebu. By late evening, the ship was unloaded, Pollak sorrowfully having to refuse Evans' offer of a ride south. *Anhui* made it through Surigao Strait that night. But there still was a long, long road ahead. Although her routing was known to our submarines, Adm. Hart had ordered unrestricted submarine and air warfare on 8 December. Any ship afloat was highly suspect to our subs in those seas which the Japanese all but privately owned. An American sub skipper's enthusiasm might dull his sensibilities at recognition.

Anhui's cruise was a fearsome trip at slow speed in a friendless ocean. She passed within 100 miles of the enemy base at Palau. Four days later, she dodged what might have been an enemy destroyer off the Admiralties. By 26 March, close to the Solomons, all hands breathed easier. But it was premature. A single-engined, unidentified plane roared over at low altitude. On a second approach, the soldier-gunners took no chances and opened fire. Four bombs came spiraling down. Their straddle drenched the ship but left her undamaged.

Several days later, there was another scare. Two float planes drew near. But these were unmistakably U.S. cruiser scouts. There was mutual recognition and the planes flew off.

On 3 April 1942, after a close-to-12,000 mile round trip in enemy-infested seas, *Anhui* gratefully found the Sydney dock. It was Good Friday by the calendar, but to those sorely tried men board *Anhui*, it was the *Best* Friday in their lives to date.

In George Pollak's case, the orange soda, "square face" gin and luck all ran out together. When the Japanese landed on Cebu, he and several others dived into Sudlon Forest. Deep inside, a missionary establishment refused them sanctuary, lest in the eyes of the eventual Japanese occupiers they be tainted by association with the American military. Barely avoiding enemy patrols, the little party made it by 'banda' across Tanon Strait to the island of Negros, George riding an outrigger of the overloaded little cockleshell, his .45 Colt around his neck for dryness.

Among natives that still hunted wild boar with spears, Pollak, Lt. Cmdr. Edward Dockweiler, and Lts. Richard Anderson and James Davis moved into a 'nipa' shack on the mountainside. Soon thereafter, the white flag went up over Corregidor, covering all U.S. forces in the Philippines.

The four argued at length. Should they surrender, or melt into the hills as guerrillas or hunted men, or try the almost hopeless run for the south—even Australia? Their only weapons were .45 Colts. Without medicine, more bouts with tropical ulcers and malaria could soon bring them all to a miserable, wasting death. One could not be sure of the natives, valiantly though they had fought throughout the islands. In a thousand, 999 could be faithful, but it required only one faint heart or money-hungry traitor to arrange the hangman's noose. Colonel Landon, second in command on Negros, courageously went to meet the Japanese advance party, made the surrender arrangements and led the Americans into town. For George and friends, the fighting part was over.

FURTHER READING

Further details on Pollak and similar operations in the early days of the war in the Far East can be found in the author's *Cruise of the LANIKAI*, published by the Naval Institute Press, Annapolis, Maryland.

Battles for the
Central Philippines

September 1944

First published in 1948

THUS far in the American and Allied operations in the Pacific our efforts had been concentrated on two objectives, the liberation of the Philippines and the defeat of Japan. The long and extensive preparation for the accomplishment of these two missions was tedious and it was thorough. The science of warfare on both land and sea reached its highest point of efficiency in the build-up of forces and preparation of land and sea areas covering almost one-fifth of the globe. Let us consider once again certain of these preliminary and preparatory operations before the great blows could be struck that would accomplish our missions.

EXPERIMENTAL BEGINNING OF STRATEGIC BOMBING OF JAPAN

On or about 15 June 1944 the United States began its program of increasingly concentrated air bombardments of Japanese war plants and shipyards. Up to this the Japanese homeland had experienced only slightly the impact of the war, due to the fact that the European Theater had first call on our resources, and to the further fact that distance was hitherto too great for effective bombing. Now that our air force was superior in every way, and that we occupied bases within easier reach of enemy targets, we were ready to launch upon the Japanese home islands all the fury necessary to produce total surrender or destruction.

The Doolittle raid of 18 April 1942 was only a suggestion of what was to follow, when time and circumstance would permit.

Our submarines for two and a half years after Pearl Harbor were our most potent instrument in Japanese home waters. By the summer of 1944 our submarines had sunk a total of 687 Japanese vessels and damaged 115 more. Japanese communication and supply lines were thrown into confusion, and her ocean traffic was seriously crippled. But Japanese war production was as yet scarcely touched.

The newly created Twentieth Air Force under the direct control of General H. H. Arnold was given the mission of destroying the Japanese war supply system at its source. This force was equipped with improved bombers capable of global operations if necessary.

On 16 June 1944, the day after the landing of Americans on Saipan, the Japanese got their first view of America's latest great achievement, the B-29 Superfortresses of the Twentieth Air Force. Striking from a base somewhere in China, the Superfortresses carried fear and distress to the Japanese homeland, an accentuated reminder of the Doolittle Raid in 1942.

The first Superfortress raid hit Yawata on Kyushu Island. On 10 August 1944, they bombed Nagasaki, the longest bombing operation in history. Tokyo was stunned by the new super-bomber, but plaintively consoled the Japanese people by saying: "We should not think that we have been passively attacked, but that we have pulled the enemy towards us."

On 15-16 June 1944, the program was initiated out of the west by hurling bombs on the Yawata steel works on Kyushu Island. Three weeks later, on 7-8 July 1944, the second raid occurred on Yawata and the naval base at Sasebo. The air attacks were then carried to the Asiatic mainland, where on 29 July 1944, we struck at Anshan in Manchuria and Tangu, the port for Tientsin in occupied China. In the fourth operation on 11 August 1944, two formations struck at widely separated targets with demolition and incendiary bombs—the Nagasaki area of Kyushu and the Pladju oil refinery at Palembang, Sumatra. These were some of the preliminary and experimental strategic bombing attacks, a foretoken of what was yet to come.

WESTWARD ACROSS THE PHILIPPINE SEA

In the southwest Pacific, General MacArthur's American and Australian forces had already made rapid strides on the long road back to the Philippines. By spring of 1944 two Japanese armies had been neutralized and isolated on Bougainville, New Ireland and New Britain; but a third enemy army of some sixty thousand men still held the northern coast of New Guinea from Madang to the Moluccas. An amphibious expedition prepared in and proceeding from the Admiralty Islands, landed behind the enemy lines cutting his only communications. The enemy's only escape would be to the jungles and mountains of the interior of New Guinea where food would be insufficient to maintain an army for any length of time.

In support of our plan, on 27 April 1944, the United States 41st Division, escorted by a strong American fleet and carrier planes, landed with little opposition at Tanahmera Bay, Hollandia and Aitape, and in four days' time, captured all three airfields and a beachhead of 175 miles along the northern New Guinea coast. An Australian division, landing near Madang, advanced some eighty miles towards Wewak and Aitape and on 15 June 1944, occupied Hansa.

Meanwhile the 41st Division, with naval and air support, sailed two hundred miles west of Wakde to Biak, landing on 27 May 1944. Biak is the largest of the Netherlands East Indian Schouten Islands, and lies about nine hundred miles southeast of the Philippines. Fierce enemy resistance was encountered as we moved in to take the first of three enemy airfields, our main objectives. Here the first tank engagement of the Pacific war was fought but the Japanese were repulsed by our Shermans. Our troops occupied a beach head and on 2 June 1944, landed on Owi and Wundi, two small islands to the south of Biak. The Japanese made a desperate effort to reinforce their troops but were frustrated on 8 June 1944 when our Mitchell bombers sank four enemy destroyers. Capturing Mokmer, all organized enemy resistance ended on 20 June 1944, and for two weeks our troops were busy mopping up remnants of the enemy. On Biak, 3,268 Japanese were killed and fifteen taken prisoner.

Allied troops landed on Noemfoor Island on 2 July 1944, and with the aid of paratroops, captured the air field on 6 July 1944, killing and capturing 871 of the enemy.

On 11 July, the Japanese Eighteenth Army, isolated near Wewak in British New Guinea, attempted a breakthrough. The Americans succeeded in splitting the enemy forces into three parts on 2 August, the Japanese suffering 18,000 casualties.

Hence, General MacArthur's troops in eleven weeks had advanced more than eight hundred miles. The Japanese in New Guinea were now in small isolated segments. The general now commanded the southeastern approaches to the Philippines only five hundred miles away.

The United States Third Fleet made a carrier-based air attack on Mindanao on 9 September 1944, sinking or damaging eighty-nine Japanese vessels and destroying sixty-eight planes. On 12-14 September 1944 the Third Fleet attacked Cebu, Negros and Panay Islands in the central Philippines, destroying 156 enemy planes in the air and 277 on the grounds, besides sinking or damaging eighty-four enemy surface vessels.

From 12-13 September, the Far Eastern Air Force swept targets all the way from the Celebes to the Palaus with 384 tons of bombs, after intensive air and naval preparation over a radius of six hundred miles.

The first landing on the Palaus was made on 15 September 1944, when the 1st Marine Division established a beachhead on the southwestern shore of Peleliu Island. Japanese counterattacks were repulsed; by nightfall we had captured an airfield and counted 1400 dead Japanese. On the same day troops of General MacArthur's command, under General John C. Persons, landed on the southwestern coast of Morotai Island, in the Dutch Halmahera Group, five hundred miles southwest of the Palaus, met slight resistance and captured an airfield.

On 17 September 1944 the 81st Infantry Division under command of General Paul J. Mueller, landed on Anguar Island, the southernmost of the Palaus and six miles southwest of Peleliu. Here organized resistance ceased on 20 September 1944. The American Marines on Peleliu were strongly opposed at Umurbrogol Mountain (Bloody Nose Ridge) on 19 September 1944. Elements of the 81st Division reinforced the Marines, cutting off the enemy on Umurbrogol Mountain on the 26th. Fighting on Peleliu continued until 13 October when organized resistance ceased.

Admiral Mitscher's Task Force 58 made the first air raid on airfields in the Manila Bay area of Luzon on 21-22 September 1944, sinking or damaging 103 Japanese ships and destroying or damaging 405 enemy planes. Two days later, on the 24th, six islands of the central Philippines were bombed, destroying twenty-two enemy ships and thirty-six planes. Attacks were repeated on 11 October 1944 and on 14, 15 and 17 October.

On 21 October 1944, elements of the 81st Infantry Division occupied without opposition the Ulithi Atoll in the western Carolines.

On 21 September 1944, United States Marines from Peleliu Island invaded and quickly subdued the enemy on Ngesebus and Kougarur Islands to the north.

Through the month of September the Far Eastern Fleet and the Seventh Air Force had been reaching out in all directions. The first, striking enemy positions at Ceram, Celebes, Halmahera, Dutch Borneo and Java; and the second striking at Yap, Paramushiro in the Kuriles, Iwo in the Volcanos, Chichi and Haha in the Bonins, Rota and Pagan in the Marianas, Truk and Ponape in the Carolines, Marcus, the Marshall and Nauru Islands.

On 9 October 1944 the casualties of the fight for the Palaus were estimated to be: Japanese 11,380 dead, and 228 captured. Americans: 1,105 dead, 6,439 wounded and 245 missing.

The Third Fleet penetrated to the Japanese home waters on 9 October 1944 to bombard the coastal batteries on Marcus Island, 1,150 miles from Tokyo. On 10 October it attacked Okinawa and other islands of the Ryukyus, damaging 127 ships and small craft and 119 planes.

On 9 October 1944, elements of the U.S. 81st Infantry Division landed on Garakayo Island two miles north of Peleliu, and on the 11th occupied Bairakaseru Islet seven miles northwest, and Arimasuko on 12 October.

On 14 October 1944 the Far Eastern Air Force made their fourth raid on the Japanese oil refineries at Balikpapan in southeastern Borneo.

On 17 October 1944, the Third Fleet attacked Luzon in its ninth day of sustained operations in the western Pacific.

The stage was now set for the invasion of the Philippines. The "Road Back" had become shorter.

PREPARATION FOR INVASION

On 7 September 1944 the Southwest Pacific Command began operations preparatory to an invasion of the Philippines. General Douglas MacArthur and the troops of the U.S. Sixth Army commanded by General Walter Krueger had been waging a successful fight against the Japanese troops "holed-up" in the Dutch New Guinea area and the Halmahera Islands.

The Southwest Pacific Command on 7 September moved in on Soepiori Island in Geelvink Bay. And on the 15th troops of the U.S. 31st Infantry Division and the 126th Infantry Regiment of the U.S. 32nd Infantry Division under command of General John C. Persons landed on Morotai, about four hundred miles from the Philippines. Morotai was soon conquered, and as a result the Sixth Army had possession of air bases from which it could dominate our approach to the Philippines.

The first plan of our high command was to land on Mindanao Island in the Philippines in the month of November, but in our carrier plane sweeps over the Philippines it was discovered that the enemy in the central Philippines put up very little opposition, and the Filipino guerrillas gave us secret information that the enemy was weak in that area. It was then decided to advance the date of invasion to 20 October, and that the first landing would be on Leyte Island.

The island of Leyte, in the central Philippines is situated about midway between the island of Luzon in the north and the island of Mindanao in the south.

THE BATTLE OF LEYTE, 20 OCTOBER 1944-26 DECEMBER 1944

For the re-conquest of the Philippines, the Central Philippine Attack Force was under the command of Admiral Thomas C. Kinkaid, and was composed of the Seventh Fleet greatly augmented by units of the Pacific Fleet. This large naval force was divided into the Northern Attack Force under command of Admiral Barbey, and the Southern Attack Force under command of Admiral Wilkinson. In addition, there were surface and air cover groups, fire support, bombardment, minesweeping and supply groups. The Attack Force comprised a total of more than 650 ships, including battleships, cruisers, destroyers, destroyer escorts, escort carriers, transports, cargo ships, landing craft, mine craft, and supply vessels. The mission of this Attack Force was to prepare the way and land four Army divisions on D-day.

The Third Fleet under command of Admiral Halsey was given the mission of covering and supporting the landing operations by long range air strikes at the enemy over Formosa, Luzon and the Visayas, and to protect the invasion forces from the Japanese Fleet that might be in hiding awaiting a favorable moment to attack.

For eleven days, 9-20 October 1944, preparatory flights and strikes were made in order to destroy enemy air and surface strength wherever found. A cruiser-destroyer task group bombarded Marcus Island on 9 October and damaged enemy installations. At the same time ships of another fast carrier force were approaching the Nansei Shoto (Ryukyu Islands) destroying enemy search and observation planes and picket boats so that our heavy forces might achieve a tactical surprise in the landing operation. Carrier aircraft attacked Okinawa Island in the Nansei Shoto on 10 October, where the Japanese were taken by surprise and many of their ships were sunk and airfields damaged. Then came on 12-13 October an attack on Formosa and the Pescadores, where we found important air facilities, factories, warehouses, wharves, and much coastal shipping. Here we met stiff resistance. A large number of enemy planes opposed us and anti-aircraft fire was intense. In spite of this opposition, on the first day we shot down 193 enemy planes and 123 more were destroyed on the ground. On 13 October an enemy air force damaged two of our cruisers, but they were taken in tow and returned safely to base for repairs.

For six days from 14 to 20 October our carriers launched repeated fighter sweeps over Formosa, northern Luzon and the central Philippines, destroying or neutralizing as much as possible every fragment of enemy power that might interfere with our plans for landing on Leyte. Even on 20 October, the day of the landing, while some of our fast carriers furnished direct support to the landing operations, other fast carrier forces were conducting long range searches for units of the enemy fleet. In this way, the enemy power to prevent our initial assault on Leyte was neutralized.

The American pre-invasion air attacks on enemy installations in the Philippines were far more successful than was at first thought. After we had recaptured most of the islands in the Philippine Archipelago, General George C. Kenney, commander of the Far East Air Force declared that wrecks of nearly 3000 Japanese planes littered the airfields of the Philippines.

This explains why our initial landings were not so difficult as they might otherwise have been.

LEYTE LANDINGS

During the nine days of clearing the way referred to above, our forces were assembling in the area, coming from all parts of this Pacific. For three days prior to the landing, the eastern entrance to Leyte Gulf had been secured; approach channels and landing beaches cleared of mines and reconnaissance of the main beaches had been made.

Troops of the X Corps and the XXIV Corps were landed on schedule on 20 October 1944. The landings were made without difficulty and were in every way successful.

Damages to our ships in these initial operations were as follows: *YMS 70* was sunk in a storm, and tug *Sonoma* and *LCI (L) 1065* was sunk by enemy action. On the 19th the destroyer *Ross* struck a mine and the light cruiser *Honolulu* was seriously damaged on the 20th by an aerial torpedo.

The Navy had convoyed and landed American troops on Leyte. Now the Navy was to protect our rapidly expanding beachheads from attack by sea and air in the Battle for Leyte Gulf, on 23 October, the Battle of Surigao Strait, on 25 October, the Battle off Samar, on 26 October, and the Battle off Cape Engano, on 24-25 October 1944.

AMERICA RETURNS TO THE PHILIPPINES

On 20 October 1944, General Douglas MacArthur waded ashore on Leyte in the Philippines, accompanied by President Sergio Osmena of the Philippine Commonwealth. On the road back to the Philippines, MacArthur as head of the Southwest Pacific Command had relentlessly yet patiently fought his way through 2500 miles of land and water from Milne Bay in southern New Guinea.

On 17 March 1942, two years and seven months and nine days before, he had landed in Australia under orders from the President of the United States to organize and command a counteroffensive. When MacArthur left Corregidor in early March 1942 he left a message for the Filipino people, "I shall return." Now on 20 October 1944, stepping on shore at Leyte he issued a challenge to the Filipino people: "I have returned. Rally to me. Let the indomitable spirit of Bataan and Corregidor lead on!"

The United States Sixth Army had been given the task of invading, re-conquering and occupying the Philippines. It consisted of the X Corps under command of General Franklin C. Sibert and the XXIV Corps under command of General John R. Hodge. The Army troops as well as Admiral Thomas C. Kinkaid's U.S. Seventh Fleet were under the direct control of General MacArthur, while Admiral Halsey's Third Fleet operated in direct support. The landing on Leyte had been prepared for by the heaviest concentration of air and naval power yet seen in the Western Pacific.

After the Navy's preparatory bombardment, the X Corps consisting of the 24th Infantry Division and the 1st Cavalry Division, landed south of Tacloban. The XXIV Corps consisting of the 7th and 96th Infantry Divisions, landed near Dulag. Beachheads were secured, deepened and widened.

Our troops pushed inland against rather light opposition from the Japanese 16th Division. The Americans captured Dulag on 21 October and Tacloban with its airfield on 22 October 1944, and now that the Leyte plain was in our possession, it looked for the moment as though the conquest of Leyte was near at hand. But the Japanese high command, realizing the importance to them of the Philippines, determined to reinforce the Leyte garrison. As a result a long drawn out battle for control ensued.

Then the rains began to fall in torrents. Tanks bogged down in deep mud, just as the Japanese were reinforced and became more menacing.

Additional American units were called into the battle of Leyte: the 32nd Infantry Division, the 77th and 37th Infantry Divisions, the Americal Division, the 11th Airborne Division, the 112th Cavalry Regimental Combat Team, the 503rd Parachute Infantry Regiment, the 20th Armored Group, and the 1st Filipino Infantry.

The Japanese were all driven from southern and northeastern Leyte by 30 October 1944, with an estimated loss of 24,000 men. Still not willing to relinquish control of the island, the Japanese high command sent in additional troops as follows: the Japanese 34th Army consisting of the 1st, 30th and 102nd Divisions under command of General Tomoyuki Yamashita. In addition, new Japanese planes were brought into the fight from neighboring islands. Suicide attacks were made on American shipping in Leyte Gulf on 14 November-7 December. Japanese paratroopers were landed near American airstrips at Tacloban in an attempt to destroy our planes and interrupt our air operations.

The American troops had tough going, and against such strong opposition, slow progress was made.

On 6-7 December the 77th Division executed an amphibious operation by landing three miles south of Ormoc, an operation which must have startled the enemy, for the Japanese attempted to bring in several transports into Ormoc Bay at the same time the Americans were landing on the shores of the bay. Six Japanese transports loaded with troops and supplies were sunk by our protecting force, and three additional transports were sunk northwest of Leyte the following day.

On 11 December the 77th Division captured Ormoc and made a junction with the 7th Division which had captured Albuera on the 10th. The 77th captured Cogon on 16 December and occupied Valencia on 19 December. The 1st Cavalry Division captured Kananga on 20 December.

Organized resistance on Leyte was declared at an end on 26 December 1944, but mopping-up operations continued for many weeks.

The Japanese losses in Leyte are estimated to have been 54,833 killed and 493 taken prisoner.

The American losses were 2,623 killed in action, 8,422 wounded, and 172 missing.

EXTENDING OUR FOOTHOLD

During the progress of the fighting on Leyte, our forces whenever opportunity afforded, crossed over narrow straits to invade neighboring islands. A combat team of the XXIV Corps landed on Panaon Island just south of Leyte.

Troops of the 1st Cavalry Division invaded Samar Island and secured solid beachheads on both sides of San Juanico Strait on 30 October 1944. The island of Samar had no enemy garrison, and its occupation was accomplished with comparative ease and there we found a well organized army of Filipino guerrillas ready and waiting to join with us in the fight against the common enemy.

On 15 December the Americans made a landing on Mindora Island, some two hundred miles northwest of Leyte, and in easy striking distance of Manila Bay and the island of Luzon.

THE SECOND BATTLE OF THE PHILIPPINE SEA

The landing of the Americans on Leyte brought the crucial moment in Japanese history. It presented a challenge that could not be ignored. Japanese leaders had long insisted that possession of the Philippines was absolutely necessary for the perfect victory they hoped to achieve in their East Asia Co-Prosperity Sphere. So the landing of the Americans brought the challenge: it was a case of fight now or never. On 23 October 1944 the Japanese Fleet came out from hiding and steamed forth into the jaws of death.

The advance of the Japanese Fleet brought on three naval engagements which taken together may be spoken of as the Second Battle of the Philippine Sea, although each was an important battle in itself. The Japanese Fleet moved out in three columns, southern and central and northern, and the three battles occurred almost simultaneously. As early as 23 October American planes and submarines had warned of the approach of the enemy fleet. The submarines *Darter* and *Dace* sank two heavy cruisers and our air force damaged two additional.

THE BATTLE OF SURIGAO STRAIT

Surigao Strait lies between Leyte Island and the northern tip of the island of Mindanao, lying to the south. In the early morning hours of 25 October 1944, the enemy's southern naval force, consisting of two battleships, one heavy cruiser and four destroyers, entered Surigao Strait. Admiral J. B. Oldendorff, in tactical command of the U.S. Seventh Fleet units so deployed his strength that the enemy was struck first by our PT boats, then by destroyer torpedo attacks, and finally by our heavy cruisers and battleships. This was what is known as "crossing the enemy's T," an expression with which Navy men are familiar. Before the Japanese fleet could extricate itself from this trap, it lost two battleships and three destroyers. The remaining heavy cruiser was sunk by our planes on the following day. Thus the entire Japanese southern force was annihilated, while the U.S. Seventh Fleet sustained damage to only one ship, the destroyer *Albert W. Grant* by enemy gunfire.

THE BATTLE OFF SAMAR

The central force of the Japanese Fleet headed eastward out of the China Sea for the Strait of San Bernardino lying between the northern tip of Samar Island and the extreme southern end of the island of Luzon. The enemy's central force consisted of five battleships, eight cruisers, and thirteen destroyers. While it was approaching its destination, it was encountered by U.S. Third Fleet carrier planes in the Strait of Mindoro, far to the west of Leyte. These attacks sank the new Japanese battleship *Musashi*, one cruiser and one destroyer, besides damaging other units. When the enemy fleet, still pursuing its eastward course, reached the coast of Samar, it had only four battleships, five cruisers, and eleven destroyers.

This still powerful enemy fleet struck a group of six American escort carriers, three destroyers and four destroyer escorts under command of Admiral C. A. F. Sprague. Our air force sank one enemy heavy cruiser and one destroyer, but in the surface engagement which followed the U.S. escort carrier *Gambier Bay*, the destroyers *Hoel* and *Johnston* and the destroyer escort *Roberts* were sunk by enemy gunfire. The escort carriers *Suwannee*, *Santee*, *White Plains*, and *Kitkun Bay* were damaged. And on the morning of 25 October enemy kamikazes sank the escort carrier *Saint Lo*.

The Battle off Samar had a strange ending. The strong Japanese force after pounding a comparatively weak American force, suddenly broke off the engagement and retired through San Bernardino Strait, leaving the American transport fleet in Leyte Gulf unscathed. Planes from Admiral Sprague's remaining carriers and planes from the Third Fleet pursued the enemy and sank two additional enemy cruisers and one destroyer, while our battleships sank one cruiser, on 26 October 1944.

A Doctor in Bataan

by Lt. Col. Ralph W. Hubbard, Medical Corps, U.S. Army

First published in 1949

THE following is an eyewitness account of Dr. Ralph W. Hubbard of Oklahoma City, of whom *Time Magazine*, for 12 February 1945, spoke as one of the "Heroes from the Grave." Colonel Hubbard tells us in vivid language of his experiences on Bataan and of his three and one-half years in a Japanese prison camp.

The entire story of the ill-fated force of American troops in the Philippines at the outbreak of the war cannot be told from the viewpoint of one of the members of that force. This statement is made from the observation of a medical officer who served in that force. The story is necessarily a chronicle of his personal experiences and the conclusions that he was able to draw. It is not an official document from the viewpoint of the military authorities of this country, and it is not substantiated by proof in the legal sense.

*

Oklahoma was represented by five hundred to nine hundred men who were in the Philippines at the outbreak of the war. These figures are broad and not specific because at the present time an official list of the Oklahoma citizens has not been released. An unofficial roster prepared by the writer and Major W. R. McNeil of Oklahoma City while we were prisoners of war is the only evidence we have of the exact number. Our figures of those who survived the ordeal are also similarly vague. As near as we can determine, about two hundred have returned to this country since the termination of the war.

We in the Philippines were a small outpost in the front yard of a major Asiatic power. Our total forces, excepting 26,000 Americans, consisted of less than 60,000 members of the Philippine Army. This army was untrained and ill-equipped. It had not been inducted by the time the war began. Our total air force consisted of some 250 planes of all descriptions—a few modern airplanes and the others either observation planes or obsolete bombers and fighters. Our supplies were inadequate in all respects. Much of our ammunition and weapons dated

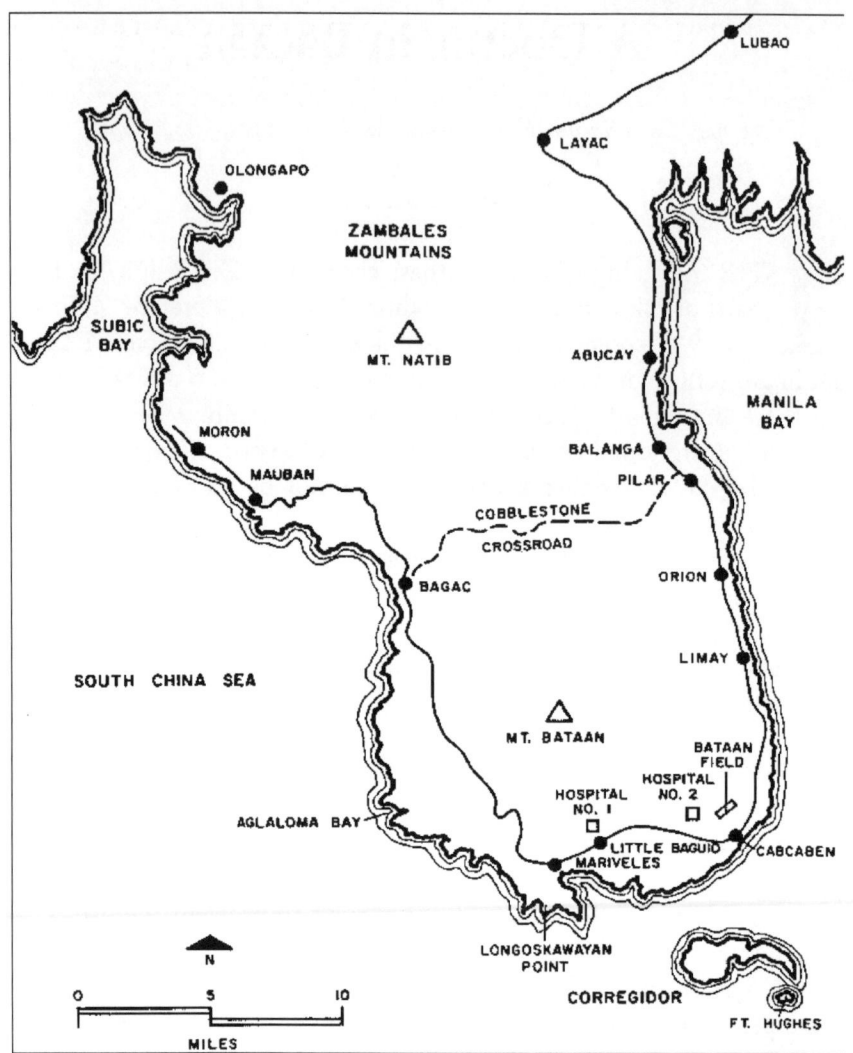

from 1917 and 1918, and many of the weapons we were forced to use had been in the Philippines since the Insurrection in 1902.

I was stationed at Sternborg General Hospital in Manila at the beginning of the war. It was an old wooden structure built in the sixteenth century by the Spanish and maintained by the American forces throughout our occupation, more as a historical landmark than as a modern hospital. Many of our troops were housed in such buildings, and training facilities were not of the most modern character. This was in line with the policy that the outpost in the Philippines was a token force—a token of the commitment that the U.S. had made in the Far

East. We have no criticism for any person or any department of this government for the sacrifice of this outpost, but the catastrophe overtaking the forces in the Philippines is the ultimate conclusion of a policy which commits a nation to certain responsibilities and at the same time fails to provide for the enforcement of these commitments. The people of the United States are peaceful in their attitude and have always avoided entangling themselves in the affairs of others. During the years preceding the war we overlooked the storm clouds of Europe and Asia and went blissfully about our business of solving our own personal problems and our domestic economy without looking at the dangers from overseas.

We were notified in the early morning hours of 8 December of the attack on Pearl Harbor, and immediately began our preparations that had been planned in advance. Our units started out to their assigned positions in the field, our air force was alerted, and we were placed upon a war basis as rapidly as possible. This fact was completed in a miraculously short time. To us who were immediately involved, it was a period of heartache and worry, because things seemed to us terribly slow and chaotic... The sudden change from a life of peaceful living to war. Alertness is of such magnitude that the uninitiated cannot comprehend the problems involved.

Our medical plans in Manila called for the establishment of a hospital center of three thousand beds and more. We had made arrangements with various schools and buildings in Manila to use them as hospital annexes. The morning of the 8th was spent in a feverish and very hurried effort to accomplish this task in the least possible time. It seemed that the problems of the world had fallen upon our shoulders at one moment, and everything had to be accomplished at once with only a few available to do the work.

I was called out that afternoon to Fort Stotsenburg to care for the casualties inflicted by the Japanese air raid on Clark Field. The Japanese were able to put so many thousand airplanes in our skies at once that our air warning system was completely befuddled. We were unable to tell whether they were American or foreign planes, and as a final result our pitifully small air force was destroyed during the first two days of the war. Air attacks produced so many casualties at once that no medical force was large enough to care for the casualties as they came in. Accordingly, the first week of the war was one of an intense effort by the medical department, fighting against time. We had casualties from Clark Field, Iba Field, Cavite Naval Base, Nichols Field, all pouring in during the first three days of the war, and it took about a week of serious and sustained effort to get things under control and discover the course of the war.

It was soon apparent that it was impossible to defend the Philippines from attack. There were over seven thousand islands with many possible landing places, and our small force could not hope to defend them all. The enemy, having the choice of attack, could concentrate his forces at will, being able thereby to pile up an overwhelming force against the thin cordon of defense we could throw around these landing places. It was thus apparent that the only thing possible was a delaying action. We were to hold as many Japanese forces and as much Japanese equipment as possible in the Philippines to prevent them from being used elsewhere. We were to force the enemy to expend as much material and as many men as possible in order to diminish his power to attack in the south. We reverted to the "Orange Plan," calling for a last stand on the Bataan Peninsula.

Bataan is a peninsula forming the northern arm of Manila Bay, and together with the fortified islands of Corregidor, Fort Drum, Fort Wint and Fort Frank, was to prevent the enemy from entering Manila Bay. Bataan was an ideal defensive position from a geographical standpoint. It was mountainous with heavy jungles, and chains of mountains ran east and west which forced the enemy to go over one chain after another in their forward movement. We had several defensive lines planned which afforded us observation of the enemy though we had no air force to carry out aerial observation. By a miracle of military strategy and the personal heroism of the units in the field, particularly Philippine Scouts and the 31st Infantry Regiment, the Japanese were held in the north until all of our forces reached Bataan. During all of this time, the Japanese had a field day from the air. There was hell from the skies day and night, and we were unable to fight back with the exception of a small amount of anti-aircraft, which was entirely insufficient to accomplish the desired result. The Japanese were over us day and night, observation planes flying around without any opposition, bombers releasing their bombs at random and at will, and the futility experienced by us is something that we will never forget as long as we live.

Manila was declared an open city on 24 December 1941, and all of our forces left in order to prevent the destruction of this historical and beautiful city. I was ordered from Manila to Corregidor and was made chief of the Surgical Service in the tunnel hospital at Fort Mills. This tunnel had been built in 1932, but had not yet been made ready for occupancy. By working our men day and night we got everything ready and our supplies in order, so that when the first major bombing of Corregidor occurred on the 29ᵗʰ of December, we were ready for it.

On the 29ᵗʰ, about noon, the Japanese came to Corregidor. We had clouds overhanging the island, and the Japanese were able to come in from the edge of the clouds and drop their bombs before our anti-aircraft could get them under observation. This attack lasted a little over three hours, and it was full evidence that our 1918 plans of defense had not taken into consideration war from the air. This attack did not produce any serious military damage but certainly gave us a forewarning of our fate.

After arranging things in this hospital, and after this bombing had occurred, I was transferred to Bataan where I worked in General Hospital No. 2. This hospital had no buildings. It was completely open-air, and consisted of about a mile of jungle on both sides of a small mountain stream. It was in a valley, which made it safe from air observation, but also made it difficult to get in or out with patients. All movements had to be made after dark and without lights because of the constant aerial activity of the Japanese. I remained at this hospital until 2 March 1942. During this time our forward lines made two movements toward the rear, and we reached the last ditch line between Orion and Bagac, knowing that from this point there could be no retreat. By this time it was very evident that an army remaining in Bataan very long would be destroyed. Geographically it was a good defensive position, but the diseases of Bataan had defied the efforts of industry and agriculture during all the history of the islands. Amebic dysentery and malaria were prevalent through almost the entire peninsula, and our troops rapidly sickened and died from the effects of these diseases.

Adding to our problem of being in a disease-ridden area, we were practically without medicine and without food. We were placed on a two-meal-a-day schedule on the 1ˢᵗ of January, 1942, and those two meals consisted of a small amount of rice with infinitesimal amounts of salmon or sardines or corn-beef and occasionally a very small amount of sugar and canned milk. Our ration dropped from approximately 2,500 calories in the early part of January to 900 calories during the month of March 1942. On this starvation diet, our forces were carrying on a war in the jungle. Their movements were made on foot because of lack of transportation and fuel. The fox holes and trenches and the gun emplacements were all built by starving men. There were no post exchanges, no Red Cross, no place for relaxation. There were no soft drinks, no cigarettes, no candy—no relief from front line duty. Our ammunition was old, cartridges would fail to fire, grenades would fail to explode. Army Ordnance did everything it could to remedy this situation, but it was beyond the power of humans to solve at the time.

On 2 March 1942, I was transferred from General Hospital No. 2 to command a collecting company which was serving the so-called Provisional Air Corps Regiment. We had not the forces to defend our short front line on this, our last-ditch defense. The regiment we served was composed entirely of air force personnel who learned infantry tactics in actual combat. The company under my command had been detached from the Philippine Army and assigned to this infantry regiment. While there were many serious problems involved in this new assignment and many insurmountable obstacles, I considered it a privilege and an honor to be able to serve in this forward position, and learn first-hand the true facts of human conduct under fire. I discovered that our troops, both Filipino and American, although starved, sick, and discouraged, were filled with an indomitable courage and a willingness to die for a cause.

When the Japanese overwhelmed us on 9 April 1942, they overwhelmed a sick, starved remnant of what had once been free citizens of the United States and the Commonwealth of the Philippines. We could realize that General King made the only possible choice in surrendering Bataan, but I personally witnessed many brave and strong men break into tears over the humiliation of surrendering to the Japanese, the all-despised and distrusted.

The Japanese can not take any honor for having overwhelmed us in Bataan. They lost many thousands of troops. They expended many airplanes. They had every advantage of modern warfare, but they could not break the heroic will and courage of the defenders of Bataan until sickness and starvation had overtaken and defeated them.

This is not a criticism of the size of our force. Were we to have had more divisions in the Philippines, a larger number of men would have been lost. The entire problem was a lack of supply lines and reinforcements for our troops, and the Japanese controlled the entire Pacific Ocean immediately after Pearl Harbor.

The Japanese attack beginning on 3 April 1942 pulverized our forward area by artillery and aerial bombardment and massing of troops. Our sick and starved forces were cut to pieces during the first two or three days, and when our lines finally broke there was nothing between the Japanese and southern tip of Bataan except disorganized, sick, weak and dying soldiers. Malaria, dysentery, beriberi, scurvy, and general starvation had decimated our forces until we could no longer resist.

Thus, Bataan surrendered on 9 April 1942 and closed a chapter of a heroic defense of an untenable position. When the forward lines collapsed, I led my company back to Hospital No. 2, where we found over six thousand patients in a hospital planned for one thousand patients. Our duties were clear-cut; although we had no organization to support, no commitments to remain in Bataan, none of us desired to go to Corregidor or make an attempt to escape. We all went to work caring for the wounded and the sick in Hospital No. 2. We were there at the time the Japanese came in and officially took over the hospital.

On 9 April 1942, we were free men. Sick, starved, beaten to be sure, but still maintaining the dignity of the individual as a member of the human race. One day thereafter, we were forced to begin our adjustment to a period of slavery where the individual had no rights, no privileges, no honor; and we were driven and cajoled, threatened and beaten by the lowest members of the Japanese Army. The indoctrination was simple. General Homma had expended so many of his forces and so many of his supplies in order to capture a handful of Americans that he was humiliated. Because of his humiliation in the eyes of his government, he vented his spleen upon the Americans and the Filipinos whom he had been fortunate enough to capture, by reason of our weakness and sickness.

The first things done by the Japanese were to take away from us all of our clothing, our medical supplies, our food, and to deny us the rights of existence as prisoners of war. The march from Bataan to Camp O'Donnell will long be known as a peak of brutality, baseness, and dishonor on the part of the Japanese. After having deprived the individual Americans of canteens, head coverings, mess kits and personal possessions, the Japanese forced them to march twenty hours out of the twenty-four, in the broiling sun on the plains of Luzon, during the hot season, without being fed, and subjected to all forms of brutality. Those who were sick and disabled and were not physically capable of continuing the march were killed without ceremony by the Japanese. The rest periods were taken in open rice paddies in the broiling sun, in front of Japanese artillery positions. The Japanese would take this time to fire at Corregidor expecting the return fire to kill Americans, and it did.

During the six weeks the American forces remained at Camp O'Donnell, 1,500 men lost their lives from starvation and disease. The Japanese punishment for moderate infractions of discipline, including escape and fictitious charges of escape, was execution. Each execution was preceded by a minimum of forty-eight hours of some form of physical torture. The victims of this practice were invariably happy and anxious to face the firing squad in order to end their misery.

I remained at Hospital No. 2 during this march and missed the ordeals of that sad chapter of our history. The Japanese came into our hospital and removed our food and medical supplies, but kept us in our area while they pursued their activities against Corregidor. They placed their artillery upon all sides of our hospital, used our main road through the hospital as a military highway, and started their operations. It was necessary for Corregidor to fire back, and although the Americans on Corregidor did not know whether or not we had been removed, they could not remain defenseless and were forced to fire in the immediate vicinity of the hospital. Due to their impeccable marksmanship and ability in directing fire, there were very few casualties inflicted upon Americans in our hospital area.

Of the 6,600 patients in No. 2 Hospital at the surrender of Bataan, about 4,500 were Filipinos. The Japanese ordered us to release them, stating that they were being allowed to return home, and that the Philippine Army was being disbanded. These patients left the hospital in droves; there were so many that we could not control them, and hundreds of Filipinos left the hospital with malaria, with dysentery, with fractures, with amputations. Men were on crutches and had their arms and legs in casts. When they reached the highway, the Japanese ordered them into line and marched them to the infamous camp at O'Donnell. I saw the bodies of many of our patients who failed to make the march. And in the Filipino camp at O'Donnell, where the Filipinos were segregated from the Americans, more than thirty thousand lost their lives before February of 1943. That is more than half of the original force of the Philippine Army that died because of the Japanese brutality and revenge.

On the first day of June 1942, No. 2 Hospital was transferred to Cabanatuan, about forty miles north of Manila and toward the east side of the island. It was in the middle of the plains and rice paddy section of the island of Luzon, and one of the great rice producing areas of the island. The rainy season had just begun. Mud and rain were with us night and day. The area in which we moved had been built primarily as a training ground for the Philippine Army by the U.S. government but had not been completed. Sanitary facilities were absent. The buildings were of bamboo and so-called sewalli, which is a split vine similar to bamboo, and of which walls are woven in the manner of basket weaving. These buildings had been planned for forty Filipinos by our Army. When the Japanese ordered us into this area, 100 to 125 large

Americans were crowded into the area originally planned for forty small Filipinos. The floors were made of split bamboo, that is slats of bamboo, and we were forced to sleep upon these floors. No bunks and no beds were allowed.

About the 5th of June 1942, the camp of O'Donnell was evacuated into our camp, and within three or four days five thousand sick and dying Americans were brought in. Water was scarce. We had to stand in line for hours to obtain a canteen of water. We were limited to one canteen of water a day for drinking, washing our dishes, bathing, and toiletry. Food consisted of about three cups of rice gruel and water weeds, which the Japanese called greens, a day. Men were dying at the rate of thirty to fifty a day.

By the middle of June we prevailed upon the Japanese to allow us to segregate a hospital area. We had no medicine with which to treat the illness of these men, and the Japanese were not furnishing us with enough food to nourish them. Segregating the seriously ill and dying men from the rest of the camp was a very important thing toward building morale of the Americans. We established this hospital area about the middle of June, and by the first of July had a hospital population of over 2,300 separated from the rest of the camp. During that month over eight hundred men died from starvation, malaria and dysentery. Many of the patients were hurried to their death because of exposure. The rainy season had started and the wind and rain of the tropics during the rainy season is very, very miserable. It was cold and wet, and about one-third of the men from Camp O'Donnell had not one stitch of clothing nor one single blanket to shelter them from the rain, wind and mud of this particular season. The Japanese commander told us in the hospital each morning at roll call that he didn't care whether the Americans were dead or alive, but he had to have an accurate count. So, each morning before daylight, we who were in charge of the hospital wards had to get out through the tall Cogan grass and under the buildings, look for the bodies of our patients who had crawled away during the night to die, and then pile them up in front of the buildings so that the Japanese officer could count the dead as well as the living to satisfy his requirements for the day.

This condition prevailed during the long rainy season from June until November 1942, and each day brought further oppression and brutality upon the part of the Japanese. About twenty-six men were executed for fictitious causes during this time, and each one was tortured for forty-eight hours preceding. A daily parade of the dead occurred each evening about five o'clock. Four men carrying home-built litters made of wood or bamboo or any kind of scrap available would carry each body out to the cemetery. In the driving rain, wind and mud, this line would start out in the evening, wind its way through the camp and leave toward the south. The men carrying the litters looked scarcely better than the bodies they carried. Many were the times when a man carrying a litter one day would be carried out the next. The situation was hopeless. The Japanese were winning in all of their efforts. America had not started to fight back. We in the medical department had no medicine, no treatment to offer in the face of mass starvation and mass tropical diseases. About five thousand men died by the first of the year.

After General Homma of the Japanese Army had been relieved, conditions began to improve, and in December 1942 we received a shipment of Red Cross supplies which included some medicines, some bulk food and a few personal packages for each man. This stopped the death rate, and during the year of 1943 the death rate had been cut down to only about twenty times the normal rate for men in such a precarious predicament.

We learned during the year of 1943, the mental attitude of the Japanese toward the Americans. They took great delight in humiliating the so-called arrogant, proud Americans. They bragged in their newspapers of making them work as coolies and slaves. They used the prisoners as examples to the Filipinos of the superiority of the Japanese over the Americans. We were not only slaves; we were subjected to the ridicule and the humiliation of every Japanese whether he be a private or a general. The futility and hopelessness of our position was reflected in our death rate, hundreds of men giving up all hope and all desire to live and dying because they refused to eat the stinking rice furnished them. Those who remained to carry on were the unusual and more fortunate individuals who maintained an optimistic attitude. This condition prevailed for thirty-four months for those who remained.

The Philippine Inland Seas Defense Project

by Charles H. Bogart

THE year 1898 found the United States—with the acquisition of the Philippines—joining that select group of nations having colonies in the Far East. Once the Army and Navy had captured the Philippines they set out to develop and implement a plan for its defense. Soon, as a result of recommendations made by the Taft Board on coastal defense, a system of fortifications were built from 1905 to 1914 to defend the entrance to Manila and Subic Bay. With the completion of these fortifications most Naval and Army officers adopted the attitude that the Philippines could be held against any enemy. This attitude was further reinforced during World War I as the U.S. developed its industrial and military might.

The 1920s saw a gradual change in the belief that the U.S. could defend the Philippines against all nations. America, following World War I, demobilized her Army and by treaty abandoned her fleet. Adopting the philosophy that disarmament lessens the chance of war, the U.S. agreed not to update what were now obsolescent fortifications in the Philippines. This obsolescence was due to the advent of airplanes and long-range naval gunfire. As a result of these facts professional naval and military opinion examining the defense of the Philippines brought forth a revised estimate of the ability of the U.S. to hold the islands. The new plan, War Plan Orange 3, now called for the Philippines to hold out for six months while a rescue force was raised Stateside and sailed the 6,800 miles to regain the Philippines.

The decade of the 1930s saw a new military appreciation of the ability to defend the Philippines. Further cuts in the American defense budget coupled with Japan's increased naval and military preparedness led many Army and Navy leaders to doubt if the Philippines could be defended. This was followed in the late 1930s by the philosophy that the Philippines were undefendable and should be abandoned. This philosophy was based on actions of Congress which called for economic re-entrenchment, defense cutbacks, neutrality with a vengeance, and independence for the Philippines on 4 July 1946. In addition, the fact that Japan, only 1,500 miles from the Philippines, possessed an army and navy equal to the United States weighed heavily on some minds.

That Japan possessed an army and navy more than equal to the U.S. was due to the failure of Congress to fund the Army and Navy to full war strength as provided by law and treaty.

As the year 1940 brought with it the fall of France, Norway and the Low Countries, England fighting desperately for her life, China slowly being conquered and Japan, Germany and Italy flexing their military muscles, all but the most optimistic of the American military leaders lent any credence to the thought that the Philippines could hold out against a Japanese military assault until an American fleet arrived to relieve them. It was a foregone conclusion as far as the Army General Staff was concerned that the Philippines were to defend themselves as long as possible, thereby tying down Japanese troops and ships while America mobilized. The U.S. forces in the Philippines sole mission was to deny Manila Bay to the enemy as long as militarily possible and then surrender.

The year 1941, however, saw a complete reversal of the official and unofficial line of the defensibility of the Philippines. That year saw the reinstatement of Gen. Douglas MacArthur back into the U.S. Army by his appointment as commander of U.S. Army troops in the Philippines. Since 1936 MacArthur, who had retired from the U.S. Army, had been serving as military advisor for the Philippine Commonwealth government. During this period he had formed a plan that called for the raising of ten Filipino Army divisions plus an air force and a coast defense navy to defend the islands from an invader. Though the Philippine government had at first wholeheartedly supported the plan, by 1941 most political leaders in the Philippines considered the islands undefendable and had cut the defense budget accordingly. MacArthur, however, refused to consider the islands undefendable.

Once appointed commander of all U.S. Army and Philippine troops, MacArthur began to implement a beachhead resistance plan in place of the existing passive defense of Manila Bay. So active a lobbying campaign did he press for this concept that the War Dept. soon found itself pouring troops and equipment into the Philippines at the expense of other commands. The official policy now was that the Philippines could be defended. Further, USAFFE Headquarters claimed that if the Japanese waited until the summer of 1942 to attack, the islands would by then have been so reinforced that no Japanese attack could succeed.

The plan developed by USAFFE called for the main center of American/Philippine resistance to be located on Luzon. Supplies and reinforcements would be funneled from the other islands to Luzon over the Sibuyan and Visayan Seas. To protect this supply route from attacking Japanese surface ships the channels leading into these "inland seas" from the South China, Subu and Philippine Seas would be fortified by the emplacement of 8-inch and 155-mm guns.

Sometime in 1939 there were shipped to the Philippines seven 6-inch railroad guns and twenty-four 155-mm (GFP) guns. These guns, on arrival, were placed in storage at the Ordnance Depot in Manila. The 8-inch guns were Model M1888 which had originally been mounted Stateside at coastal defense forts. In 1917 some fifty of these guns were uprooted for conversion to railroad guns to provide mobile heavy artillery for the American Army in Europe. The war ended, however, after only three had reached France. The remaining guns were thus retained Stateside as mobile coast artillery guns. Now seven of these guns less their railroad platform cars but still mounted on the M1918 Carriage Barbette were in Manila. Along with the guns had arrived a number of sets of coastal defense fire control gear. Range of the 8-inch gun firing its 240-pound shell was 23,000 yards while range of the 155-mm (GFP) 100-pound shell was 17,000 yards.

Though the guns had arrived in Manila in 1939, few steps were taken to utilize them until July 1941. At that time Capt. Steve Mellnik, serving with the 91st Coast Artillery (PS) was seconded to USAFFE Headquarters. There Col. William Marquat, G-1, after meeting Mellnik pointed to a wall map of the Philippines and said:

Those colored circles represent artillery fields of fire around important channels. About two years ago Washington sent twenty-four 155-mm guns and seven 8-inch railway cannon to seal those channels. But Washington did not provide construction funds, and the cannon are now in a warehouse. USAFFE plans to install those guns. Your job is to convert the circles on the map and the cannon in the warehouse into Philippine Army firing units on the ground! You'll stake out the location of each gun, observation station, and barracks area; requisition the necessary fire control equipment; schedule the induction and training of Filipino personnel, and supervise all elements of the program. We call this the "Inland Seas Defense Project."

Captain Mellnik, commenting later, stated:

I was astounded at the magnitude of the task. A few months indeed—the project would take a year! Dozens of questions leaped to mind. I asked them. Bill's answers were not encouraging. The project consisted of circles on a map, cannon in a warehouse, a Washington promise to provide construction funds, and a Commonwealth commitment to provide manpower on call.

Assigned to work on the project was Maj. Guy Stubbs.[9] Working together the two officers, using field manuals, maps and technical manuals, laid out a work schedule that projected a completion date for the Inland Seas Defense Project of April 1942. Though the gun positions had been located on maps each of the twelve proposed sites would have to be visited on foot to confirm the sites' suitability and to physically lay out the battery. Due to the primitiveness of transportation in the islands and the location of most sites some distance from an urban area it was projected that twelve weeks would be needed just to visit the sites.

While selection of the firing sites was up to Mellnik and Stubbs, who were now assigned to the Philippine Coastal Artillery Command, actual construction was to be overseen by the Philippine Army Engineers under the command of Lt. Col. Max Janairo. To assist the two officers in laying out the sites and starting preliminary design work, Lt. Col. Janairo assigned one of his officers to accompany them on the field reconnaissance.

The positions surveyed, running in a counterclockwise direction from Manila, were located in general terms at: [see map]

1. Cape Santiago on Luzon
2. Mananao on Mindoro
3. Southern tip of Mindoro
4. Semirara Island
5. Caluya Island
6. Pucio Point on Panaya
7. Nampulugan Island
8. Santander on Cebu
9. Panglao on Panglao Island
10. Massin on Leyte
11. Allen on Samar
12. Southern tip of Luzon

---

[9] Major Stubbs, though captured at the fall of Corregidor, survived captivity and testified at the Tokyo War Crimes Trials. He died shortly thereafter.

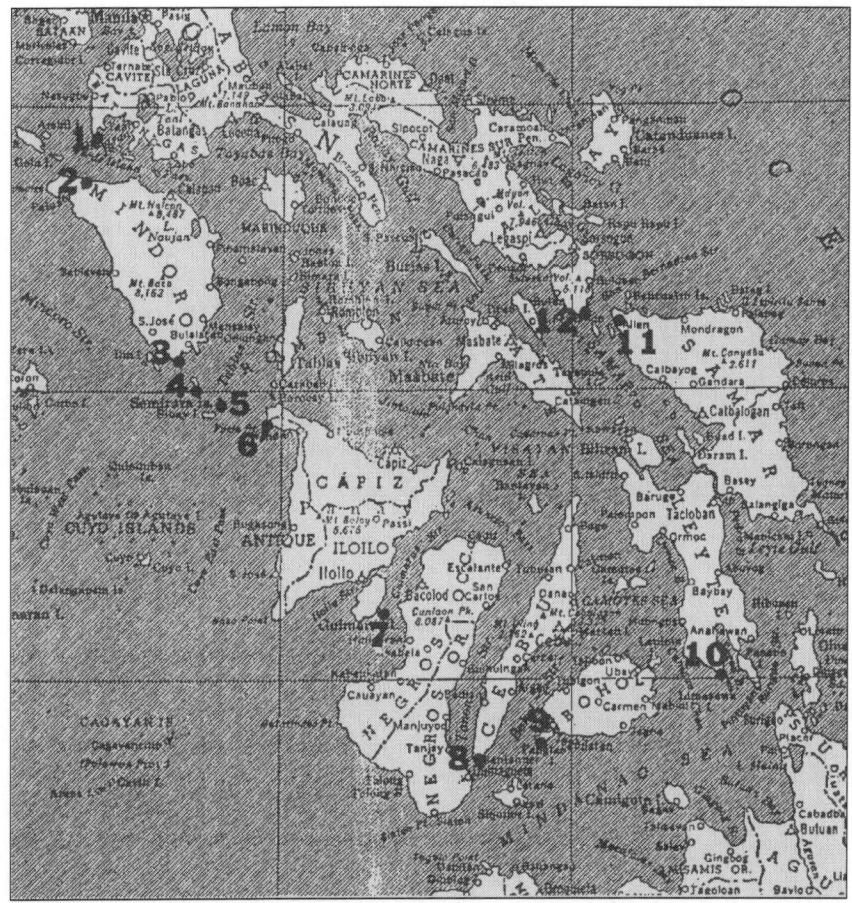

First battery under construction was the 8-inch gun at Cape Santiago.[10] The morning of 8 December saw construction at the 8-inch gun battery having progressed to the stage of being ready for concrete pouring.[11] That day Stubbs and Mellnik inspected the position and authorized pouring of the concrete. This pouring, however, was not to take place because before the day was over the Japanese struck the Philippines. The following day after the two officers had returned to

---

[10] General Mellnik stated in regard to the proposed location of the other 8-inch guns, "Sorry, I do not recall precisely where 8-inch and 155s went. We put 8-inch in places where 155s did not have the reach."

[11] As to the best he can recall, Gen. Mellnik said the batteries were to be constructed by digging a pit and pouring two slabs of concrete to ground level. The guns were mounted "more like barbette. Guns came with own support."

USAFFE Headquarters, Maj. Stubbs was called before Col. Constant Irwin, G-3, to justify continuance of the Inland Seas Defense Project and report on possible completion dates. In response, Stubbs stated, "By cutting corners we can make the first battery operational by mid-February."

Colonel Irwin, after evaluating this information in connection with a study of available manpower, recommended to USAFFE Headquarters that construction be stopped because

> Things are so uncertain, that no one can predict our situation even two weeks from now. And since eleven of the twelve positions are south of Luzon, the enemy can capture them at will! General Sharp's force has only enough small arms ammunition for guerrilla warfare. Let's not spend our limited resources on things we can't hold.

In response to this recommendation, Maj. Gen. Richard Sutherland, MacArthur's chief of staff, ordered "Scrub the project and turn its assets over to Maj. Gen. Edward King," who was in command of the Field Artillery. The twenty-four 155-mm (GFP) were a welcomed long-range addition to King's artillery park. These guns served by Filipino soldiers were to be the backbone of the Field Artillery on Bataan.

Since the 8-inch guns lacked mobility, Stubbs was ordered to destroy five of them and transfer the other two to the Manila Bay Harbor Defense Command. One of the guns was sent to Corregidor and the other to the west coast of Bataan. Due to the rugged terrain of Bataan the only position Stubbs and Mellnik could locate in the short period allowed was near Bagac. This position, half-way up the west coast of Bataan, near the proposed Rear Battle Position, would have provided a seaward defense against any Japanese ship trying to bombard Bataan's west coast and add a punch to I Corps artillery support.

The fate of the Bataan 8-inch gun is uncertain. It is claimed that this gun was destroyed after being mounted by enemy action, or destroyed by American troops when they fell back to the Bagac–Orion line on 26 January 1942. Since only six weeks had passed since orders had been issued to mount the guns, Mellnik states that he doubts that it was mounted as the engineer troops were spread thin and their major concern was building the main line of resistance between Mauban and Mabatang on Bataan.

The 8-inch gun sent to Corregidor "was mounted on a prepared concrete base near RJ43 east of Malinta Hill—and [had] all-round fire except to the west which was screened by Malinta Hill." This gun was proof fired on 4 March 1942 and passed all stability tests. Though now ready for combat use, the gun was never again fired as the troops that were to man it were never evacuated from Bataan. This gun was later destroyed by the American troops on Corregidor before they surrendered.

As far as can be determined only a few of the twenty-four 155-mm guns sent to Bataan fell into Japanese hands in working order. Most were destroyed by enemy action or by their crews before surrendering. Thus ended the Inland Seas Defense Project. Yet a number of questions remain to be answered. When and by whom was the Inland Seas Defense Project originally conceived?[12] Were the guns originally sent to the Philippines for carrying out the Inland Seas Defense Project or were they sent for some other reason? Were the 155-mm guns used to arm Forts Mills, Frank and Hughes in 1941 also drawn from this source?[13] To whom did the guns belong, the American or Philippine Army? Who was to have manned the Inland Seas Defense Project, as not enough existed to man all the existing coast defense batteries at Manila Bay?[14] Who authorized sending these guns? How effective would they have been?

SOURCES

This article is based primarily on General Steve Mellnik's book, *Philippine Diary*, a conversation with him, an exchange of letters, and a review of this article by him. All quotes in the text are from his book.

---

[12] General Mellnik, in regard to this question, stated "I doubt if the Inland Seas Defense Project was ever conceived by anyone. Most likely MacArthur's office (1936) asked the War Dept. to ship some cannon to the Philippine Islands to seal off the Inland Seas eventually. Colonel Marquat was on that [MacArthur's] mission and was a Coast Artilleryman so the idea was a logical one for him to develop. However, the material had to be available before anything else. Obviously, neither Washington nor Manila was willing to spend the money to make the guns operable."

[13] General Mellnik stated that as far as he knew "the 155s used on Corregidor came from the U.S. but were not part of the Inland Seas Defense Project shipment."

[14] General Mellnik stated that he understood "... Philippine Army troops were to be included to man artillery of ISDP."

Corregidor

An Airborne Assault

by Charles E. Heller

DURING World War II a significant number of the airborne assaults that were attempted either failed entirely or did not justify the high percentage of casualties that resulted from them. A few of them, however, did achieve varying degrees of success. The most successful, and perhaps the most spectacular airborne combat assault of the global conflict, occurred during the latter stages of the war in the Pacific on the island of Corregidor.

SITUATION

On 9 January 1945, elements of the Sixth U.S. Army landed at the Lingayen Gulf in the north of Luzon, the major island in the Philippine chain. These landings were followed by secondary amphibious assaults on the east coast of Luzon, above the Bataan Peninsula at San Antonio, and south of the entrance to Manila Bay, at Nasugbu. By the end of January the capture of Manila had become crucial because the engineers could not construct enough port facilities at the Lingayen Gulf.

The Japanese forces in the city had received orders from General Tomoyuki Yamashita to abandon it, but Admiral Sanji Iwabuchi, commander of the Manila Defense Force, had disobeyed. As a consequence, Sixth Army units encountered stiff resistance in the city and found Japanese garrisons still manning the harbor fortifications.

Corregidor, known since pre-war days as the "Rock," held no value for the Japanese in their defense plans, but until it could be neutralized it posed a threat to any Allied shipping that might try to enter Manila Bay. Well before the invasion of Luzon, the Sixth Army commander, General Walter Krueger, and his G3 section had considered the possibility of capturing the island. As a result, when General Douglas MacArthur informed General Krueger of his desire to take Corregidor by amphibious or airborne assault or by a combination of the two, it took General Krueger's G3 section only two days to come up with a plan. It was to be conducted by elements of the Sixth Army, code named Rock Force.

ROCK FORCE

The 503rd Regimental Combat Team (Parachute), supported by elements from the 462nd Parachute Field Artillery Battalion and a company from the 161st Airborne Engineer Battalion, would make a parachute assault. An amphibious assault would be conducted by the 3rd Battalion, 34th Infantry, and by the 151st Regimental Combat Team (RCT). Aircraft of the 317th Troop Carrier Command would transport the airborne forces while the 592nd Engineer Boat and Shore Regiment would be responsible for landing the infantry.

This force, the planners believed, would be adequate to deal with the Japanese garrison on Corregidor, which they estimated at no more than 850 to 1,000 men. This turned out to be a significant intelligence error; there were in fact more than 5,000 Japanese on the island under the command of Naval Captain Akira Itagaki.

To the planners, the island of Corregidor resembled a tadpole with an oversized head facing east out of the bay. The widest point measured one and a half miles. The end abruptly narrowed to a softly curving tail. The total length of the island was about three and a half miles. The head—except for three steep ravines which led to the sea—had cliffs that plunged to the narrow beaches from heights of four to five hundred feet. This part of the island, known as Topside, had a relatively flat surface.

The bombed-out shells of the buildings and gun emplacements that had been built and occupied by U.S. forces before the war marred the island's surface, and amid the rubble were splintered trees and bomb craters. The only areas that were moderately clear of debris were an old parade ground and a golf course. The parade ground was only 325 yards long and 250 yards wide, while the golf course was 350 yards long and 185 yards at its widest.

At the neck of the tadpole, called Middleside, steep slopes led to a saddle, some five hundred yards wide and about one hundred yards above sea level. This area, Bottomside, contained the ruins of a small village, San Jose, as well as docking facilities on the nearby beaches. Black Beach, on which the amphibious landing would be made, was to the south. Malinta Hill with its pre-war tunnels was west of the saddle. Then, from Malinta, the terrain gradually sloped to the tip of the island not more than 150 yards above the sea. A single-strip airfield occupied a portion of the wooded terrain at the tip.

The planners wanted to use airborne forces to obtain surprise, so they made two assumptions: The Japanese, having taken the Rock themselves by an amphibious assault in 1942, would not expect an airborne invasion; and the enemy, scanning the sea approaches from underground bunkers, probably would be distracted by the approach of the amphibious assault forces and would not see the paratroopers in time to react to them.

The selection of drop zones thus became of primary importance. Colonel George M. Jones, who commanded the 503rd Regimental Combat Team, after making an aerial reconnaissance, recommended Kindley Field, a small landing strip at the tail of the tadpole. Because of the rugged terrain and the debris and ruins on the rest of the Rock, he believed a jump anywhere else would cause a high percentage of injuries, enough to render his force ineffective. General Krueger, however, vetoed the suggestion, explaining that a drop on Kindley Field would not secure key terrain. Besides, troops dropping there would draw as much fire as if they had come from the sea. (In 1942, when the Japanese had landed by sea in this area they had suffered many casualties.)

The only other way to achieve surprise, therefore, was to land the troops on Topside. But steep cliffs to the south and west bordered the area, and a strong or shifting wind could bring the paratroopers onto the cliffs or into the sea below. The advantages of a landing on Topside outweighed the disadvantages, though, and the parade ground was designated Drop Zone "A" and the golf course, Drop Zone "B."

The troops of the first serial were to secure and hold both drop zones in preparation for the second lift. With the additional troops they would then clear Topside, provide covering fire for the amphibious assault, and then establish contact with the 3rd Battalion, 34th Infantry. The entire force would then conduct mopping up operations.

MAIN AIRBORNE ASSAULT

At 0700 on 16 February the C-47s of the 317th Troop Carrier Command rose from airfields on Mindoro, circled, and then headed in a wide westerly sweep north to Corregidor. A half-hour later a second flight followed bringing the total to fifty-one aircraft. At 0830 the first wave of aircraft was ordered to proceed with the drop.

Two columns of C-47s, one for each drop zone, flew on a course from southwest to northeast, and the 'V' formation used in the flight from Mindoro broke into an "in trail" formation. Aircraft trailed six hundred feet apart at a speed of one hundred miles per hour, flying 650 feet above Topside. Given that speed, each aircraft had only ten seconds over its designated drop zone, a time that did not allow all of the troopers to exit in one pass. This meant that each plane had to make three passes, releasing a stick of six to eight men each time.

Because of the prevailing winds over the bay the jumpers could not use a prearranged "go" count when the green light flashed on. Instead, the pilots counted seconds after passing the "go" point. This became especially necessary when the wind speed increased. Also, since the approach headed into the wind, an increased count allowed the troopers to drift back onto the drop zones instead of falling short onto the cliffs or into the bay. Accordingly, the jumpmasters paid attention to the green "go" light and not to the drop zone below. A verbal warning indicated ten minutes from the objective, and when the aircraft was three minutes out the red light went on.

As the first stick of chutes blossomed from the doors, the command aircraft noted that the twelve-knot wind from the north-northeast was causing the troopers to drift short of the "go" points and onto the cliffs. As planned, the pilots increased the count, first to six and then to ten seconds after the "go" point. As a consequence, troopers left the aircraft past the drop zone. The pilots, concerned about getting their troopers within the drop zone, cut their airspeed from one hundred miles per hour to eighty-five and dropped from a height of 650 to 500 feet above Topside. According to the pilots, jump discipline, except in one or two cases, was excellent. As it turned out, ninety per cent of the men who landed outside the two drop zones fell short either on the cliffs or into the sea, where PT boats braved Japanese fire to pick them up.

The airborne assault came as a complete surprise to the Japanese. The first troopers drew no fire as they floated down at 0833, three minutes late, and only sporadic rifle and machine gun fire met those who followed. The first lift consisted of the 3rd Battalion, 503rd Infantry; Battery C and a platoon of Battery D, 462nd Parachute Field Artillery; Company C, 161st Airborne Engineer Battalion; and a portion of the regimental headquarters and headquarters company.

By 0945 Colonel Jones had assembled the men of the first serial. They had three missions: Secure the drop zones, prepare to secure Topside after being reinforced by the second serial, and establish positions to provide supporting fire for the infantry landing on Black Beach. All of these missions had been accomplished by 1028 when the first of twenty-five landing craft, carrying the 3rd Battalion, 34th Infantry, lowered their ramps on Black Beach. Distracted by the parachute assault, the Japanese ignored the first four waves. By the time they reacted, tanks of the 603rd Tank Company were already ashore, and at 1100 several companies of the 34th Infantry stood on top of the key terrain feature, Malinta Hill.

At 1240, twenty-five minutes late, the second aerial serial, made up of the 2nd Battalion, 503rd Infantry; Battery B, 462nd Parachute Field Artillery Battalion; Service Company of the 503rd; and the balance of the headquarters floated to the ground, meeting only scattered sniper fire. By nightfall the united airborne elements had enlarged the existing perimeter while several companies moved down Middleside to within 250 yards of the 34th Infantry.

SECURING THE ROCK

The clearing of Corregidor consisted of numerous small-unit actions against disorganized and scattered Japanese defenders. When a jump on 17 February was canceled, the 1st Battalion, 503rd Infantry, reached Bottomside by landing craft to aid in clearing out the remaining bunkers, pill boxes, and tunnels.

The most serious challenge to the U.S. occupation of the island came on the 24th when more than six hundred Japanese launched a counterattack, but more than half of them succumbed to the artillery and small arms fire of the infantry and dispersed.

On 26 February at 1100 a tremendous explosion, a suicidal tour de force, marked the end of the organized resistance. On 2 March Colonel Jones reported the island secure.

Jump casualties had been amazingly light. As it turned out, only twenty-five per cent of the men in the first drop had jump-related injuries. Even with the increasing wind, the second drop had even fewer injuries as the pilots became more adept at dropping their sticks. Out of the 2,019 paratroopers who jumped, 279 suffered jump-related casualties, or 13.8 per cent. Twelve died; one man's chute failed to deploy and the remaining eleven were shot while descending or while still in their harnesses after reaching the ground.

The success of this airborne operation can be credited to a number of factors. The first was the element of surprise. The Japanese, as a result of their experience in 1942, had surmised that the only way the island could be taken would be by amphibious assault. The terrain as it appeared in 1945 was certainly not conducive to parachute landings, especially not on Topside, and the Japanese did not believe anyone would attempt such a maneuver. As a result, the airborne forces were able to trap the large garrison below ground in caves and tunnels or in positions that had been situated to repel an amphibious assault in the ravines leading to Topside and on the tail of the island. Captain Itagaki had even stationed his reserves, as the Americans had in 1942, in the tunnels of Malinta Hill.

Meticulous planning also contributed to the victory. The close working relationship of the men of the troop carrier group and the paratroopers, along with the fact they had trained and previously gone into combat together, were essential ingredients in the success of the operation.

Another reason for success was the use of a command ship that circled the objective; it alerted pilots if they deviated from the approach path and gave instructions for the jumpmasters to increase the count before releasing the troopers. This control measure certainly helped keep the number of jump casualties relatively small.

The human factor must also be mentioned. The officers and men of the 503rd Regimental Combat Team (Parachute) exhibited a great deal of spirit and courage. Because they did, their operation stands as an excellent example of the successful use of airborne troops.

The 3rd Field Artillery Battalion (Provisional) in the Philippines

1941-1942

by George R. Reed, Captain, Field Artillery, U.S. Army

THIS was originally prepared as a manuscript by the author in 1948 and submitted to The Adjutant General (Historical Section), Washington, D.C. Copy obtained from the National Archives, Washington, D.C.

PROVISIONAL FIELD ARTILLERY, SELF-PROPELLED MOUNTS, FORT STOTSENBERG, PAMPANGA

First Battalion
Commanding Officer:
  Major D. S. Babcock
Battery Commanders:
  Captain John Curtis
  Lieutenant Murray M. Day
  Lieutenant Brunette
  Lieutenant Corrigan

Second Battalion
Commanding Officer:
  Major Joseph Ganahl
Battery Commanders:
  Lieutenant William Jones
  Lieutenant Travis Perrenot
  Lieutenant Daniel W. Cranford
  Lieutenant Peck

Third Battalion
Commanding Officer:
  Major J. R. Lindsay
Battery Commanders:

Lieutenant Wayne Fisher
Lieutenant George A. Reed (the author of this work)
Lieutenant Van de Lester
Lieutenant Svobodny

The self-propelled mount was the only piece of modern artillery materiel in the Islands. Fifty of them had arrived in Manila the previous month (November) and had only been brought to Stotsenberg four days before war was declared. Two of them were still in Manila. Essentially, the self-propelled mount is a French 75-mm gun mounted on a half-track scout car. The car is stiff and unwieldy in handling as well as being very vulnerable from the front. In spite of this these guns proved to be very valuable during the retreat into Bataan.

The personnel of this group was drawn from a number of sources: battalion and battery commanders were American officers; junior officers were from the Philippine Army; the firing battery was from the Philippine Army; the half-track drivers were from the 14th Engineers (Philippine Scouts); and the ammunition truck drivers were from the 200th Coast Artillery Corps (National Guard).

My assignment at Fort Stotsenberg was to Battery E, 24th Field Artillery (Philippine Scouts), as the battery executive. For a short period before the war I was attached to the 21st Field Artillery (Philippine Army) as adjutant of American instructors. The camp was located at Sta. Ignacia, Tarlac. Colonel Catalan was the Philippine Army commander and Col. R. C. Mallonee was the commanding officer of American instructors.

On 6 December 1941, Col. H. N. Lockwood, S-3 of the Field Artillery Brigade, arrived in camp at Sta. Ignacia with orders to report to the brigade commander without delay. That same day I reported to Col. Louis R. Dougherty who ordered me to report to Maj. D. S. Babcock. That evening Maj. Babcock gave me command of the Fourth Field Battery. The next day, 7 December 1941, being Sunday no work was scheduled, however, Maj. Babcock suggested I go to the gun park and familiarize myself with the weapon, which I did.

On the morning of 8 December, we heard by radio of the bombing of Pearl Harbor and the declaration of war.

FOURTH FIELD BATTERY, 3ᴿᴰ PROVISIONAL BATTALION, FIELD ARTILLERY (SPM)

Commanding Officer:
First Lieutenant George A. Reed, USA

Executive Officer:

  Second Lieutenant Amador Lim, PA

Supply Officer:

  Third Lieutenant Amado Santiago, PA

Liaison Officer:

  Third Lieutenant Romero, PA

I reported to Maj. Babcock at the half-track park opposite the ordnance shop immediately after hearing the news over the radio. The drivers of the tracks from the 14th Engineers, Philippine Scouts, were also present. With their help I began to draw equipment for the guns and tracks. These guns were to be completely equipped. At 10:00 a.m. Maj. Babcock received the following message from brigade headquarters: "Japanese planes have been sighted over Lingayen Gulf." Battery commanders were ordered to take their guns and place them under cover in various parts of the post and then return for further orders. I took my battery to the rear of 2nd Battalion, 24th Field Artillery, and on returning to Maj. Babcock I was told that I could pick up my ammunition trucks and drivers in the rear of the brigade motor shop, after which I was to draw 300 rounds of ammunition for each gun at the magazine. I found the trucks behind the motor shop, but the drivers were absent. I found they were having lunch at their barracks. At approximately noon Lt. Langlois and I watched sixty-four planes bomb Clark Field. After the bombing the drivers returned. We then took the trucks, drew the ammunition and returned to the rear of the 24th Field Artillery barracks. Returning to Maj. Babcock I was ordered to take my guns and trucks to the forage farm under cover of darkness. This order was carried out and all elements were placed under cover. On the completion of this move I reported to Col. J. T. Tacy at Camp Del Pilar where I received my quota of Philippine Army personnel.

The time until 20 December was spent in training and equipping the Philippine Army personnel of the battery. These men had had six weeks of training at Camp Del Pilar before the war. During this period also, Maj. Ganahl with three batteries left for north Luzon, Lt. Perrenot was attached to the 26th Cavalry, Philippine Scouts, and Maj. Babcock with four batteries left for southern Luzon.

On the evening of the 20th of December Maj. Lindsay ordered all battery commanders to place their guns so as to be able to repel an attack of parachute troops on Clark Field. I placed my guns under a line of trees on the east side of the buildings of the forage farm and established an observation post on Lone Hill.

Early on the morning of 21 December, I received orders to proceed to Carmen, Pangasinan, where I would defend the bridge over the Agno. This move was completed without any difficulty and the guns were placed as shown in Figure 1. [*Editor's Note: None of the figures mentioned in this work were available.*] In the afternoon Gen. W. E. Brougher, Commanding General, 11th Division, Philippine Army, visited the line at Carmen and named Capt. Robert Besson as combat team commander. We encountered some trouble in getting the half-tracks over the levee and into their positions. I asked Capt. Besson if he would like a tank block on the road to Rosales. He replied in the affirmative and that night we moved the guns on the right of the bridge to the positions marked 1 and 2. Two Japanese planes dropped bombs at the bridge that afternoon but failed to hit it. On the 22nd, Maj. Lindsay passed through Carmen on his way to Rosales to see Lt. Van de Lester. I saw Lt. Fisher, who had a badly infected foot, trying to contact the battalion commander.

On the 23rd of December two Japanese planes dropped five bombs at the bridge, one of which struck the span next to the bank dropping that span, which had been prepared for dynamiting, into the river. I made an inspection of the guns immediately after the bombing, and when I reached number four gun I found that a piece of steel from the bridge had gone through the hood of the track, taking off a corner of the cylinder head, passing through the instrument panel, the door, and then dropping to the ground. In addition, steel from the bridge had punctured the radiator and tires of an ammunition truck which was nearby. I sent both back to Stotsenberg to the ordnance shop, telling them to stop at Maj. Lindsay's command post on the way back. Later in the day the battalion commander contacted for a report in order to find out what had happened to the mount, and before leaving promised to replace the ammunition truck. I moved the gun by the hotel to the position formerly held by the damaged gun.

24 DECEMBER

Lieutenant Van de Lester was reported killed in action at Binalonan. Knowing Lt. Van de Lester to be dead I stopped an SPM which was on its way to him. The track was stripped. There was no sight, ammunition, equipment or oil in the recoil cylinder and the gun was full of cosmoline. The driver and I cleaned the gun. We furnished it with a panoramic sight and ammunition, but had no filler pump with which to fill the recoil cylinder. The tanks had none and I was unable to find one anywhere since there are no other SPMs near. Repair of the bridge to permit traffic was begun with Maj. S. Malevich, Gen. Wainwright's staff, in charge of construction.

Generals J. R. N. Weaver, tank commander, J. M. Wainwright, Northern Luzon Force Commander, and G. M. Parker, Southern Luzon Force Commander, had a conference in Carmen on Christmas Day.

I received the information too late to contact Lt. Perrenot who was over the river and was unable to cross as bridge repairs were incomplete. I sent the extra SPM back to Maj. Lindsay. There was a great amount of motor traffic moving to the rear. Major Lindsay inspected the gun positions and approved of them. Bridge repairs were completed. Lieutenant Perrenot picked up members of his battery who had been dropped off at my position that morning.

At dawn on 26 December we received our first hostile machine gun fire from the north bank of the river. During the day we received 40-mm fire from a tank which was eventually put out of commission by Lt. Lim's gun. For a time we were under fire from what I believe was a self-propelled mount, possibly one of Lt. Van de Lester's guns. A shell from this gun struck our ammunition truck on the road. The driver, Pvt. Robert Arledge, 200th Coast Artillery Corps, was killed. Captain Besson received orders from Gen. Brougher to retire at nightfall. During the afternoon we received heavy mortar fire which soon had Carmen in flames. Shortly after noon friendly, indirect, artillery fire from the right rear was directed at the bridge over the river. This fire fell short of the target. Most of the shells fell in the area between the river and the road running parallel to it. I ascertained later that this fire had been directed by the 91st Field Artillery, Philippine Army. Lieutenant Lim's gun was hit in front by a 40-mm shell, the driver, Pedro Sarabia, 14th Engineers, Philippine Scouts, was killed and the tracks torn from the mount. Lieutenant Lim destroyed the gun and set it afire. We retired at nightfall as far as San Miguel looking for Maj. Lindsay's command post as my rear echelon had gone there that morning. We fed the battery with the maintenance company of the 192nd Tank Battalion and then started north again. I found the command post north of Tarlac, Tarlac, and was ordered to report to Gen. Brougher at Victoria, Tarlac. We had hardly started when the driver of the SPM drove it off the road into a dirt bank. The motor refused to start, so I hitched the track on behind one of my 6x6 ammunition trucks and towed it to Victoria, where we arrived about dawn. We traveled about eight miles an hour.

I reported to Gen. Brougher who gave me orders to report to the combat tea commander at the road intersection north of Guimba, Nueva Ecija. On arrival at the road intersection I saw Capt. Dysterhoff who told me to use my gun as I saw fit. (See Figure 2). I asked Capt. Dysterhoff what he would do if he were hard-pressed, since the bridge to the south which had been bombed by the Japanese several days before, cut off al retreat to the direct rear and left only the road to Pura as a way out for us. This road, which lay directly across the front of the Japanese advance, was not open to me for retreat since my maximum speed was only eight miles an hour. So we pioneered a road down to the creek and winched all our trucks across. About this time my other gun was pulled to a point one kilometer south of the bridge by A Company, 192nd Tank Battalion. The engine had no power because of a torn gasket on the cylinder head. I was able to obtain one from Lt. Hurd, commanding officer of A Company.

During the afternoon artillery to the east on the road to the Cagayan Valley moved from our front to our rear. I contacted Lt. Howard Amos, liaison officer of the 91st Field Artillery, Philippine Army, whom I had known at Stotsenberg. It was his opinion as well as my own that the attack would not be pushed along the road we were defending. Orders were received from Gen. L. R. Stevens, Commanding General, 91st Division, to retire at 9:00 p.m. About sunset I was contacted by Lt. Robert McDowell, commanding officer of the Second Platoon, Company B, 192nd Tank Battalion, who had been sent by Gen. Brougher to pull my foremost gun out by way of Pura to Stotsenberg to be repaired. Lieutenant McDowell had no extra cable and would not split his platoon to pull my other gun out, so I arranged with Lt. Hurd for one of his tanks to pull the track out to Baloc Junction. Lieutenant Amos and I in my sedan led A Company out to Baloc Junction. I took the gun there, dropped Lt. Amos at Santa Rosa, and proceeded to San Isidro, arriving there about 5:00 a.m. The motor sergeant began to put the new gasket on the cylinder head while I reported to Gen. Stevens who told me that I would find Gen. Brougher at Magalang. I proceeded to Magalang, but found that the 11th Division command post was not there. After gassing all motor vehicles I picked up Maj. Joseph Ganahl who was also looking for the division command post and we proceeded north to Concepcion where he located Gen. Brougher's headquarters. I was ordered to join other elements of the Provisional Field Artillery at La Paz, Tarlac. The following morning (29 December) I placed my gun in support of a gun under Lt. Peck on the road to Cabanatuan. (See Figure 3.)

During the day we heard considerable artillery fire to the north. Major Lindsay contacted me in the later afternoon, ordered me to turn my gun over to Lt. Peck, locate the Fifth Battery somewhere north of Capas and to take over from Lt. Fisher who would go to the hospital. I contacted Lt. Fisher that night at San Miguel, Tarlac.

FIFTH FIELD BATTERY, 3RD PROVISIONAL BATTALION, FIELD ARTILLERY (SPM)

Lieutenant Fisher left immediately for the hospital. I made an inspection of the gun positions before turning in and found them to be satisfactory. (See Figure 4.)

Early on the morning of 30 December I inspected the guns and found them to be in a deplorable mechanical condition. There were only thirty-five rounds of ammunition, none of which were even ready to be fused. The bodies of all the tracks, which should have been kept clear, were piled high with unopened ammunition boxes, duffel bags, food and other impediment. The ammunition cylinders beneath the breech were covered and it would have been difficult to fire the gun. I had the duffel bags and all impediments, which could be spared, placed in the supply truck. I supplied each gun with one hundred rounds of ammunition stored in opened boxes ready for firing.

I found Lt. McDowell with three tanks present in the barrio. We heard considerable firing well to the north.

On 30 December I received a note from Col. R. C. Mallonee, senior American instructor of the 21st Field Artillery, Philippine Army, to the effect that I was attached to the 21st Division, Philippine Army, Gen. Capinpin, commanding. I reported to Col. Mallonee at the division command post, who ordered me to report to Col. G. H. McCafferty, senior instructor of the 22nd Infantry, Philippine Army, and coordinate my retreat with the last element of the 22nd Infantry. I contacted Col. McCafferty and then arranged with Lt. McDowell for the defense of the road until the infantry was well to the rear. In the retreat the SPMs took up positions one kilometer apart and leap-frogged front to rear all the way to the next defense line. The first elements of the 22nd Infantry began to pass through San Miguel at sundown. The last troops had passed by 12:00 a.m. That night we retired to the Bamban River line without incident. (See Figure 5.)

On 31 December, we are out of contact with the Japanese. All was quiet. The Japanese seem to have a policy of limited objectives. If they had only known what was holding up their advance they wouldn't have hesitated but would have pushed us back into Bataan immediately. The bridge over the Bamban was dynamited on the night of the 31st of December.

1 JANUARY 1942

There was a conference at the division command post in Mabalacat to coordinate the retreat which was to take place the following night. My policy would be the same. There was a division of elements at Angeles, some were to go by way of the San Fernando-Guagua road while others were to retire by road. On the morning of 1 January, I leap-frogged number one gun to the rear. It was too close under the heights of the north bank of the Bamban. The gun fired on Japanese machine gun patrols before moving. There was heavy fire on the hills to the left flank. They are the only point of observation within our lines and they overlooked the Japanese advance. The retreat was carried out without incident, and on the morning of the 2nd I placed my guns in depth along the road south of Hacienda Pio. (See Figure 6.) I reported to Col. Mallonee at the division command post, San Jose, and was informed there would be no move tonight. On the way to the command post I had noticed a tank platoon, Lt. McDowell commanding, off the road in some trees a good distance behind the lines just east of Kalantas. While in San Jose I found Capt. Donald Haynes, commanding officer, B Company, 192nd Tank Battalion, who was using his radio to maintain contact with his platoons, of which Lt. McDowell's was one. I asked him for a note placing his platoons at my disposal and received the same.

Just west of Pio I picked up Lt. Grover C. Richards, an instructor with the 3rd Battalion, 21st Infantry, Philippine Army, who told me that the command post of the 21st was surrounded. I parked my car on the line of 2nd Battalion, 21st Field Artillery, Philippine Army, guns, and Sgt. Hagedorn, Lt. Richards, and I started to walk forward. As we did so, a platoon of tanks passed us going forward. We had not walked 200 yards when the same tanks came charging back. I turned to Richards and said, "Those tanks should have stayed up there." He replied, "They're not doing my command post any good." I told him to go forward to my first gun and wait there while I went back and contacted the tanks.

I went back to the woods and after some persuasion and showing the note from Capt. Haynes, Lt. McDowell agreed to bring his tanks up with my guns. I started back and was a good distance in advance of the tanks when I was fired on by a Japanese machine gunner at the bamboo line. I jumped out of the car, threw a grenade, and got my rifle. The tanks had come up by this time and they began to throw 37-mm, .50- and .30-caliber into the bamboo. I climbed on top of the leading tank and used the turret gun until it jammed. I then jumped off the tank, got them to stop firing, and lead them up the road on foot and placed a tank with each of my guns.

With some of the men from the tanks I made a scouting trip to where the ground dropped off in order to be sure there were no Japanese nearby. When I returned to my first gun, Lt. McDowell stuck his head out of the turret and asked me if I expected him to stay where he was that night. I replied in the affirmative.

He said, "But we are vulnerable at night."

"So are my guns," I replied.

"I won't stay," he answered.

"Oh, yes, you will."

"No, I have a platoon coming up to relieve me. We don't stay in the front line more than twenty-four hours."

"Well," I answered, "the man who relieves you will."

Sergeant Hagedorn and I then drove to Hacienda Pio to meet Lt. Harrison. While there firing broke out nearby and Filipinos began to run past. Hagedorn and I drove out to the road. There was much confusion; only one machine gun was firing; the personnel of the 21st were lying down behind their guns; whereas one shell would have ended the Japanese penetration.

At the intersection to the main road I found the tanks, 2nd Platoon, B Company, retreating. I stopped them and asked Lt. Jennings where he was going.

"To the rear. The Japanese have broken through."

"How about staying with my guns?" I asked.

"No!" he replied.

I threatened him with a court-martial, but it didn't do any good and he went on to the rear. I stopped the sergeant of the next tank with a few hard words and put his tank and the other two in position with my guns again. Not long afterwards Lt. Jennings returned and asked me where I wanted his tank. After that things quieted down. The 21st command post had been relieved in the afternoon when the tanks came up with my guns.

4 JANUARY

There is heavy artillery fire on the main road to the south. The Japanese have apparently given up their attempted flank movement here. Firing is sporadic. There is Japanese and Philippine Scout cavalry in the mountains to the north. Captain Fowler, 26th Cavalry, Philippine Scouts, contacted me to tell me of the presence of his troops in the vicinity so that my guns would not fire on them before ascertaining their identity. When on the Bamban Line I had received orders to fire on any cavalry, since none of ours was in the vicinity at the time. Colonel Mallonee ordered me to follow my same procedure in covering the retreat of the infantry tonight.

The retreat began at nightfall and by noon next day we were in Dinalupijan, Bataan. At the command post Col. Mallonee ordered me to place my guns on the road to Guagua at nightfall and to follow the 26th Cavalry across the Lyac Junction Bridge into Bataan, at which time I would revert to the command of the Provisional Field Artillery (SPM). He did not know the rendezvous area of the SPMs. I crossed the bridge some time around 11:00 p.m. and met Maj. Ganahl who was looking for some SPMs that had gotten lost. He told me the rendezvous area was on the Pilar-Bagac Road near Bagac. I found the area the next day and reported to Col. Babcock.

Two days later, 8 January 1942, I turned the battery over to Lt. Daniel W. Cranford and became S-1 and S-4 of the 1st Provisional Battalion, Field Artillery (SPM), Maj. Joseph Ganahl commanding.

M16 Half-tracks in the Philippines

After Action Reports of the 209th Anti-Aircraft Artillery Automatic Weapons Battalion

U.S. Army

THESE narrative reports were obtained from the National Archives, Washington, D.C.

BATTERY A, 209ᵀᴴ AAA AW BATTALION
0320, 17 FEBRUARY 1945

Corporal James Robinson was on guard duty at No. 12 machine gun position on the Pasig River when at 0320 hours on 17 February 1945 he spotted a canoe coming down river about 25 yards away. He immediately opened fire with a Tommy gun from a position in a foxhole. The first two short bursts of four each wounded one of the three visible men in the craft. One man from the rear of the boat ran forward to help the wounded man and at this point Corporal Robinson could plainly hear the occupants of the boat jabbering. He then emptied his Tommy gun on the canoe which caused it to blow up with a tremendous explosion. Corporal Robinson was knocked down by the explosion and received a slight cut over the eye from a flying piece of bone. Private James McCarthy, who was on the half-track, was knocked off by the force of the explosion but was uninjured.

Corporal John Holmes ripped his way out of his hammock and leaped on to the half-track and into the gun turret. He immediately raked the river and banks expending eighty rounds of .50-caliber ammunition. Small arms were fired spasmodically until daylight at every floating object on the river. The gun section expended sixty rounds of small arms ammunition altogether.

The area around the gun was inspected at daybreak and fragments of human bodies were found all over the area. Bone fragments, pieces of flesh, skull fragments, and human entrails were found on the gun itself, in the hammocks, and all over the area in general. The force of the explosion broke window panes for 150 yards around and one piece of flesh was found 200 yards from the immediate scene of the action. The only damage incurred was the ripping of three jungle hammocks caused by the men themselves in their haste to get out. It is assumed that the enemy was attempting to blow up the pontoon bridge close by our position.

BATTERY A, 209TH AAA AW BATTALION (SP) ATTACHED TO 3RD BATTALION, 63RD INFANTRY REGIMENT, 21-30 JUNE 1945

21 JUNE

At 0700, Provisional Platoon Battery A, consisting of seven M16 and two M15 Special half-tracks departed Luna, arriving at 6th Division command post at Solano at 2200. The battery was quartered at division command post that night and attached to 3rd Battalion, 63rd Infantry Regiment, which was located five miles north of Bagabag. Battery arrived at 3rd Battalion at 1300, 22 June, and reported to commanding officer, Colonel Mueller. There was no action on this date.

23 JUNE

Supply trains had been ambushed on the morning of 22 June and our first mission was to accompany the supply train along with an armored car on the morning of 23 June. We used a personnel carrier half-track and two M16s. Major Samusson, S-2 of 63rd Regiment, and Major Wells, Executive Officer of 3rd Battalion, rode in a gun track. The enemy action of the previous day had everyone on the alert. There was no enemy action en route. Destination was the forward area of I and K Companies, 11 miles north of Bagabag on Highway No. 4. At this location the commanding officer of the 3rd Battalion designated an area that he wanted strafed. Working in shifts, two M16s strafed the area thoroughly. During the firing an explosion was heard and it is believed an ammo dump was hit by our fire. Firing was completed at 1230 and all tracks returned to our command post at 1300 hours. There was no enemy activity and we sustained no casualties or damage to material.

24 JUNE

No action occurred.

25 June

1ˢᵗ Battalion requested two M16s for the morning of the 25ᵗʰ. Vehicles arrived at forward command post, 1ˢᵗ Battalion, located eight miles north of Bagabag on Highway No. 4 at 0700. At 0800 both half-tracks moved north up Highway No. 4 with squads of infantry covering both flanks. A pillbox was sighted at 800 yards. We opened fire and set it ablaze. At a point nine miles north of Bagabag, Company C, Captain Rainville commanding, joined us. Company C dispatched a patrol to take a hill on our right front. Captain Rainville directed one of our machine gun squads to strafe a draw on our forward left flank. Just before we opened fire an enemy sniper's bullet ricocheted off a scout car and all took cover. As we opened fire a Japanese machine gun hit our track. The infantry patrol was pinned down by the machine gun and later withdrew 500 yards to reorganize. We returned to 1ˢᵗ Battalion command post and the two half-tracks remained there all night by order of Lieutenant Colonel Brunevolt, commanding officer of 1ˢᵗ Battalion. The damage to our half-track was negligible and there were no casualties.

26 June

No action occurred.

27 June

At 0800 the two half-tracks proceeded up Highway No. 4 to a bridge one-and-a-half miles north of 1ˢᵗ Battalion command post. One section strafed the bridge approach and a mined area. The mined area was then cleared by engineers. The other half-track went past approximately one mile north and met Company G. From this point they strafed a hill designated by commanding officer of Company G. Both half-tracks returned to battery command post at 1530. No casualties or damage to material occurred.

28 June

Two half-tracks were sent north on Highway No. 4 to a point 11 miles from battery command post. An M4 tank was operating in this area and our mission was to support and cover the tank. There was no enemy action, however, a position thought to be an enemy machine gun was fired on by one of our half-tracks. Both half-tracks returned to battery command post at 1400. No casualties or damage to material.

29 JUNE

Two half-tracks were sent north 11 miles on Highway No. 4. Due to impassable roads and difficult terrain vehicles were unable to continue with the infantry. A suspected enemy cave was sighted and fired upon at 20 yards range by one half-track, with unknown results. The half-tracks returned to battery command post at 1430. No casualties or damage to material.

30 JUNE

Two half-tracks were sent north 11 miles to a point where a bridge had been washed out and vehicles could not pass. Half-tracks were relieved at 1600 and returned to battery command post. No enemy action.

World War II's Last Bitter Battle

by Howard Apter

DESPITE the impression everyone has that the war against Japan ended, for all practical purposes, with the dropping of the A-bomb on Hiroshima and Nagasaki, the heart-breaking truth is American GIs were still dying on such blood-soaked slopes as Mayayao Ridge in the Philippines at the precise moment Emperor Hirohito's peace emissaries were flashing word to Washington that they agreed to surrender unconditionally. Here, for the first time, is the agonizing story of the last bitter battle of World War II.

During the early evening of 19 July 1945, an American soldier was carefully moving along the bank of a swiftly moving stream in the mountains of northern Luzon. Suddenly he stopped. Footsteps ahead! The soldier quickly slid into the water behind a growth of reeds and crouched. Just in time. Twenty yards away a squad of Japanese soldiers was moving toward him. For a moment the American was tempted to fire—the lead man was already in the sights of his carbine—but he left the temptation pass. He was on a vital mission that did not include a firefight with the enemy. Instead he moved deeper into the water. Just as the eight Japanese soldiers stopped he tore off a piece of reed, put it to his mouth, and disappeared in the stream. Only the reed, like the snorkel of a submarine, remained above the surface.

The enemy squad, as the man in the water heard, not only stopped but sat down. Soon the tropical night fell like a curtain, and the soldier knew what lay ahead of him, for the Japanese stretched out to spend the night. Two guards, a few feet away, kept whispering. The American knew he would have to stay submerged all night breathing through the reed.

Why was this soldier, S/Sgt. Wayne Brodle, spending all night in the water in an inaccessible mountain wilderness of the northern Philippines? During the afternoon his platoon of M Company, 3rd Battalion, 148th Infantry Regiment, 37th Division, had reconnoitered a Japanese pocket on a nearby mountain slope. It seemed like a routine mop-up, but Nambu machine guns had opened up and cut down eight men at once. Soon there was firing on both flanks of the platoon. A counterattack! The Americans quickly formed a perimeter and raked the thick undergrowth with their weapons. Then all was quiet. But it was obvious they were surrounded, and the wounded needed medical attention, so Brodle volunteered to slip through enemy lines to contact the nearest American unit. That's why he found himself submerged in the stream while the nightly downpour of the wet season beat on the surface above him.

Officially, Brodle should never have been in that stream hiding from the enemy. Neither should his platoon have been surrounded on that date. For the war in the Philippines had officially ended over two weeks ago. On 28 June, Gen. Douglas MacArthur had issued a communiqué in which he "closed out" the Luzon Campaign, and on 5 July, he issued another communiqué of an even more assuring nature. MacArthur declared the Philippine Campaign "virtually closed" and estimated "that only some minor isolated action of a guerrilla nature in the practically uninhabited mountain ranges may occasionally persist." Virtually "all" of the enemy's 450,000 men had "been annihilated" and only thirty thousand troops remained, isolated in small pockets without food and ammunition throughout the vast Philippine archipelago. Obviously, it was all over.

MacArthur had an extremely complex personality. What his mimeograph machines produced for public consumption was often quite different from his practical military actions. On 1 July, he changed command of the Philippines from the U.S. Sixth to U.S. Eighth Army. The former was to prepare for the coming invasion of Japan. Fortunately, MacArthur had withdrawn only a handful of Sixth Army divisions for rest and amphibious training. The rest, all veterans, remained. Thus, on Luzon alone no less than seven American divisions, the 37th, 6th, 32nd, 43rd and 38th Infantry, plus the 11th Airborne and 1st Cavalry maintained their positions. In addition, they were backed by twenty-one thousand Filipino guerrillas under Col. Russell Volckmann (USAFIP-NL) and the U.S. Fifth Air Force. In charge was MacArthur's number one Pacific clean-up hitter, Lt. Gen. Robert Eichelberger.

It was just as well. For an incredible intelligence blunder was being committed. Before leaving the scene, Sixth Army had estimated that only twenty-three thousand scattered Japanese remained in all of Luzon. The rest, seven thousand, were all over the many Philippine islands. MacArthur concurred in these estimates. So did Eichelberger. Years later, the official Army historian was to remark ironically that it appeared to be "a relatively easy mopping-up and patrolling operation." By that time Eichelberger had already admitted in his memoirs how wrong he had been.

The general discovered the truth very soon after taking command. On a visit to his various divisions he ran into a strange situation on 12 July at the headquarters of the 38th Division, which was located only one hour's drive east of Manila. The Philippine capital had been retaken about six months ago. This area, from which the enemy appeared to have been cleared long ago, was teeming with action. During Eichelberger's visit 259 Japanese soldiers were killed and twenty-nine captured before the day was over. Quite a toll for a single day considering that the enemy had supposedly been "annihilated."

This was a mere skirmish compared to the action farther north in the mountains where Sgt. Brodle was trying to rescue his platoon. There it was obvious that the officers and men, from generals down, of the 6th, 32nd and 37th Divisions, as well as Volckmann's guerrillas, had not paid enough attention to MacArthur's communiqués; possibly because they were involved in some of the roughest mountain fighting of the Philippine campaign.

It was also obvious that Gen. Tomoyuki Yamashita, the man they were going to "mop up" and "patrol" had not paid close enough attention to MacArthur's communiqués, either. The "Tiger of Singapore," as he was known to the Japanese (the Filipinos nicknamed him "Old Potato Face" because he was so ugly) was very well placed indeed. He had executed a brilliant withdrawal into the virtually inaccessible and unsurveyed wilderness of the Cordillera Mountains in northern Luzon. And there he sat, not with twenty-three thousand scattered troops as the American High Command believed, but with nearly seventy thousand men, all fanatical veterans ready to die to the last man.

Yamashita had taken over from the incompetent Field Marshal Terauchi in 1944. Terauchi had been exiled to Saigon. Shortly thereafter American troops landed on Leyte. Yamashita had no illusions that he could eject the Americans from the Philippines, especially after they hit Luzon in January 1945. But he had a plan. He moved 150,000 of his best troops north of Manila while the rest of his 390,000 men battled American forces elsewhere. The concentration in northern Luzon was named the "Shobu Group." With it he hoped to tie down American troops in the Philippines as long as possible, inflict maximum number of casualties and prevent their employment elsewhere.

Interestingly, one American, Col. Volckmann, the leader of the Filipino guerrillas on Luzon, had seen through Yamashita's plan at once. When Volckmann reported to Gen. Krueger, the Eighth Army commander, shortly after the Luzon landings and told him about

Yamashita's strength, Krueger roared: "Damn it, Volckmann. If there are that many Nips left, why don't they drive me back into the sea?"

"Sir, they're going to sit and force you to dig them out of the mountains," replied the colonel. And that's exactly what was to happen during the next six months. True, by 1 July, Yamashita had taken terrible losses and had been cleared from the rest of the Philippines, but he was quite ready to continue his game in northern Luzon. His plan was to hold out until September 1945 and then continue with guerrilla action, which might last for years.

By western conventional warfare standards, his situation was catastrophic. The "Shobu Group" was now surrounded by three American divisions and Volckmann's guerrillas, all under the command of XIV Corps. Each of Yamashita's soldiers was rationed a few spoonfuls of rice and a cup of water a day. Medical supplies and salt, vital in the heat of the tropics, were nearly gone. Dead and wounded lay about unattended. When one of his staff officers inspected forward positions he had to report to Yamashita that he found dead Japanese everywhere in the jungle and on the slopes, their swollen bodies and faces covered with flies and maggots. Other corpses were floating in the mountain streams. Thousands of the survivors were suffering from malaria, dysentery and beriberi. His staff officers lived on snakes and mice. Yamashita himself was living in a simple grass hut atop Mount Prog, nearly 10,000 feet high; the mountain tribes regarded it as holy. There he ate the same rations as his men and refused to bathe because his soldiers lacked water. Yet he still had plenty of men, weapons and ammunition, and these very same starving, disease-ridden troops were fighting like fanatics. Whenever bad news came to him he comforted his staff with the following words: "The enemy attacks my stomach. I must hug him close to me to strangle him."

The men of the XIV Corps who were fighting in this wilderness soon found themselves stymied. The terrain was not only the roughest in the Philippines, it was the roughest American troops had fought in except New Guinea and Burma. Mountain rose after mountain, with slopes thickly covered with brush or jungle. There were gorges and deep rivers. There were no roads, only a few trails.

Finally, there were the rains. It was the wet season in July, and tropical cloud bursts broke every afternoon. At night it was cold, and a steady rain poured down. Men who perspired during the day shivered at night. Many came down with colds, the flu, and pneumonia.

The rains also flooded the river banks, washed out the few trails, and sent mud sliding down the slopes. The 37th Division had to send its wounded down the streams on rafts since jeeps couldn't operate in the interior. The rains also washed out the air support. Yet on each jungled hill, on each elevation, in each cave sat Yamashita's men and their guns covering every approach. During the first three weeks of July the American advance in northern Luzon was crawling ahead at a snail's pace.

The outside world knew nothing of this. Germany was now occupied. Okinawa had fallen finally on 22 June, and the Philippines, according to MacArthur, were "liberated." True, the war still continued in Burma and China, and B-29s and Halsey's Third Fleet battered Japan itself. But there was a great pause in the world's consciousness. On 17 July all eyes were fastened on the Potsdam Conference of the "Big Three," which would undoubtedly usher in the final act of World War II, the surrender or invasion of Japan. From the Philippines only an occasional paragraph reached the American newspapers. The correspondents had gone elsewhere.

If the world didn't know about the Philippines, then the Americans, Filipino, and Japanese soldiers there didn't know about the world. Not even MacArthur and Yamashita knew what was transpiring behind tight security curtains. Tremendous events were being set in motion behind the scenes.

On the same day, 12 July, that General Eichelberger discovered that there was still lots of action taking place near Manila, Japanese Foreign Minister Togo sent a most significant cable to Ambassador Sato in Moscow. Its first line told the story:

> His Majesty is extremely anxious to terminate the war as soon as possible, being deeply concerned that the further continuation of hostilities will only aggravate the untold miseries of the teeming millions, innocent men, and women of the countries at war.

Togo ordered Sato to ask the Soviet government, still a neutral as far as Japan was concerned, to receive a special envoy, Prince Konoye to "negotiate for a speedy restoration of peace."

After a long silent struggle the "Peace Party" in Japan, headed by the Emperor, the Premier, and Foreign Minister Togo, had gained the assent of the warlords to ask the Soviet government for mediation.

Several hours later the text of this message was in the hands of the top men in Washington. The U.S. had broken, even before the war, the Japanese diplomatic code, as well as several naval codes.

The Japanese warlords were already out of the game. Washington did nothing, and Sato couldn't even get to see Molotov, the Soviet Foreign Minister. His deputy said he was on the way to Potsdam but he would forward the message to him.

Four days later a mushroom cloud rose over the desert of New Mexico near Alamogordo. A "special bomb" of tremendous force had been exploded. The results were flashed in code to President Truman and his closest advisers in Potsdam.

On 19 July, the day Sgt. Brodle's platoon had been ambushed in northern Luzon, Molotov's deputy told Sato in Moscow that the message of the 12th was not clear. What precisely did the Japanese government have in mind? Sato had to cable home for further instructions.

Meanwhile the war continued. In the northern Philippines while fog still sat above the rippling water, Sgt. Brodle rose like a dripping ghost out of the mountain stream and moved ashore. He had heard the enemy depart, and it was time to continue the mission. The wet GI, shivering in the cold, his stomach in knots because of hunger, once again moved carefully along the jungle trail. When he finally reached the nearest American unit, help was already underway. A patrol had been sent out to probe for the encircled platoon, and a task force was being assembled. After gulping down some food, Brodle returned with the relief column. By noon of the 20th, the Japanese ambushers of his platoon were themselves ambushed and killed to the last man.

About an hour before dawn on 25 July on a drenched slope near Bunhian, north of the Shobu pocket, a few men were huddled under some ponchos spread against a rock. A mist-like drizzle was still falling after the tropical rain of the night had exhausted itself. The wet men were shivering in the cold air. Even the few field mice and snakes had sought refuge during the miserable night.

Under the cover of the ponchos, Capt. Deogracias Caballero was whispering instructions. He wanted his provisional battalion of the 11th Guerrilla Regiment to attack shortly after dawn when the rain had stopped and had turned into thick fog. It was their best—perhaps their only—chance to dig out the Japanese defenders of the ridge several hundred feet above them.

Caballero's officers and senior non-coms grunted. There was no conversation for there was no need to discuss anything. They had just spent a miserable night clinging to the wet slopes after being tossed off the ridge during the previous afternoon. Few of the men had blankets or ponchos, and some of the wounded had drowned during the downpour, so the conference ended quickly. The men moved out from the shelter of the ponchos to see to it that their troops got ready for the attack. Soon small clusters of men, often supporting each other but perfectly noiseless, crept silently through the night up the slope.

Light came up quickly as it always does in the tropics. The Japanese on the ridge coughed in their foxholes as they awoke in the thick fog. There was no breakfast again but there was hope. They were to counterattack later in the day with their Nambu machine guns, their mortars, and their hand grenades, and chase the Filipino guerrillas out of the area. Best of all, they would capture those marvelous American K-rations with which the Filipinos were gorging themselves.

As the Japanese soldiers stretched, rubbed their eyes, or drank some rainwater in their foxholes, about one hundred men shielded by the fog, listened nearby. Captain Caballero had once again placed the Igorot Co. in front, and the men of that company were ready. Their naked brown bodies—their only clothing was a loin cloth—hugged the ground. They silently prayed to their gods and grasped their favorite weapon, the bolo knife. They also had M1s, some Thompsons, grenades, and even spears—but they liked the bolos best. The Igorots, the feared mountain tribe of northern Luzon, were very fond of enemy heads as decorations.

A shout broke through the fog. Suddenly a volley of bullets hit the Japanese line. Before the Nambus could reply the Igorots jumped into the first line of foxholes.

This time the savage shouts of the Igorots were drowned by cries of the Japanese as the bolo blades found their mark. Fountains of blood spouted as bodies and heads fell to the muddy ground.

A Thompson cut down the crew of the first machine gun. The second Nambu crew was blown up by a grenade. The mortar got off three rounds before its crew was jumped. A Japanese officer rushed forward with his samurai sword but a bolo blade struck his neck from behind and head and sword flew through the air. Caballero's men were swarming all over the ridge, and Igorots and Japanese fought each other with spears, bayonets, rifle butts and knives.

Thousands of miles west, in Moscow, Ambassador Sato finally got in to see Molotov's deputy again. The Japanese diplomat pressed the Russian for a speedy answer to his government's request for mediation. He was promised a "quick reply." And what a reply Sato and Japan would eventually get! For at the very same time Stalin and Molotov in Potsdam were clearing the last formalities with Truman and Churchill to enter the war against Japan three months after the surrender of Germany. That meant either 8 or 9 August depending on whether you counted V-E Day Western or Soviet style. At the same time the two Soviet leaders were studying a copy of a declaration drafted by Truman, Churchill and Chiang Kai-shek. Its final sentence contained the gist and a mysterious threat:

> We call upon the government of Japan to proclaim now the unconditional surrender of all Japanese armed forces, and to provide proper and adequate assurances of their good faith in such action. The alternative for Japan is prompt and utter destruction.

Allied radio stations were getting ready to broadcast it around the world.

Not even Stalin and Molotov knew that on the very same day across the Atlantic in Washington one of the most momentous orders in American history had been issued to Gen. Carl Spaatz, commander of the U.S. Army Strategic Air Force in the Pacific. This order directed Spaatz to have the 509th Composite Group, 20th Air Force, "deliver its first special bomb as soon as weather will permit visual bombing after 3 August 1945 on one of the targets: Hiroshima, Kokura, Niigata and Nagasaki." Spaatz, still in Washington, was asked to deliver one copy personally to Gen. MacArthur and Adm. Nimitz.

On 4 August the heavy cruiser *Indianapolis* was anchored off Tinian. Components of the "special bomb" were unloaded under extreme security measures. In Tokyo the Japanese government was pondering the meaning and intent of the Potsdam ultimatum.

On 24 July, the 20th Regiment relieved the 63rd. The rains eased up, and some Filipino companies of the 14th Guerrilla Regiment had been put into the lead since they were more familiar with the terrain. But the total advance toward Kiangkiang remained a mere two miles since 12 July. A commanding ridge barred the advance of the 20th Regiment and the Filipinos as it had barred the 63rd. The Japanese were well dug in. Their machine guns were firing from hidden caves while mortars and artillery from rear positions plastered the trail. All attempts to take the ridge failed. By the afternoon of the 28th the ridge was still firmly in Japanese hands.

During the same afternoon, in Tokyo, Premier Suzuki expressed himself somewhat imprecisely regarding the Allied Potsdam declaration. He used the word *mokusatsu* which has several meanings. Historians and linguistic scholars are still debating it; however, it is generally believed now that Suzuki meant "withhold comment." But his militaristic enemies and the controlled Japanese news media saw it otherwise. "Treat with silent contempt" or "laugh it off" was the way the government reaction to Potsdam was presented to the Japanese people and the watchful Allied world.

So the debate about *mokusatsu* still goes on, and it is no irrelevant ivory tower discussion, for with that one ambitious word Suzuki condemned over two hundred thousand Japanese men, women and children to death.

Next morning, Company D of the 20th Regiment and two Filipino companies tried it again. Once more they got to the base of the ridge before the heavy Japanese fire pinned them down. As a matter of fact, they had gotten closer than ever but were worse off as they frantically sought cover in shell holes. They were completely exposed and could neither advance nor retreat. Machine guns from the caves were already raking the shell holes.

At that moment Sgt. Melvin Mayfield decided he'd had enough. He grabbed his carbine and some grenades, leaped out of his hole, and jumped into the one ahead of him. Then he tried the next. The men behind him fired frantically at the caves to divert the Japanese gunners because Mayfield, crawling and sometimes running in a crouch, was advancing from shell hole to shell hole up the barren slope. It was only a matter of seconds before he would be cut apart by the machine guns. What happened next is simply incredible.

While firing his carbine with his left hand, the West Virginian tossed a grenade into the first cave, silencing the Nambu. Before the gunners in the second cave could cut him down another grenade sailed in. A third cave was blown up in the same way. One more cave and one more machine gun to go!

Then a bullet broke Mayfield's carbine and shattered his left hand; but the indestructible sergeant still had his right hand. He threw his last grenades into the fourth cave while blood dripped from his wound. This cave also was knocked out. Mayfield lived to receive the Medal of Honor, the last American in World War II to receive it.

Unfortunately, there were more ridges and more caves ahead on the road to Kiangkiang, and several hundred Americans were to die in the Philippines before 29 July came to an end.

It was a moonlit night as the *Indianapolis* neared Leyte after delivering its terrible cargo to Tinian. Captain Hashimoto of the Japanese submarine *I-58* spotted the warship in the periscope. The heavy American cruiser was a perfect target in the silver-sheeted sea. Several torpedoes hit its unprotected side and in twelve minutes it went down. A few dazed survivors were finally picked up four days later. The *Indianapolis* had gone and returned in utmost secrecy and the U.S. command on nearby Leyte had simply "forgotten" about her. Her 833 American sailors died in the shark-infested waters off Leyte.

On the morning of 31 July, while the sailors were floating in the bloody waters of Leyte, a combat patrol of the 145th Regiment, 37th Division, left the barrio of Penablanca in the Sierra Madre Mountains east of the Shobu pocket to probe for a trail reaching to another mountain barrio called Malabag. Its thirty-two men were under the command of Lt. John J. Rodman. At eleven a.m., Rodman reported over his radio that everything was "okay."

A few minutes later the patrol passed some boulders flanking the trail. Two Japanese machine guns opened up. The first half of the column went down like a string of puppets. The two camouflaged machine guns worked their way up and down, scything the men with streams of bullets. When a rescue column arrived it found only a handful of wounded survivors.

By then Don Blackburn and two battalions under Capts. Caballero and Bill Burch had reached the Mayoyao ridge. It had been a tortuous trek, and on the way they had overrun Bunhian and Barangbang. The former had been easy. The Japanese had preferred to blow themselves up with grenades rather than face the terrible Igorots. Barangbang, however, was cleared only after six Japanese counterattacks had been repulsed. But the Mayoyao ridge was a tougher nut than Melvin Mayfield's ridge in the 6th Division area. Once again, Blackburn's men were clinging to the wet slopes.

It was a jagged piece of mountain, dominated by an apex, rising to 5,000 feet above sea level. In front of the ridge was a saddleback about 125 yards long and 50 feet deep. To outflank the enemy on the ridge was impossible. The saddleback turned razor-thin with steep sides and Blackburn estimated only two men could crawl on it abreast. The ridge would have to be attacked frontally, across the saddleback in face of Japanese machine guns and mortars firing from caves.

Once again the first attempts failed. Blackburn had no artillery on the scene since only mortars could be carried into this terrain. The only artillery available was miles away. So his men were once again spending rainy nights on a bomb-blasted slope.

But this time their situation was critical. They had neither blankets nor ponchos. Food was short. They were now subsisting on a third of a K-ration a day plus one cup of water. Medicine was also scarce. Everything had to be carried from Blackburn's base by porters and mules over terrible trails for nearly 30 miles. The steady rains and the terrain were too much for man and beast, and many of the wounded died on the way back.

During the first hours of 6 August, three B-29 bombers took off from Tinian, about 1,600 miles east of Mayoyao. "No. 91," carrying cameras, was under the command of Capt. George Marquardt. "The Great Artiste," filled with instruments, had Maj. Charles "Chuck" Sweeney in the pilot's seat. Finally there was the "Enola Gay," flown by the commander of the 509th Composite Group, Col. Paul Tibbets. In its bomb bay was a single narrow bomb of unusual design. It was "small" by the blockbuster standards of World War II and weighed only five tons. Therefore it had been named "Little Boy." Its components consisted of pieces of U-235 (uranium) metal. The target was the sprawling city of Hiroshima on Honshu.

At 7:30 the trio of B-29s crossed the Japanese coast. A weather plane under Maj. Claude Eatherly, which had preceded them, radioed that conditions over the target area were excellent. Shortly after 8:00 a.m. they moved in over Hiroshima. At 8:15 Maj. Thomas Ferebee aboard the "Enola Gay" dropped "Little Boy." The equivalent of 13,500 tons of TNT exploded less than 2,000 feet above the ground, and an enormous boiling cloud rose from a Hiroshima that was no more. Over eighty thousand people were killed and thirty-seven thousand injured.

That awful event gripped mankind at once. It overshadowed all other events taking place at the time and created the illusion that this single terrible blow knocked Japan out of the war for good and that only surrender formalities followed. Far from it. The war continued. And even worse was to follow.

Next morning while Hiroshima was still burning and radioactive dust was settling on the survivors, Blackburn, at the Mayoyao Ridge heard heavy firing nearby. He thought friendly forces were on the way, but the firing eventually died down. The company of the 6th Division never showed up. Later a radio message informed him that it had been thrown back. So Blackburn was on his own again. He would have to storm the apex the hard way.

During the day 117 B-29s struck at Japan again but hardly anyone paid attention. It was the "Atomic Bomb announcement" from Washington by President Truman, apparently drafted and pre-recorded at Potsdam, that was reverberating around the world. It is quite possible that Yamashita in his hideout had picked it up for we know that his radio was receiving short wave broadcasts from Saigon and San Francisco. But if he heard the bulletin it is quite certain he was not impressed. He would stick it out until September. His military superiors in Tokyo were not impressed either, but they took the precaution of keeping the extent of the damage to Hiroshima from the Emperor and the Cabinet.

On the 8th, Blackburn attacked the apex. He had infiltrated men on the enemy flanks and rear; and another company of Igorots had arrived on the scene. The concentrated attack overran the apex; the caves were finally taken after hand grenades had blown up the defenders. Then Blackburn came off the ridge and moved into Mayoyao. This was a great blow to Yamashita and it eased the pressure on the 6th Division still stuck near Kiangkiang.

During the battle for the apex no less than 420 B-29s struck at various targets in Japan, but this was another interlude. During the afternoon crews of the 509th Composite Group on Tinian were told they would head for Japan again early next morning. The primary target was Kokura; the alternate, Nagasaki.

Before the day ended Ambassador Sato was to present himself to Molotov in the Kremlin at 6:00 p.m. sharp, Moscow time. The Japanese diplomat strode toward Molotov with a smile. At last the long-delayed Soviet reply would be read to him by the Foreign Minister himself.

Molotov did not smile. He waved the Japanese to a chair. Then he began to read a statement. Sato's smile vanished. It was the Soviet Union's declaration of war, to be effective at midnight.

A little before 2:00 a.m. on Tinian, while Soviet artillery was pounding the Kwantung Army in Manchuria, three B-29s once again roared off the runway. "The Great Artiste" had a new commander, Capt. Frederick Bock. The camera plane was piloted by Maj. James Hopkins and had two British guests aboard, Dr. William Penney and Group Capt. G. L. Cheshire.

Captain Bock's own aircraft, "No. 77," or "Bock's Car," had been taken over by Chuck Sweeney. It carried a single 10-foot long bomb. The bomb's five-foot width made it look almost like an onion. Its name was "Fat Boy." But "Fat Boy" was not identical to his "Little" brother. It was a plutonium bomb that produced a new form of power release. A new word had been coined, "implosion," to describe it. The term itself remained an official U.S. secret until 1951. The scientists of the Manhattan Project believed that "Fat Boy" with its plutonium content was far more destructive than the uranium-containing "Little

Boy." The crew had the strictest instructions to drop it by visual observation only.

The B-29s reached Kyushu around 9:00 a.m. Kokura was only partially in view. The aiming point, the Japanese Army arsenal, could not be seen. The planes circled for fifty minutes under growing flak and then fighters appeared. Sweeney decided to pull out and head for Nagasaki.

Nagasaki was also under cloud cover; besides, fuel was running low, and there was just enough left for one bomb run and the return trip to Okinawa. Tinian was already beyond fuel range. The bomb would have to be dropped at once regardless of visibility or they would have to drop it later in the ocean. Navy Commander Fred Ashworth of the Manhattan Project finally made the decision aboard "Bock's Car"—drop the bomb on Nagasaki.

A little before 11:00 a.m. bombardier Kermit Beahan let loose "Fat Boy." It "imploded" 1,540 feet above the city. Nagasaki died in a mushroom cloud even more powerful than the one at Hiroshima. It almost caught "The Great Artiste" and "Bock's Car." Five minutes later radio operator Sgt. Abe Spitzer sent word to Tinian that the results were "technically successful." Possibly as many as one hundred thousand persons were dead. We shall never know the true figures.

The destruction of Nagasaki set off a series of fantastic events in Tokyo which historians are still unraveling. Shortly before midnight Emperor Hirohito met with the top eleven men of the government in his underground concrete shelter. It was an unprecedented Imperial Conference, and the "Peace Party" was ready to throw the gauntlet to the militarists. But War Minister Anami and Army Chief of Staff Umenzu were still full of defiance. Not even Nagasaki and the Soviet attack on Manchuria had shaken them. They were prepared to fight one last "decisive" battle on Japanese soil.

But Emperor Hirohito had heard enough. He issued his decision—the Potsdam Declaration would be accepted. Then he strode from the shelter. During the night cables were sent to Japanese ambassadors in neutral Switzerland and Sweden to contact the Allies. On 11 August, Washington replied asking for a formal surrender affirmed by the Emperor's signature.

Was the war over? Not at all. While people were dancing in New York's Times Square men were still dying on land, in the air, and on the seas. Certainly for Yamashita it wasn't over. He had picked up a San Francisco broadcast telling of the Emperor's decision but this appeared to be more a symbolic than concrete finality. Perhaps Yamashita sensed that events in Tokyo still hadn't run their course. After all, he knew the fanaticism of the younger Army and Navy die-hards and those officers were already in full revolt. In fact, they were moving on the Imperial Palace itself.

Two days later, when still no official reply had been received from the Japanese government, Gen. Spaatz threw another thunderclap at Japan. He mounted a maximum effort, 828 B-29s, accompanied by 186 fighter escorts, a total of 1,014 aircraft. They hit targets in the Tokyo area. It was the last great mass raid of World War II but by no means the last air battle.

Next morning, the 15th, Halsey's Third Fleet standing off Japan sent 176 planes from its carrier toward Tokyo. After the planes had disappeared a sudden message from Adm. Nimitz arrived for Halsey. "Suspend all air operations." Halsey's officers radioed for the planes to return. Only seventy-three could be contacted. The rest were already over Japan battling forty-five Japanese fighters. None of the airmen, Americans or Japanese, knew that Japan's surrender reply had been received in Washington and that President Truman had announced the cessation of hostilities.

The Japanese troops in the Philippines did not get the word either. On that very same morning Blackburn lost no less than four company commanders killed along with other casualties. Even when the news did reach the Americans on Luzon it made no difference to the other side. Within hours a company of the 32nd Division had to beat off a fierce Japanese counterattack. Yamashita's men were still firing from hills, ridges and caves. No wonder. The "Tiger" had received no orders to stop shooting.

The shooting continued although there was pandemonium in New York, Chicago, London and Paris. San Francisco went completely wild, and there were riots in the streets. At five o'clock that evening in Tokyo shots were still being fired as the revolt against the Emperor's decision was being crushed. A group of eleven kamikaze naval bombers, led by Adm. Matome Ugaki, took off against orders. The goal of their mission was Okinawa. What happened to them is still not clear. They simply vanished.

There were other die-hards. Two days later four B-32 reconnaissance planes were attacked by fifteen enemy fighters near Tokyo. The B-32s fought them off and when they returned next day they were again attacked. Three Japanese planes were shot down.

In the meantime, the desperate Japanese High Command, in response to a message by Gen. MacArthur, was trying to contact its commanders in the field to stop shooting. A mission headed by Gen. Kawabe took off in specially marked planes for Manila on 19 August to start the difficult task of winding up the hostilities. The same day Yamashita received orders from Field Marshal Terauchi to stop shooting. One by one Japanese generals and admirals acknowledged those orders, and by the 22nd all of them in Southeast Asia had so notified Tokyo—except for one man, Yamashita. Japanese officers and men were beginning to surrender to Allied forces everywhere but the "Tiger" was in no hurry. A fantastic play was about to begin in the Philippines.

On 23 August a small party of Japanese soldiers arrived at an outpost of the 148th Regiment near Tumauini with a strange request. They wanted to know what was happening. The American reply was classic: "The sooner you guys get in here, the sooner we get back to the States—so hurry up."

Next morning two Japanese officers returned. They were ready to negotiate the surrender of an engineer regiment of 550 men including its colonel. That was excellent news. It had to be exploited. So that same day a pilot flying an L-5 liaison plane, was sent to the area of Yamashita's headquarters to drop a letter written by Gen. Gill of the 32nd Division. The letter asked for a parley.

On the following day, the 25th, a Japanese captain appeared at the lines of the 129th Regiment, 37th Division, in the Paret River Valley east of the Shobu pocket. The captain explained that he had come on behalf of a Gen. Iguchi who was ready to surrender 8,500 men. The American commanders, of course, accepted. But Iguchi could not deliver. He had jumped the gun on his own, and Yamashita jumped on him. The "Tiger" was by no means ready to surrender as long as he had no orders, and he made this quite clear in a most unusual fashion. On 26 August an officer delivered his reply to Gen. Gill. It was written in a stilted but very polite English, and it stated in part:

> To date of writing, however, I have failed to receive order from Imperial Headquarters authorizing me to enter into direct negotiations here in the Philippines with the United States Army concerning the carrying out of the order for cessation of hostilities, but I am of the fond belief that upon receipt of this order, negotiations can be immediately entered into. Presenting my compliments ...

The "Tiger" was not only polite and proud, he was stalling. True, he was one of Japan's senior commanders, but he was also acting like an independent power. According to the 8th Army after action report he never acknowledged to Tokyo that he had received the order to cease fire.

On 28 August the first American party under Col. Charles Tench arrived at Atsugi Airfield, an important kamikaze base near Tokyo, and formally took it over from Gen. Seizo Arisue, the Japanese Army G-2. Next morning the 11th Airborne Division landed to add muscle, which was badly needed, although the Japanese were polite and accommodating. A few hours later, at 2:19 p.m., Gen. MacArthur stepped from his C-54 "Bataan" and drove towards Yokohama, about fifteen miles away. Thirty thousand Japanese soldiers, standing at attention, lined the road; they had their backs turned to MacArthur's column of cars, but this was no sign of disrespect. On the contrary, it was a mark of deference.

So the Allied Supreme Commander was already on Japanese soil. American GIs and Marines were landing at various points and taking over installations, but all this was not good enough for Yamashita. The iron warrior was waiting. He had promised to hold out until September, and he would keep that promise.

At 9:00 a.m. on 2 September, Gen. MacArthur, flanked by Admirals Nimitz and Halsey, stepped on the main deck of the battleship U.S.S. *Missouri* anchored in Tokyo Bay. A glittering assembly of Allied generals and admirals surrounded a table covered with green cloth. Facing the table was a Japanese delegation headed by the new Foreign Minister Mamoru Shigemitsu. MacArthur told the Japanese to sign the surrender document on the table. At 9:04 Shigemitsu signed. He was followed by firebrand, Gen. Umezu. Japan had formally surrendered to an enemy for the first time in its 2,600-year history.

Later, when the sun was already hot, the "Tiger" finally came down from Mount Prog. The night before he had written a poem:

My men have been gathered from the mountains
Like Wild Flowers
Now it is my turn to go
And I go gladly

So on 2 September 1945, Yamashita, followed by his chief of staff, Lt. Gen. Muto and Vice Adm. Okochi, senior Navy commander in the Philippines, and about thirty officers, walked toward the lines of I

Company, 32nd Infantry Division. He walked with a cane. He was ugly but his tall, powerful frame looked impressive. He was taken to Baguio, the Philippine summer capital. And there, on 3 September, the capitulation was made formal as British Gen. Percival, who Yamashita had taken prisoner at Singapore, looked on. MacArthur had Percival and Gen. Wainwright of Bataan fame flown from the *Missouri* to Baguio. After the ceremony Yamashita was taken to prison. Japan had surrendered on 2 September but the "Tiger" formally capitulated on the 3rd. The old samurai warrior had outlasted his empire.

As his men came out of the mountains American staff officers began to scratch their chins, rub their eyes, and heave sighs of relief. They had already accounted for 20,311 Japanese dead and 2,300 prisoners between 1 July and 20 August. That should have taken care of all the Japanese soldiers on Luzon according to their earlier estimates. But now thousands of Japanese soldiers came out of the valleys, mountains and caves. A good many were not much more than skeletons, but all were well disciplined. At least 50,500 men surrendered in northern Luzon alone. But that wasn't all. On eastern Mindanao where all had been quiet since 1 July, 34,150 Japanese troops came out of the jungles! All in all, over 114,000 of the enemy surrendered in the Philippines after 15 August. And that is by no means a conclusive figure. Soldiers were being taken prisoner for years afterward. It was enough to turn many an American Army G-2's head gray. Such a force could have held out for years.

'The "Tiger of Singapore" had done it. He had held out until September. There was no question, as the official U.S. Army history put it years later, that he "had indeed executed a most effective delaying action." He had brought out 50,500 men alive out of the original 150,000 of his "Shobu Group." Almost all of them would see Japan again as he had promised them. Thus it appears that Yamashita had the last laugh; but not quite, for he was never to see Japan himself except in his spirit. On 7 December 1945, he was sentenced by an American War Crimes Tribunal in Manila for the sack and destruction of the city during its fall in February 1945. MacArthur upheld the sentence. On 23 February 1946, Yamashita was hanged.

Perhaps he sensed his fate when he wrote that poem.

The Battling Bantams
of Leyte Gulf

by Steve Damien

A T 6:38 a.m., 25 October 1944, Rear Admiral Clifton Sprague's "Taffy 3" force—six escort carriers and a screen of three destroyers and four destroyer escorts—cruised in a calm sea 60 miles off Samar, the large island northeast of Leyte where 150,000 American troops had begun the invasion of the Philippines.

Northernmost of the three carrier groups of the Seventh Fleet's Task Force 77.4 supporting the beachhead, Sprague's baby flattops headed into the wind to launch planes for combat and anti-submarine patrol, and to protect the armada of transports and freighters unloading in Leyte Gulf.

Aboard the screen destroyer *Johnston*, Lieutenant Robert Hagen, the gunnery officer, stood watch. Visibility was still good but closing in with scattered rain squalls to the west over the Samar Mountains. Neither Hagen nor the lookouts saw any sign of the enemy. The dawn alert had ended and the ship was secured from general quarters. Hagen ordered a fried egg sandwich and coffee from a mess attendant. It looked like a routine day.

But within minutes the *Johnston* was pitched into an ordeal of agony. In the most gallant action in U.S. naval history, the destroyers and other screen ships slugged it out with a mammoth Japanese fleet which threatened the entire invasion of Leyte. The Japanese made a bold surprise thrust that was met by a deliberate suicide attack from the tiny U.S. force. Against overwhelming odds, and suffering appalling casualties, they made the enemy break off and run when it was only 70 miles—a little more than two hours' sailing—from its virtually undefended target.

At 6:40 a.m., the *Johnston* made an unidentified surface contact on its radar. Simultaneously, a radioman aboard Sprague's flagship, the carrier *Fanshaw Bay*, heard what sounded like "Japs gabbing" on the American interfighter radio band. It was dismissed as a clumsy attempt at jamming since there was no Japanese striking force in the area. Search planes had sighted enemy columns (beaten in an earlier phase of the battle the previous day), abandoning wounded ships as they ran, steaming west through San Bernardino Strait to the Sulu Sea.

The only Japanese ships roaming loose were Vice Admiral Ozawa's carriers, far to the north off Luzon, breaking radio silence and making smoke, still trying to decoy Admiral Halsey's Third Fleet from the gateway to San Bernardino Strait. Hours before, the aggressive Halsey had taken the lure and radioed Admiral Kinkaid, Seventh Fleet commander:

Central enemy force heavily damaged according to strike reports. Am proceeding north with three groups to attack carrier force at dawn.

At 6:45 a.m., 18 minutes after sunrise, Ensign William Brooks, flying anti-submarine patrol, radioed Sprague:

Enemy surface force of four battleships, seven cruisers, eleven destroyers sighted twenty miles north your task group and closing at 27 to 30 knots.

Sprague was annoyed. "Now there's some young screwball reporting our own forces. He probably spotted some of Halsey's fast battleships. We've got the whole damned Philippines between us and the Nips now." He shouted into the squawk box: "Air pilot, tell him to check his identification."

At 6:48 the verification came. Brooks's voice was strained as it came through the static:

Identification of enemy force confirmed. Ships have pagoda masts.

On the *Johnston* bridge Hagen picked up a spyglass and peered to the north. His sharp features went slack. Looming on the horizon, plunging swiftly ahead on a southwesterly course, were the high superstructures and pagoda masts of Japanese ships. Puffs of anti-aircraft fire dotted the sky as Brooks went in on an enemy cruiser with his anti-sub load—two depth charges.

For brief moments the men in Sprague's Taffy 3 group were paralyzed with disbelief—Where was Halsey, the main cover for the invasion force?

Unmistakably, this was the central force of Vice Admiral Kurita, in Halsey's estimation a thoroughly pounded and crippled fleet in full retreat. But they had regrouped, repaired damage, and reversed course during the night. Kurita had navigated the hazardous San Bernardino passage undetected, covering 150 miles in seven hours, and slipped through the mists into the open sea off the Samar coast. Halsey had exaggerated the strike report and was gone—with all his ships, including three battleships which he was supposed to leave to defend Leyte.

Sprague suddenly realized that only his puny force stood between the Japanese and Leyte Gulf—only baby flattops and the screen of "small boys"—the weak protecting the weaker. His carriers, designated CVEs, were thin-skinned merchant or tanker hulls with flight decks slapped on them. Half the size of the average carrier and armed with only one five-inch gun, they didn't have the last recourse of the vulnerable—speed: their maximum was 18 knots.

Kurita's force was deployed in four columns: destroyers on the flanks, heavy cruisers in the middle. Behind the cruisers were the battleships, and 15,000 yards off either flank was a screen of destroyers and light cruisers.

Seventy-two warships only two hours' sailing time from Leyte Gulf—hawks sweeping down on the chickens.

At 6:52 a.m. Sprague radioed urgent messages for help. The other two CVE groups were 30 and 90 miles south, and the battleships and cruisers to the south were low on fuel and ammo. Admiral Kinkaid had to give the landing force first priority—transports, amphibious and land forces, even the Seventh Fleet itself, were now in peril. He couldn't afford to strip them of even a small force. Sprague was trapped cold. Except for planes from the nearest CVE group, Taffy 3 had to fight it out alone.

Sprague figured the Japanese would detach a few heavy cruisers to maul his force and send the rest on a direct run for Leyte. He might delay them if he could provoke an attack. But he knew that, inevitably, his own ships would be slaughtered.

At 6:59 a.m., the Japanese opened fire from 17 miles with salvos from the 18-inch guns of the super-battleship *Yamato*, committed to its first wartime action. Sprague ordered all ships to lay smoke from their stacks and from the chemical tanks normally used by planes. Black and white clouds billowed over their sterns as the commander ordered the carriers to change course. They turned right on a southerly course, churning along at top speed. They could only head in the same direction the Japanese steamed—toward Leyte Gulf. Sprague wanted to lead the enemy where someone would smack them. He didn't think his ships could last 15 minutes against such odds. But if his group was expendable, he wanted to make it count.

At Leyte, Admiral Kinkaid, stunned at the news of the surprise attack, sent off his first uncoded message to Halsey:

Enemy battleships and heavy cruisers of Kurita's center force firing on Taffy 3.

The *Johnston*, patrolling the sector nearest the enemy, leaped into action as soon as the Japanese were sighted. Her skipper, Commander Ernest Evans, a stocky, burr-voiced Cherokee Indian, rushed from his cabin to the bridge, shouting orders: "All hands to General Quarters...Prepare to attack major portion of Jap fleet...All engines ahead flank...Commence making smoke and stand by for torpedo attack...Left full rudder."

Lieutenant Hagen thought the skipper was out of his mind. No destroyer could close to effective torpedo range of a battleship or cruiser in daylight—and live. Evans saw his puzzled look. "Mister Hagen," he said, smiling, "all we need is a bugle to sound the charge and we'll come running."

Trailing great plumes of smoke, the *Johnston* fishtailed between the main body of Taffy 3 and the Japanese fleet, putting out a smoke screen over a 2,500-yard front. For the first minutes, Hagen felt "completely, sickeningly impotent." The big Japanese guns now had Taffy 3 in range, and the *Johnston*'s five-inchers were useless. Hagen checked his gun stations and waited. Evans gave him a general order to commence firing at any available target as soon as it was in range. Every hand stayed cool as Evans's words came over the bullhorn.: "This is a fight against overwhelming odds from which survival cannot be expected."

It was a curiously formal, graceful statement, but the tough crew of the *Johnston* (famous for actions at Kwajalein, Guam, Bougainville, Eniwetok, Peleliu, and Ulithi) knew that Evans was telling them they would probably die.

An unnerving quiet swept the *Johnston* as she made a flanking run at the cruiser *Kumano*, 18,000 yards away. The angle of her approach brought some of the Japanese ships into echelon so that only their forward guns could fire without interference. At first the enemy's salvos landed harmlessly off the destroyer's stern. Then bunching fire bracketed the *Johnston*, but she kept boring in, her guns pumping. Hagen counted three flaring explosions on the *Kumano*'s bridge.

Sprague had feared that Kurita would cut across the semi-circular arc Taffy 3 was traversing, and blast them. But the Japanese commander foolishly split his forces trying to box in the carriers from three sides instead of forming a battle line with his fast heavy ships so his enormous superiority in firepower would be decisive.

Sprague was being boxed and had to do something fast; his order went out.

"Small boys...launch torpedo attack!"

On the *Johnston*, Evans had anticipated the order by several minutes. As four Japanese cruisers poured lashing fire all about the destroyer for five minutes while she closed on the *Kumano* at 27 knots, the destroyer got off 200 rounds as she darted in, then her spread of ten torpedoes slid into the sea at 10,000 yards. They were observed to run "hot, straight, and normal" tracks—a torpedoman's dream.

Two rumbling underwater explosions were heard, then, seconds later, a third. In the confusion of the attack the *Johnston* streaked in closer and gunned the nearest enemy ships, then whipped about and retired making heavy smoke. As she emerged into a patch of clear sea, Hagen saw the *Kumano* dead in the water. She had taken two hits. The third torpedo had hit the battleship *Kongo* on its starboard quarter, but there had been no time to change the depth setting of six feet, so the hit was ineffective.

The *Johnston* had opened the battle by charging cocksuredly at the enemy. Kurita was bewildered, and for the first time concluded—from the hellbent charge of a single 2,100-ton flush-deck destroyer—that the American force was far more powerful than he had first thought.

When the first dispatches on the *Johnston*'s action came in to Leyte, Kinkaid was encouraged, but he knew the carriers couldn't last long against the enemy's brute power. Bitter at Halsey's action, he suddenly saw the entire Leyte battle plan disintegrating. Another uncoded dispatch went out to Halsey:

Request battleships proceed top speed to cover Leyte. Request immediate strike by fast carriers.

This reached Halsey at 8:22 a.m.

At 7:30 the *Johnston* was hit—three 14-inch shells from a battleship, followed 30 seconds later by three six-inch blasts from the light cruiser *Noshiro*. Many of her crew were killed as her aft engine room and fire room were knocked out. The steering engine went dead. All power to three five-inch stern guns was lost. The ship's speed was reduced to 17 knots, and her gyro-compass and radar on the mast were smashed. Three officers were killed on the bridge. The deck was torn with gaping holes and littered with dead and wounded. Men trapped in the burning, twisted steel began to scream.

Commander Evans lost most of his clothes and his helmet in the bridge explosion. His body was badly burned and shell fragments had ripped open his face and neck. His left hand was blown off. He waved a medic away and wrapped a handkerchief around the bloody stump. Hagen had been slammed to the deck but suffered only a bad knee gash. He stumbled to his feet and shouted into the phone: "All stations...control testing!"

A sudden squall swung in over the *Johnston* and gave her a respite in which to estimate damage and make quick repairs. Hagen's No. 4 gun had no communications and had to fire by local control, almost worthless guesswork at long ranges. Enough power was restored to Nos. 3 and 5 for partial fire control from the director and plot.

Steering was shifted to manual aft, tremendously difficult in that heavy sea. The strongest men still alive on the ship worked doggedly at steering but even they had to change shifts every 15 minutes. While the *Johnston* lay concealed in the rain, part of her radar was repaired and targets appeared on both sides of the ship. Hagen's crews pumped 100 rounds at a cruiser and a destroyer.

Two other screen destroyers, *Hoel* and *Heerman,* raced past the stricken *Johnston* at full speed to unleash their torpedoes. Hagen thought that Evans would now order the destroyer to retire toward the CVEs. Amazed, he heard the skipper's voice booming across the smoking bridge: "We'll go in with them and provide fire support."

Hagen kept his guns bucking off quick salvos until the two lead ships had loosed their underwater missiles. The *Hoel* damaged the cruiser *Haguro*, but took mortal wounds when she attacked the *Kongo*. The *Heerman* was luckier. Her fish hit the cruiser *Chokai*, and she remained in the area to exchange fire with her target. The *Johnston* started to retire, then closed to within 6,000 yards of another cruiser and scored ten hits. With the other destroyers she then made best speed to close on the carriers of Taffy 3, making smoke and firing at the pursuing enemy.

The battle scene was an eerie mixture of light and shadow. Visibility, ranging from 100 to 25,000 yards, was constantly changing. For brief moments the dull, gray sun would break out of the clouds and every ship came in sight. Then rain squalls, black oily smoke from the funnels, and the low-hanging chemical vapor blotted out entire sections of the sea. Every carrier was wrenched in violent maneuvering to evade enemy salvos, and from the *Fanshaw Bay* Sprague could hardly locate his ships.

Just as the *Johnston* slipped from a pall of mist and smoke, Hagen spotted the *Heerman,* only 100 yards off, heading straight at them at top speed on a collision course. Both destroyers backed emergency full, but with her limited speed the *Johnston* could only crawl away from the oncoming ship. Hagen no longer saw any water between the two ships, only the *Heerman*'s bow pointed for the *Johnston*'s bridge. Their crews, transfixed, watched the two silent shapes slipping toward each other through the choppy sea. Hagen gripped the rail hard, but a loud spontaneous cheer went up from all topside hands—the destroyers missed by inches.

Halsey, far to the north, had been deluged by messages. At 7:39 a.m., Kinkaid radioed a third uncoded dispatch:

Help needed from heavy ships immediately.

This was received at 8:41.

From far-off Pearl Harbor in Hawaii, Admiral Nimitz questioned the impulsive Halsey:

Where is Task Force 34?

Sprague, too, had sent a message to Halsey for the first time, saying he was under attack by battleships and heavy cruisers, and giving his position and the bearing and distance of the enemy. He searched the sea and sky with a spyglass—no planes or ships to help. He tried to keep the carriers inside the larger circle of the destroyer screen while also trying to keep them from the heaviest fire. The Japanese, switching from their poor radar to optical range-finders, increased the accuracy and intensity of their fire—300 salvos at two-second intervals.

Plowing along at 18 knots, the carriers were overtaken by three Japanese heavy cruisers. Four carriers were covered by smoke, but the two stern ships, *Gambier Bay* and *Kalinin Bay,* were naked as the formation scudded before the wind. The *Gambier Bay,* on the exposed left flank, was the unlucky ship, hit brutally and incessantly. At 8:27 a.m., she was burning, listing 20°, and beginning to sink.

The main air strength of all three Taffy groups had taken off for missions over Leyte before the sea battle was joined. A few hours would elapse before the flights could rendezvous, return, and locate the enemy. Sprague's carriers had to launch the few available planes under heavy gunfire. There was little or no time for briefing, fueling, or re-arming when the Japanese came racing over the horizon. Planes took off through shell splashes while the decks rocked from explosions and the carriers maneuvered violently to escape salvos.

Few of the pilots had been trained to attack surface ships, but a dive bomber and a torpedo bomber scored hits on a battleship and heavy cruiser. It was a wild, confused, uncoordinated attack by ill-armed planes. When a pilot's ammo ran out, he made dry runs on the enemy ships, trying to divert them and throw their firing off for a few precious minutes. Hellcat fighters ran interference for the bombers, but too often all the planes were bluffing, boring in without any weapons.

There was no panic on the carriers. Repair parties made their rounds; deck crews and re-arming crews got the few remaining planes off; boatswain's sections worked in as much as five feet of water to plug holes below the waterline; engineers and firemen risked death from scalding steam, working knee-deep in oil, choked by the stench of burning rubber, to repair ruptures in the power plants.

At 8:29 a.m. Kinkaid sent off the last of his messages to Halsey:

Situation critical. Battleships and fast carrier strike wanted to prevent enemy penetration of Leyte Gulf.

Halsey received it an hour later and replied that he was engaged with Ozawa's force. He said he had dispatched another carrier group—hundreds of miles east—to help Sprague—but the planes didn't reach the area until two hours after the battle was over.

At 8:31 a.m., Sprague barked out another order to his flotilla: "Small boys on my starboard quarters...intercept an enemy cruiser coming in on my port quarter."

The *Johnston* went into a limping turn to obey. She had no torpe-does, the only weapon with which she could knock out a heavy cruis-er. Forty seconds later Sprague's voice sounded more urgent: "Expe-dite!"

Evans replied with a cryptic message. "Exercise completed." It was the only way he could let Sprague know that he didn't have a torpedo left. But he knew he had to take on the enemy cruiser.

Mustering what speed he could from his crippled ship, Evans cut across the rear of the carrier formation. Anything they did from that point on, Evans thought, was going to be half-bluff. Hagen's crews opened fire, and he saw three more enemy cruisers coming up behind the first. Astern of that column were two big ships he couldn't identify. He prayed for another quick rain squall.

At first the *Johnston* had one advantage, despite being faced with more than 40 large-caliber guns—the Japanese were superb targets for a destroyer's small guns at 11,000 yards, while she presented a difficult one for the enemy. Hagen's crews kept up rapid fire as Evans "chased salvos," an evasive tactic as old as naval warfare; when he saw a splash from an enemy shell he ran straight for it, on the theory that the Japanese continuously corrected range. It worked well until the enemy fired colored salvos to get the range. Then their guns began to crab up on the *Johnston* by 100-yard intervals.

The first eight-inch hit from the Japanese cruiser struck at the *Johnston*'s waterline, tearing a jagged hole seven feet wide, and flooding the forward magazines. Two more shells then struck forward beneath the water. Another hit the uptake, geysering heat and sparks from the forward boiler to the stacks. Fire broke out in the handling room. When Hagen saw flames erupting all over the ship he thought they were finished and expected Evans to abandon ship. But the *Johnston* took 30 more hits! Her agony was no longer believable. But they had diverted fire from Sprague's flagship.

The carriers were now strung out over thousands of yards of ocean, like a wagon train in full flight, and the Japanese were trying to keep them boxed in, riding along both flanks and punishing them with constant heavy fire. The *Johnston* and other screen ships were the outriders, keeping themselves between the carriers and the enemy, scooting to every trouble spot where the Japanese threatened to break through.

At 8:32 a.m., Sprague ordered his remaining destroyers and destroyer escorts to launch a second torpedo attack against the cruisers trying to head his carriers off. The assault was made, then his flagship received a message from the screen commander: "All torpedoes expended."

The second torpedo attack took tremendous pressure off the other Taffy 3 ships. The *Yamato*, the most powerful battleship ever built, spotted the torpedo tracks bearing 100° starboard. She turned to port, then almost due north to evade. This maneuver caught the dreadnought between two torpedo spreads, four to starboard and two to port, chasing her from behind. She couldn't risk reversing course, and continued in a northerly direction for almost ten minutes before the tracks vanished. This virtually removed the supership from action.

And Kurita was on the *Yamato* and was having trouble maintaining contact with his major units.

At 8:43, the *Johnston* headed southwest, trailing the main American force by several miles. Lookouts spotted the listing *Gambier Bay* under heavy fire from the Japanese cruiser *Chikuma*. Evans shouted an order to Hagen: "Commence firing on that cruiser. Draw her fire to us."

Hagen thought Evans was crazy, deliberately slugging it out with a heavy cruiser to keep her off a dying ship. But he had seen the skipper pull off too many miracles not to believe they could do it.

The destroyer closed to 6,000 yards and opened fire. The *Chikuma* immediately took five hits, and her shaken commander reacted stupidly. He could have sunk both shops, but he ignored the *Johnston* and permitted her to escape. Evans had to break off the futile encounter when another enemy cruiser and four destroyers raced in on a new sortie against the carriers. There was no ship nearby to cover them.

As she scrambled in, an eight-inch burst snapped the *Johnston's* mast. Still holding fire, she cut in and placed herself to the left of the carriers in a desperate attempt to prevent the enemy from closing. She was prepared to take on all five ships—and die!

The *Johnston* hit the lead *Terutsuki*-class destroyer 12 times at 10,000 yards. She was then engaged by the cruiser *Yahagi* as the range closed to 7,000, and was racked by eight-inch barrages. Hagen's superb gun crews scored five time son the cruiser and amazingly, the Japanese ship turned 90° to starboard and broke off the action. The *Johnston* immediately shifted her fire against the destroyers but they too turned sharply, increasing the range. For a moment Evans thought they were retreating.

The Japanese then fired torpedoes at the U.S. carriers. But Evans had bluffed them away and forced a premature attack from too great a distance. The fish, launched at 10,000 yards, had slowed considerably at the end of their long run and were moving out into the open sea parallel to the carriers. One of the last serious enemy threats turned into a fiasco. Evans was so startled and pleased he strutted across the bridge, ignoring his serious wounds: "By God!" he shouted, "Now I've seen everything."

As soon as the enemy squadron had launched its torpedoes, it concentrated on the *Johnston,* still thinking it had been thwarted by a heavy cruiser. The *Johnston's* mast hung over the bridge and fires burned everywhere on the destroyer. A 40-mm magazine exploded from a direct hit and ripped a 30-foot gash near the waterline. Sixty men were already dead.

At 9:19 a.m., Sprague again summoned the *Johnston* to lay a protective screen. The smoke was thinning out, and the enemy's main force had a clear line of vision to the bow of his leading carrier, *St. Lô.*

Evans tried to bluff his way out again. He zig-zagged slowly along the flank of two Japanese ships, firing all five guns. It was a pitiful effort: her one engine churned out just enough speed to stay near the enemy, but not enough to leap clear. Hagen watched the swiftly approaching enemy. They seemed to have sensed the kill and were warily circling the *Johnston.* Hagen thought the destroyer was beyond the point where guts—or even a miracle—could save them.

Evans was driven from the bridge by flames and shifted his command to the fantail. He bellowed steering orders through an open hatch to the men who were handling the rudder manually. In the exposed fire-control platform, Hagen and his men were choking from thick black fumes from an oil fire. Like a crippled rabbit, the *Johnston* started turning in every direction.

With every gun firing at easy ranges the Japanese still moved with caution. Two cruisers lay dead ahead of the *Johnston;* three enemy destroyers bore in on her port side. The enemy was finally getting smart: Evans had only one evasive move left, to back emergency full—but that would make his ship a sitting pigeon. For a few seconds the American ship moved forward as her attackers closed in, trading shots with whichever ship presented the most immediate threat. Every hand, witless from concussion and exhausted from the long battle was prepared to die. But they could still delay the Japanese. Every minute counted as the carriers of Taffy 3 plunged ahead toward the safety of Leyte—help had to come.

Three of Hagen's guns were knocked out; a blast had taken out the No. 1 engine and the engineering spaces were all flooded; the No. 1 magazine was afire, and the *Johnston* listed heavily to port, an inert mass of battered metal from abaft her stacks. The No. 2 gun continued to function, her crew loading, ramming, and firing entirely by hand. The men had full knowledge of the risks they ran in operating without an air supply to eject the powder gases. While they tried to get off the seventh shell, the gun exploded killing every man in its crew but Gunner's Mate 3/c Henry C. Paul, the gun captain.

Only a single five-incher, firing by local control in No. 1 turret, was left to duel with dozens of massive enemy guns, but the gun captain kept yelling for more shells, whipping his crew on.

The stench of death lay over the destroyer. She took 40 hits, mostly armor-piercing shells that ripped through the hull without exploding, but she was being punched full of holes at the waterline. Men could barely keep their footing on the deep-slanted deck as tons of seawater poured through the opening and caused the *Johnston* to list.

Evans wasn't giving up, though. He tried to feint one of the cruisers in, hoping to ram her, but three rapid salvos knocked out his remaining engine. All communication was lost on the ship. The depth charges were scuttled. Firemen and watertenders worked on the engineering plant, trying to keep the ship from exploding. But the Japanese continued to batter the destroyer's bulk with shells. Not a man aboard the *Johnston* moved from his battle station. They were afloat—and afloat they still pretended to be a threat, pinning down the Japanese forces.

By 9:45 a.m., however, five minutes after she went dead in the water, even Evans knew the end had come. But it was still difficult for him to issue the last rending order: "Abandon ship!"

Most of the men scurried down the exposed hull on the starboard side and plunged into the water. The 102 wounded were dragged off but there was only room for 45 on the three life rafts and the two floater nets thrown over the side. Evans stayed on the fantail ordering some reluctant men into the water. Two old hands were crying and refused to leave until Evans did. He maneuvered them to the bridge and pushed them overboard with his good hand.

Up in gun control, Hagen and five men were slow in getting the word because of the dense smoke and lack of communications. They were standing by quietly, helpless, wanting to continue the fight. Hagen peered out onto the deserted deck and forecastle. He realized what was happening and shouted: "What the hell are we doing here. Let's go!"

The five men raced for the rail but Hagen remained a moment, almost unconvinced by his own words. Then he saw Evans dropping over the fantail and made his way aft. He had to walk over grotesque piles of dead, and like a man suspended in a dream, he carefully and leisurely took off his shoes and dived in.

Guided by the cries of the wounded, Hagen swam through the debris and helped to keep them afloat. The current was separating the groups of struggling men. At 10:10 a.m., the smoking battered hulk of the *Johnston* began to roll over and sink. A Japanese destroyer moved in to give the 'coup de grace' at point-blank range.

Hagen thought the enemy would strafe them in the water, but as the *Johnston*'s stern rose then plunged into the sea, he saw the Japanese skipper snap a salute in tribute and back his ship off with no hostile gesture toward the survivors.

But it was only the beginning of the ordeal for the destroyer's crew. Only a few men had been able to grab lifejackets before they went over the side, and those were passed to the wounded who couldn't fit on the rafts. Only 50 miles off Samar, they expected to be picked up quickly, but they drifted for four days, fighting off sharks, the blistering heat, and thirst. A few drank salt water and died in violent paroxysms of vomiting. Some were taken by man-eaters, and others, insane with fear, slipped away in the night. They died from exposure, wounds, and exhaustion. The wounded became delirious with pain, and few survived.

In Hagen's group only sixteen men were eventually rescued by a destroyer. Evans, last seen an hour after he went over the fantail with two officers who tried to keep him afloat, was lost among the 147 others from the *Johnston*'s complement of 327.

The destroyer *Hoel* had gone down first with a loss of 253 men. The destroyer escort *Samuel B. Roberts* rolled over and sank with 109 men. With the carrier *Gambier Bay* and the *Johnston*, those were the total American losses. Japanese losses were three heavy cruisers sunk and one badly damaged.

But the fanatical resistance of the *Johnston* and the other "small boys" was no vain sacrifice.

About 10:03 a.m., when it seemed only a matter of time until Sprague's Taffy 3 would finally be overwhelmed and sunk, an amazing thing happened: the crews on the surviving American ships saw the big gray bows of the Japanese fleet suddenly wheel about and head north.

It was incredible because there was nothing to prevent Kurita from bulling through the flimsy carriers to Leyte Gulf, his primary target. But he chose to break off the action and retire.

On the bridge of the *Fanshaw Bay*, a signalman broke the stunned silence:

"Damn it, they're getting away!"

"I couldn't believe my eyes," Sprague said later. "It took a series of reports from circling planes to convince me. And still I couldn't get the fact into my battle-numbed brain. At best, I had expected to be swimming by this time."

Kurita maneuvered his ships aimlessly for a few hours, pondering like a Japanese Hamlet. He was still bent on regrouping his scattered force to hit Leyte Gulf. But as he drew farther from the battle area, he changed his mind and finally retired through San Bernardino Strait.

Many reasons have been advanced for Kurita's decision. His communications were bad, and he never knew that Ozawa had successfully lured Halsey away; the possible appearance of the Third Fleet was uppermost in his mind. The rain squalls and the zig-zagging of the Taffy 3 carriers that forced the Japanese from visual to poor radar-controlled fire were other factors. Also, the air strikes increased and intensified as the battle progressed, and some of Kurita's ships were running low on fuel.

But it was primarily the fierce and determined battle by the screen ships, and the *Johnston*'s assault in particular, that made Kurita break and run.

The heroic crews parried and delayed the powerful Japanese fleet and gave planes from another Taffy group time to reach the battle area. They also gave Sprague's planes time to reload and refuel on Leyte and fly back into action. So magnificent had been their defense that Kurita thought he had encountered big *Essex*-class carriers with heavy cruiser escorts able to make 30 knots.

His staff evaluated the force as elements of Halsey's Third Fleet, and thought there was a fast battleship lurking somewhere in the formation. The continual harassment and show of strength by the "small boys"—the simple fact that nothing that small could take that much punishment and still take on big ships—fooled Kurita and saved the Leyte invasion.

The Battle off Samar was the death throe of the Imperial Japanese Navy. After the war, Ozawa said, "There were no further operations assigned to surface vessels. They were no longer an offensive force and became strictly auxiliary."

After Leyte, the Japanese relied only on ground forces and the kamikaze pilots. There were further bloody land actions on Luzon, Iwo Jima, and Okinawa, but no beachhead was ever again menaced by battleships or carrier-based planes.

Admiral Kinkaid paid the ultimate tribute to the "small boys": "The attack of the destroyers and destroyer escorts against the heavy Japanese ships was the most courageous and effective of the war. It is an epic for all time."

Mail from Corregidor

1942

by Donald D. McPherson

First published in 1975

DURING the months that followed the first bombing of the Manila Bay area by the Japanese, on 8 December 1941, outgoing mail to loved ones was sporadic at best. The chronicle of events after the invasion by the enemy in Northern Luzon indicates an ever-tightening ring around Corregidor Island near the entrance of Manila Bay. Faced with such odds it seems miraculous that any mail could have filtered through such an encirclement, but it did.

This information and research would not have been possible if it were not for Colonel John Vance, U.S. Army (Retired), a student of history, Mrs. Vance, his charming wife, and, in Washington, D.C., the History Division of the U.S. Navy. Colonel Vance was the finance officer for the U.S. Army Forces Far East and he knew just who was being ordered off the island during the siege. Many of his friends took letters south and mailed them at locations where mail service was available. Due to the methods of travel from Corregidor, it is interesting to note that some of his mail went by air, some by surface craft and some by submarine. Upon arrival at Mrs. Vance's home in Maryland, she would record the date of arrival and save both the cover and the correspondence within. Researching this material has been a challenge to me because censorship prevented any mention of ships' names or any other mode of travel. The only concrete evidence were the postal markings, censors' names and endless research into books on the subject in general.

FOUR GROUPS OF LETTERS

All of Colonel Vance's letter seem to fall into four major groups. The *first* group would be two letters carried by a passenger on the U.S.S. *Seawolf* (SS-197) when she sailed for Surabaya, Netherlands East Indies, on 30 January 1942. Rubber stamps "Examined by Theatre Censor" or

"Soldier's Mail" was applied to these covers. A Colonel Strickland, who was an Army pilot, signed one of these covers. Upon arrival, on 7 February 1942, the colonel was reassigned to India and, as neither of the covers has any other postal marking, I assume that they went with him, then, on to the United States from east to west. [Figure 1 and 1a]

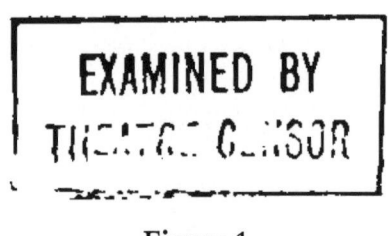

Figure 1

Figure 1a

The *second* group of covers were a bit easier to put aboard specific ships because they were all canceled with a *fancy* type of U.S. Navy cancel and had the signature of Lieutenant Stanley A. Leahigh, ONI, 16th Naval District Intelligence Unit, which was, at that time, located on Corregidor. Lieutenant Leahigh was among those who surrendered to the Japanese but he was killed while a prisoner of war when the Japanese transport, which he was aboard, was bombed in Takao Harbor, Formosa, on 9 January 1945. The specific dates on this *second* group of letters were: 5 February 1942, 14 February 1942, 19 February 1942, 22 February 1942, 28 February 1942, 14 March 1942 and 23 March 1942. The departure dates of the submarines that took all, or most all of these covers, are firm and documented. The 5th of February saw two boats leave in different directions. The U.S.S. *Trout* (SS-202) left the area with 20 tons of gold and silver as ballast bound for Pearl Harbor. The U.S.S. *Seadragon* (SS-194) headed south for Australia. It is problematical as to which boat carried the cover dated 5 February, but I am assuming that it went with the *Trout* because the boat was going to Hawaii rather than south to Australia.

On 24 February the U.S.S. *Swordfish* (SS-193) departed from Corregidor bound for Freemantle, Australia. She evacuated the American High Commissioner to the Philippines, Mr. Francis B. Sayre, and his party of twelve plus five enlisted men. *Swordfish* also carried out two of Colonel Vance's letters, namely the ones dated on 19 and 22 February. These were probably given to one of the passengers because Colonel Vance knew a number of them. The third letter in this date group was sent out with an enlisted man. It is dated 14 February and the sender was Navy Warrant Officer A. E. Salm.

Figure 2

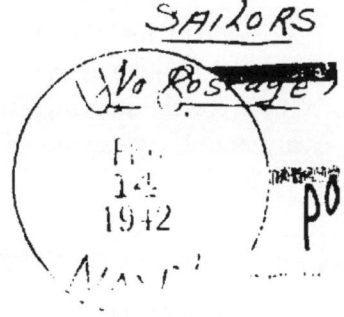

Figure 2a

Figure 2b

The next submarine to leave Mariveles and Corregidor was the U.S.S. *Permit* (SS-178). This boat was used to evacuate fifty-one Naval personnel and also brought out three torpedoes. Her departure date was 16 March and arrival, at Freemantle, Australia, was 7 April 1942. The cover dated 14 March would have been carried by this boat.

Figure 2c

The last of group *two* covers, dated 23 March 1942, would have been sent out by the *Snapper* (SS-185) when she departed 10 April after delivering twenty tons of food for the starving garrison on Corregidor Island. Twenty-seven Army and Navy personnel were also evacuated by this vessel. [Figures 2, 2a, 2b, 2c]

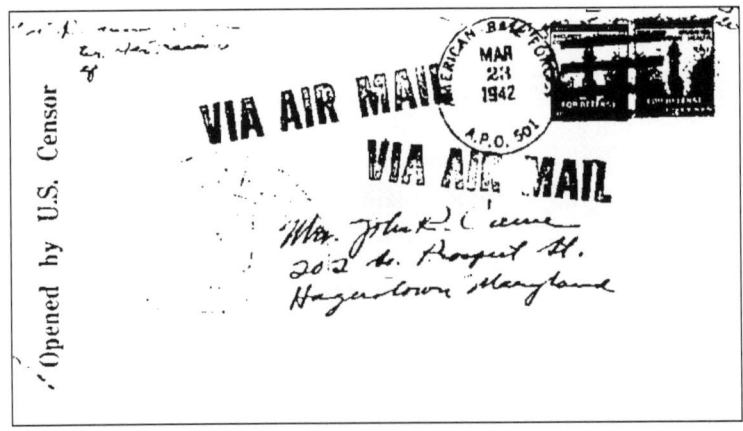

Figure 3

The *third* group of covers, carried from Corregidor, were by far the most challenging ones because every one was canceled at APO 501 located at Melbourne, Australia. All the covers have a very large circular censor mark (2 inch diameter) reading "U.S. ARMY CENSORED" containing a smaller inner circle which, in turn, contains a small shield with the number "1" within it. Below is a small rectangular box for the censor's initials. [Figures 3, 3a] These covers present problems because there is no date to go by with reference as to when they left Corregidor. It is felt that they were given to individual Army officers (Colonel Vance's friends) and that the covers were transported south in various ways. These covers are dated as follows: 20 April 1942, 29 April 1942 and 23 March 1942.

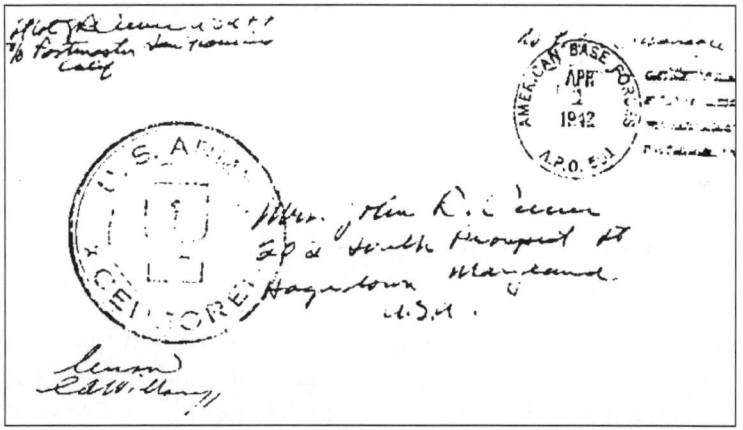

Figure 3a

After a recent talk with Colonel Vance, who checked the correspondence, we have come to the conclusion that the cover dated 23 March 1942 was taken out by Colonel "Pic" Diller, an aide to General MacArthur. The general and his party left the "Rock" on the 11th of March via PT-41 which was a member of PT Squadron 3 commanded by Lieutenant John Bulkeley, U.S. Navy. Upon arrival, at Mindanao, they were flown to an airfield south of Darwin, Australia. The next stop was Alice Springs, then on to Melbourne arriving on 21 March 1942.

Knowing approximately how many days it took to go from the Manila area to either Freemantle or to Melbourne, Australia, I tried to backdate this group of covers and found that it was not as easy as that. Some people (carrying mail) were delayed at various points along the escape route and there is *no* roster telling which person left on any specific days. Among the five covers in this *third* group, I have been able to verify only one person as to method of transportation and to have carried but one cover. That would be the envelope canceled on 23 March 1942.

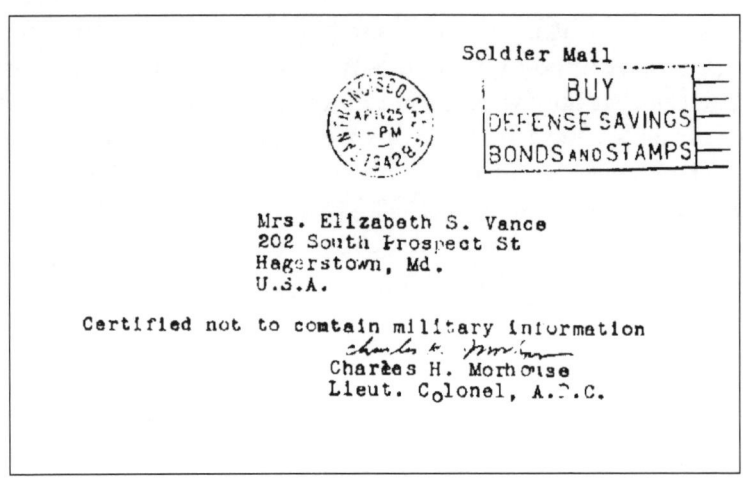

Figure 4

The *fourth* group of covers would be those that bore no markings either from Corregidor or from Australia. One such cover would be the one taken out by Lieutenant Colonel Charles H. Morhouse on PT-41. He was a flight surgeon in the Army Air Corps and Aide-de-Camp to General MacArthur. The cover is signed by him as censor and mailed on 25 April 1942 at San Francisco, California, while he was en route to Washington, D.C. [Figure 4]

Another cover had no rubber stamps on it at all nor did it have any postal cancellations. Both Colonel Vance and myself felt that it had been carried out by Lieutenant Colonel Olson who boarded the S.S. *Legaspi*, a small merchant ship that brought food from Cebu to Corregidor. This was the 18th of February and the ship sailed south to Cebu where Lieutenant Colonel Olson then sent it (the letter) south by still another carrier. Another letter was taken south by Lieutenant Colonel Joe McMicking for Colonel Vance, but I do not know which one of this group (or from group *three*) was the proper one.

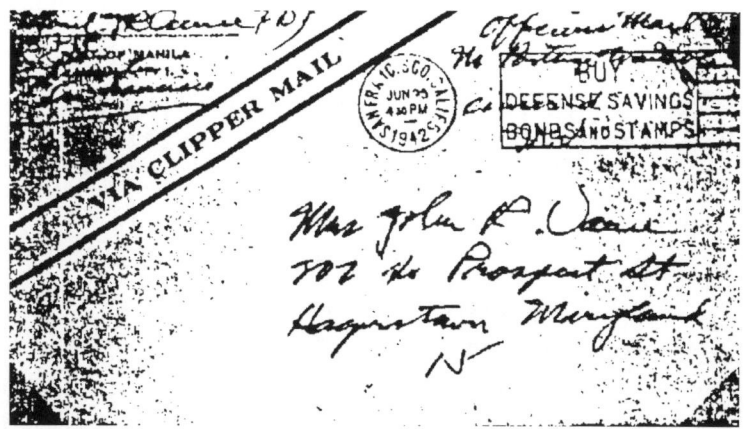

Figure 4b

Figure 4c

A high-wing Bellanca cabin plane nicknamed "Old Number Nine", piloted by Captain William R. Bradford, flew some key military people out of Corregidor at night on more than one occasion. He flew back and forth to Cebu which was 300 miles to the south. It is felt that some of the group *three* covers were taken out by this means of transportation.

The last two covers in group *four* were canceled on 22 and 25 June 1942 at San Francisco, California. One cover was carried on the U.S.S. *Spearfish* (SS-190) which arrived and departed on 3 May 1942 from Corregidor. [Figure 4b] *Spearfish* was the last contact with the besieged garrison which fell just three days later. The other cover was taken out by one of two PBY airplanes that flew a top secret mission to Corregidor arriving on 30 April 1942. [Figure 4c] They left the same day carrying some passengers that were specialists in certain specific fields which required their services elsewhere.

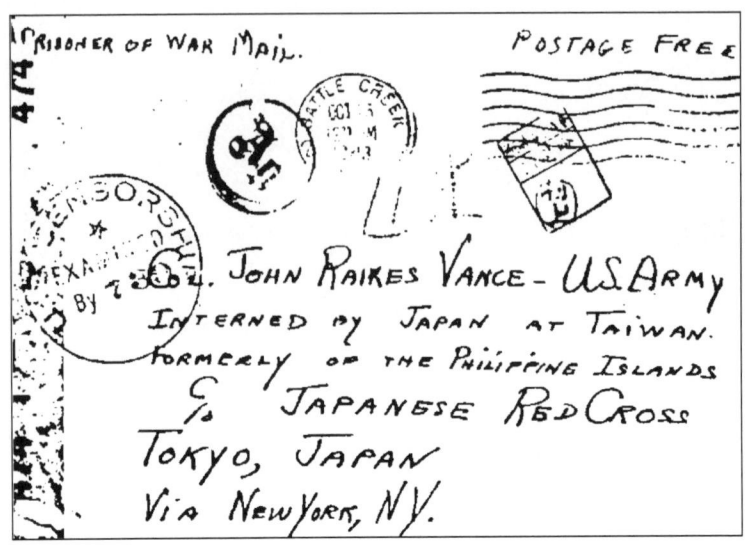

Figure 5

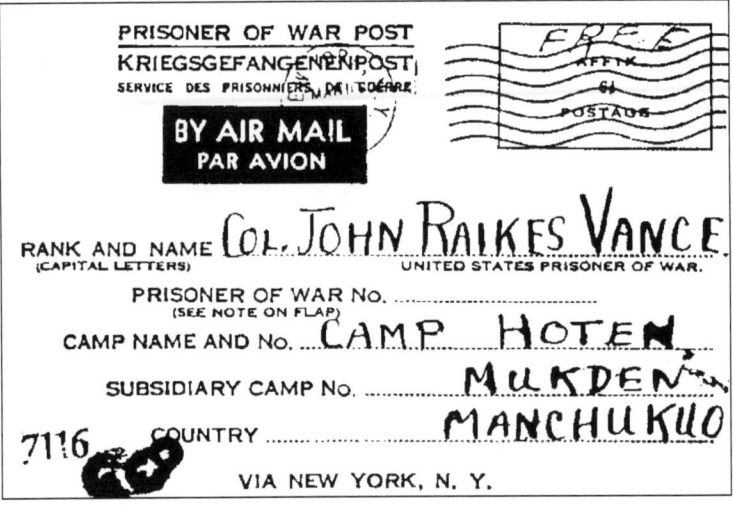

Figure 5a

After the surrender to the Japanese, Colonel Vance was taken to the island of Formosa where he worked as a prisoner of war. In October 1944, he was transferred to Manchuria. The first mail that he received from his wife and friends was given to him in July 1944. These letters were old, to be true, but most welcome. [Figure 5, 5a] A very few pieces of his mail, sent to his wife, arrived in the United States. [Figure 5b] During these years of confinement paper and envelopes were extremely scarce and what few letters arrived, for Mrs. Vance, were limited to a pitiful few words saying that he was "Okay."

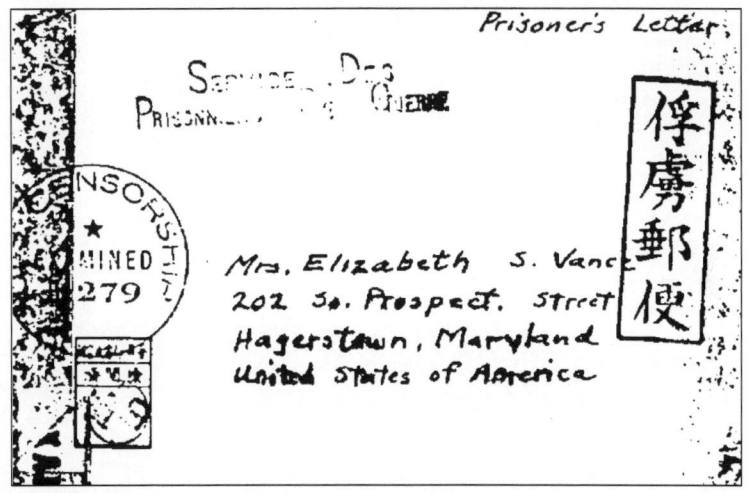

Figure 5b

Of course, there are still a few things that will never be told about this chapter of history but Colonel Vance is still very active and helpful with additional information. One thing that stands out, still unsolved, is why the mail being censored by Lieutenant Leahigh suddenly stops late in the month of March. There should be other mail that has a later date on it than Colonel Vance's letters. Colonel Vance gave his mail specifically to his friends before and after the last date recorded by the fancy type of Navy cancel. Being a colonel in the U.S. Army, he would not have to have had his mail censored through the Naval Intelligence Unit on the island.

BIBLIOGRAPHY

Vance, Colonel John R. *Doomed Garrison: The Philippines, A P.O.W. Story.* Cascade House, Ashland, Oregon, 1974.

Interviews with Colonel Vance, 1974, 1975.

U.S. Navy History Division, correspondence and records.

Minister Remembers Bataan Death March

by Richard Gill

First published 5 April 1981

THE Reverend John Morrett wasn't caring for his parishioners thirty-nine years ago Thursday. He was in the jungles of the Bataan Peninsula, marching for his life.

"It was the worst thing that ever happened to me... physically and mentally... but I put my trust and faith in God to see me through," recalled Morrett, pastor of St. Alban's Episcopal Church, 333 S. Drexel Avenue, Bexley.

In June 1941, Morrett, age twenty-four at the time, quit the Episcopalian seminary in Cambridge, Massachusetts, to become a second lieutenant in the Army.

He became part of one of the most tragic events of World War II, the Bataan Death March. The thirty-ninth anniversary of the beginning of that march is Thursday.

On that march, 70,000 American and Filipino prisoners of war were forced to march sixty-three miles in three days while temperatures soared past one hundred degrees, Morrett said.

After Bataan fell, the Japanese rounded up the prisoners at Mariveles, near the tip of Bataan. The prisoners marched fifty-five miles to San Fernando, then were taken by train to Capas. They walked the final eight miles to Camp O'Donnell, he recalled.

Starved and mistreated, only 54,000 reached the camp. Historians say 7,000 to 10,000 died on the way and thousands escaped. Morrett believes only a few hundred escaped.

Bataan Peninsula extends into the South China Sea and forms the west side of Manila Bay. About thirty miles long and fifteen miles wide, the peninsula is traversed by mountains and covered by jungle.

In the Philippines, Morrett was first assigned to a field artillery unit at Fort Stotsenburg, just north of Manila and about one hundred miles from Clark Air Base.

On 7 December, the day the Japanese bombed Pearl Harbor, Japanese warplanes also destroyed Clark Air Base.

"A few days later, I'd say about ten, they landed in the Lingayen Gulf. They landed at the port of Dagupan and headed south," he said.

"They moved steadily down the island toward Bataan," breaking through American and Philippine troops, he said.

Manila fell on 2 January 1942.

American and Philippine troops withdrew to Bataan, foiling Japanese efforts to split the forces of General Douglas MacArthur. His troops fought a fierce delaying action until 9 April, when Bataan fell.

"We simply held out as long as we could, and that was four months," Morrett said. "By the middle of January we were already on half rations. A lot of the men were suffering from malaria."

Morrett remembers the Japanese moving into the area in force.

"That morning we blew up our guns and the smaller weapons were dismantled."

He recalls being rounded up by the Japanese. Soldiers were lined up on Mariveles road and forced to march north.

"It was in the dry season and there may have been two or three inches of dust on the road. The sun was blazing and the temperature was over one hundred," he said. A Japanese guard took his canteen.

"It was a rugged march that lasted three days. And we marched one full night without rest. They didn't guard us very closely at first, but as we neared San Fernando, the guards became more watchful," he said.

"I didn't see anybody shot, but I heard shooting... mostly from the rear of the column." Still, Morrett said he knew that many were being killed.

"I did see Japanese guards beating fellows who had fallen down, with bamboo poles," he said.

"They did beat the stragglers, and they did shoot the stragglers," he said.

Morrett said many men died of starvation and disease. "There was a lot of dysentery and malaria, and no food," he said.

The prisoners spent the first night in a field. He remembers about twenty Japanese soldiers standing guard.

"The last night we stayed in an area enclosed by barbed wire. A couple thousand of us were crowded into the compound. As I recall, it was near the edge of Hermosa," he said.

"I was afraid," he admitted. "I had a fear of what might happen.

"You were just walking, like you were only semi-conscious of what was happening to you. You just kept putting one foot in front of the other.

"I guess it was like a blind determination to carry on no matter what."

Morrett said he prayed a lot. "Oh, yes, I certainly did that."

He stayed at Camp O'Donnell for five months. He spent the next nineteen months as a prisoner in Dapecol and finally Mindanao, from which he was freed.

Morrett was discharged as a captain in September 1946 and went back to the seminary. He spent eighteen months as a missionary in China and went to Honolulu from there.

He was there thirteen years, the last eight as dean of St. Andrews Cathedral. He was named pastor of St. Alban's ten years ago.

About joining the military, he said, "There were no conflicts. I'm not a pacifist."

"One should serve his country in time of severe crisis or war."

The U.S. Navy at Bataan

by Rear Admiral Kemp Tolley, U.S. Navy (Retired)

DISASTER in the Philippines rode along with that at Pearl Harbor. On the first day of war, MacArthur's modest air force was all but wiped out, mostly on the ground. Two days later, unopposed Japanese bombers obliterated Cavite Navy Yard, the headquarters of Rear Admiral Warren Rockwell, Commandant 16th Naval District (the Philippines) who shortly thereafter moved to Corregidor.

In the confusion and re-orientation the matter of mere existence took up a good bit of time. But there was plenty to do otherwise. Rockwell's little "fleet" was a wide mix, the Inshore Patrol, its mission to defend the sea and Bay flanks of Bataan. Three river gunboats, just arrived from China, U.S.S. *Luzon, Mindanao*, and *Oahu*, were as much at home on the shallow waters of Manila Bay as they had been on the Yangtze and Pearl Rivers. Three minesweepers, U.S.S. *Finch, Quail*, and *Tanager*, were available to check the channel for drifters, so that submarines could slip in and out safely. The big sea-going tug U.S.S. *Napa* was handy for towing barges and cripples.

Lieutenant John Bulkeley's Motor Torpedo Boat Squadron 3 was beginning to make history by its bold night forays and escort of blockade runners. The little boats had a wicked sting which the Japanese were well aware of. Its commander is vividly described by Admiral Rockwell's flag lieutenant, Lieutenant Malcolm "Mickey" Champlin: "Bulkeley was a wild man. Daring, courageous, admirable in many ways, but still a wild man ... a swashbuckling pirate in modern dress ... long unruly beard, two pistols, eyes bloodshot and red-rimmed from starting them out on night missions and from lack of sleep. He walked with a cocksure gait ... high-strung, temperamental, brave and gallant ... one of the most colorful figures in the Philippine campaign." Later he was to take MacArthur out of the Philippines in a daring dash through the Japanese blockade. [See the author's *Cruise of the Lanikai*, U.S. Naval Institute Press, Annapolis, Maryland.]

Floating dry dock *Dewey* lay nearly submerged on one side of the Bay at Mariveles and the old submarine tender U.S.S. *Canopus* on the other hand, beautifully camouflaged against a cliff. During daylight, skipper Commander Earl Leroy Sackett, Ensign Otter, fifteen volunteer gunners, and half a dozen engineers kept ship. All the others headed for caves and tunnels that dotted the Mariveles cliffs, there to sleep out such of the day as bombing lulls allowed.

At night, *Canopus*'s shops hummed, improvising gun mounts for anti-aircraft machine guns and repairing Army tank and vehicle parts. There were visits by grateful Army nurses, who for the first time since their last trip aboard could shuck their dusty, shapeless, sweat-soaked khakis and luxuriate under a hot shower. Dinner, with white table-cloths and linen napkins would follow, with all but forgotten delicacies such as real butter and ice cream made from milk powder in the ship's freezer.

Occasionally, *Canopus* fulfilled her proper mission, when the black, whale-like hull of a submarine slid alongside after dark. In the blackout, her cargo of anti-aircraft ammunition for Corregidor and medicines would be exchanged for torpedoes and diesel oil from *Canopus*'s dwindling supply. By dawn, she would be gone—escorted through the minefields by a PT boat, then into the depths to avoid patrolling enemy warships and planes that appeared at daylight.

Morale in the tunnels was low. They smelled nauseatingly of sweat, mold, urine, and rancid food. After a bombing, choking dust persisted inside for hours.

Mickey Champlin, the admiral's flag lieutenant, preferred to lunch in the open with buddies from the 4th Marines who were manning the beach defenses, even though there might be frequent breaks between bites, with a mad rush for slit trenches or old bomb craters when the planes came over.

This was action of a sort, but basically, it was negative. Mickey wondered how things were on Bataan. The District Intelligence Office, "Mike" Cheek, took a trip over about once a week to keep the admiral posted on how the Naval Battalion was fitting in with the Army's program. This information was important to the admiral. He rarely was invited to MacArthur's regular conferences in Malinta tunnel, even though as senior naval officer present, he commanded approximately one-third of the American military personnel on and supporting the Rock.

Major General Jonathan Wainwright, overall Bataan commander, had sent over to Rockwell asking for a liaison officer, or possibly even a naval aide. Mickey well remembered the lanky, kind-faced man who had called on his boss several months before on the latter's arrival in the Far East. He was willing and eager to volunteer. Swapping his .45 Colt for a revolver and picking up a Springfield rifle and a musette bag with one change of clothes, Mickey completed his preparations by a quick once-over of Bataan maps and the capabilities of available U.S. naval craft. He discussed motor torpedo boat operations and double-checked the extent of the minefields. Knowing the Army's weakness for identifying destroyers as battleships and mistaking tankers for aircraft carriers, Mickey took along a Navy signalman with telescope and ship characteristics booklet.

Crossing over before daylight, he tracked down the general after a brush with strafing planes. "Wainwright was tall, with sloping shoulders," wrote Mickey in his manuscript of his Bataan adventures. "He was not the strapping military figure one might expect. His movements were slow and calculated, face thin, almost gaunt. He would not particularly impress anyone on first meeting unless you became conscious of his eyes—quiet, piercing, and in moments of humor, with an unmistakable twinkle. He looked tired. His first comment was a growl: 'What do I have to do? Go through God almighty before I can talk to the Navy?'"

Rockwell had entrusted Mickey with one of Corregidor's most precious treasures, a bottle of Scotch, present for Wainwright, to help cement relations. It was a nice gesture, but not really necessary; Mickey was soon on the best of terms with the staff, members of a sister service that in those days was a deeper mystery to most Naval officers than men from Mars.

They explained that the Army was anchoring one end of its lines on the impenetrable Bataan mountain spine and the other on the precipitous cliffs overlooking the China Sea. But the Japanese were starting to infiltrate the front all along the coast. The Army had to know whether they were shooting at a seaborne enemy or the U.S. Navy.

To clarify this situation, Champlin set out to establish an observation post. "Hello, Joe!" said a voice from nowhere. It was a Filipino soldier covered with vines. "How long you on Bataan?" It was his first day, Mickey answered, when observed the Filipino, who pointed 200 yards down the trail: "I could kill you down there. I think you learn more soon or you get shot. Where you go?" Mickey told him he was headed for a 100-foot tree. From the top of this, until the Japanese spotted and bombed it two weeks later, he could observe Subic Bay, a Japanese base.

Without benefit of any substantiating documents, Champlin in effect became Wainwright's naval aide, coming to admire his new boss immensely. Once, when shells started dropping onto the road along which the two were passing, all present headed for the tall timber and foxholes except Wainwright, who calmly sat down on some sandbags in a wholly exposed position. Champlin later asked him why he had done this. "What have we to offer these troops," he answered sadly. "Food? We haven't got it. Ammunition? No. That is running low. Supplies or tanks or medicine? No. That is why I go to the front every day. Now do you see why it is important for me to sit down on sandbags in the line of fire while you all seek shelter?"

Wainwright confided some observations that revealed much by implication. Having relied on the green Philippine Army reserve divisions to stop the enemy at the shoreline was a mistake he thought. The best troops available should have been put there—Philippine Scouts and American infantry and artillery. It had been another mistake to try to defend all the islands rather than concentrate all forces on Luzon. There was veiled criticism of senior officers for not visiting the front, which could only be taken to mean MacArthur.

Danger was Wainwright's constant bedfellow. Officers wore their rank insignia on the underside of pocket flaps to avoid special attention from the ever-present snipers. On one occasion, a strafing Japanese plane coming in directly out of the sun was spotted just in time by an alert Champlin—who on graduation from the Naval Academy had been denied a regular commission for poor eyesight. Dragging Wainwright bodily out of the jeep, they hit the dirt seconds ahead of the stream of bullets that tore into the vehicle. From this episode came Mickey's second Army Silver Star, plus an award he valued almost as highly—the Springfield rifle that had become his constant companion. "It is yours," said Wainwright. "But this is government property!" protested Champlin. "To hell with government property! The rifle is now Malcolm Champlin's," the old man said with finality.

As food grew scarcer and the men weaker from dysentery, malaria, exposure and exhaustion, the few remaining cavalry and pack horses were slaughtered for food. First to go, by Wainwright's specific command, was his own beloved personal jumper, Joseph Conrad. It was a heavy blow to a man already reduced to near despair.

The pace had begun to tell even on young Mickey. Skipper Lieutenant N. M. Dial, of the tug U.S.S. *Napa,* picked him off the Mariveles dock one day and took him aboard for a bath and a meal. "This was still a ship of the U.S. Navy," wrote Mickey. "The spotless linen had a most powerful morale effect. Here were people who still lived like gentlemen—people who still had the means to do so, by God, until the ship sank. As long as the refrigerator held anything, it would be well cooked and well served, even though only beans and bread. As long as the laundry worked, there would be clean linen and clean clothes. I felt clean. Cleaner than I had for what seemed like an endless time, and I ate ravenously."

Very soon thereafter MacArthur departed for the south by "Wild Man" Bulkeley's PT boat. Admiral Rockwell accompanied him. Champlin was among the few chosen to go out via submarines; his record through the hostilities had been one of the greatest personal courage and ingenuity, not only on Bataan but in personally destroying oil supplies and stored mines. He had richly deserved the trip and his Navy Cross. The seven ships of the Inshore Patrol were either scuttled or sunk. Four of their skippers died as prisoners of war. All seven received the Navy's highest decoration, the Navy Cross. One, Lieutenant Commander J. H. Morrill, refused the prospect of capture. With seventeen volunteer crewmen from his ship, U.S.S. *Quail*, he made the most incredible journey of the war: from Manila Bay to Australia in a 40-foot open motor launch.

The word "Bataan" suggests to most Americans nothing but grim defeat and the subsequent horror of Japanese prison camps. Actually, until U.S. forces landed on Guadalcanal in August 1942, it was on Bataan and only on Bataan that Allied troops in the early phase of the Far East war fought the Japanese to a standstill. In Malaya, the British, although they outnumbered the Japanese three-to-two, were kept steadily on the run rearward, leaving hot meals on the mess tables, drums of gasoline, undamaged bridges and airfields—"Churchill airdromes," the Japanese gratefully termed the latter. As a result of a combination of American and Filipino guts and good leadership, abetted by Japanese stupidity, it was on Bataan alone that the debacle of Pearl Harbor was in any way atoned.

Ever since the beginning of the campaign the Fil-Americans had been cut to two scant meals a day, eating horses, mules, snakes, monkeys, and carabao when they were lucky enough to nab one. The men were riddled inside with dysentery and outside with jungle rot, shaking with uncontrolled malaria. There was no point in throwing them into an offensive, even though as General Homma testified later, his forces were in such bad shape from disease and casualties that the Fil-Americans could have retaken Manila. It would have been an empty triumph; the Japanese inevitably would have been back with greatly superior forces.

Not even at Valley Forge has the mettle of the American fighting men been more sorely tested. Alongside "Joe," their American comrades in arms, the little brown men of the Philippines had bled, fought, starved and died, while the Sikh police of Hong Kong had gone over in a body to the Japanese, native workmen had laid down their tools in Malaya and Javanese spit on Allied sailors who struggled ashore from sunken ships. At the same time, Filipino civilians were risking their lives to slip food and water to staggering prisoners along the route of the Bataan death march. It was all a powerful lesson in what breeds loyalty and what breeds contempt, a period of anguish mixed with justifiable pride.

I Was a Guard on the Bataan Death March

by Yasua Kata

ON 10 April 1942, I was an interpreter in the Imperial Japanese Army working out of Olongapo Base on Subic Bay. I was on Bataan for special duty at the request of the *Kempetai*, or military police. American prisoners were being sent from southern Bataan up to San Fernando Pamanga. I was with a group who would meet them at the mid-point of the sixty-mile journey and escort them to the rail head. There, others would load the prisoners on trains and ship them to Capas in Tarlac Province. From there, they would be walked to their destination, Camp O'Donnell. The officer to take charge of our area would be a Captain Umara. I knew about the captain from talk around the base. He was a member of *Kokuryu Kai*, the Black Dragon Society. He was part of the military clique that hacked up several conservatives at home. To date, he hadn't met an armed enemy.

Several men waited for the captain with me. They were members of the crack Fifth Division Tokyo Guards. They started out as a platoon but had run into a mine on the way up. There were now three. One was a youngster so new he carried a 7.7-mm rifle, which would later see service as our Model 99, and which none of the rest of us had seen until that moment. The other two were battle-wise soldiers. One they called "Ox" looked big, mean, and dumb, and carried several healed scars on his face and neck. The second, I barely saw because he kept hidden in the deep coogan grass throughout our wait, refusing to offer a sniper a target for a minute. These men were to be the captain's personal guards.

A cyclist appeared about then, and the youngster hurried over to join the crowd that formed around him. He stopped long enough for a drink of water and to stretch himself and was on his way. The boy ran back to us bringing news.

"The march has started. They started to move yesterday. They should be on us at any time." His eyes were wide. "The prisoners come in groups of a thousand each." He looked around at our relatively small number.

"Don't worry, I will protect you," the Ox grinned, and he stroked the boy's cheek. The youngster shook the hand off. The man in the grass crawled out and joined us.

"I don't like it either," he said. "We may be too few to control a thousand men."

"They would have nowhere to go if they did escape," I suggested. He shook his head.

"They might decide they are better off dead and try to take us along with them."

"The cyclist said they were sick and weak and many couldn't even walk," the boy offered hopefully.

"They once told us they couldn't fight in jungles also," the older man said grimly. The Ox started to sneer and the smaller man turned on him like a cat. The bigger man stopped grinning and backed off sullenly. The little man was cautious, but evidently very tough.

"Kata," I introduced myself.

"Tamura," he returned, surveying the area. "I would feel easier with a couple of heavy Hotchkiss guns covering those points." He gestured. "Let's hope the captain isn't a complete idiot."

"He's here, we'll soon see," I said, watching a captured jeep roll into the clearing. An officer was standing up even while it was in motion. Now, as it stopped, he was yelling orders in a harsh, rasping voice. Captain Umara was with us.

The captain was tall and very thin. He wore a sword and a heavy pistol. He informed us that several columns were moving up behind us as reinforcements. However, he pointed out that the few men we had would be enough to control the prisoners because men who surrendered in battle were cowards, and by simply being Japanese we were superior.

Tamura blew his nose loudly. The captain looked at him and showed his annoyance. Tamura returned a gaze of such innocence that it was obvious he had made the noise deliberately.

The captain went on to outline his plan for handling the Americans. It was sound and simple. They wouldn't try anything during the change of men because they faced double the number of guards. The most they might hope for at that time would be a breather. Instead, we would jump them quickly and force them into quicker paces, which we could stand as we were rested. By the time we let the pace fall off they would be too tired to start anything.

"Any breech of discipline," the captain ordered, "is punishable by death. In such cases you will use your bayonets when possible so you will have rifles ready at all times."

"What if they cannot continue to keep the pace?" someone asked.

"That is a breech of discipline," he said, pleasantly. It was obvious we couldn't leave the fallen men free behind us, nor spare our own men from guard duty to cover them. Execution was the only answer, but it wasn't the reason the captain gave.

"We will not disturb ourselves over those who will fall," he said. "They cannot expect the rules of Bushido to apply to creatures who hold themselves so low as not to fight to the death." At that point, the captain looked very noble.

Tamura blew his nose loudly again. Before the captain could take offense, a sound drew our attention elsewhere. There was an increasing rumble of sound in which yells, shots, and screams intermingled with the crashing through brush of many men. The prisoners were arriving.

The strongest prisoners came in first. They were emaciated, starved, and tattered but they were moving at a fair pace. Behind them, the line slowed in direct proportion to the weakness and injuries among the prisoners there. The guards were policing the lines, kicking and prodding them along. One of them brought up an American officer to request an audience with the officer in charge. Captain Umara motioned him over to us. The man saluted our captain, who ignored him.

"Captain," he said, "my men have been without water for nearly two days. We must have water." His own tongue was badly swollen and consequently his speech was hard to understand. The captain indicated that he should repeat his request.

"We must have water," the officer said.

"Tell him his army should have thought about that when they sent men into battle and been prepared for it." I quickly translated the captain's answer.

"The Japs took our canteens," the prisoner said indignantly.

"It is necessary to have all aluminum metal for the war effort," the captain advised him. And dismissed him with a wave of his hand. The guard who had brought him shoved him back into the moving crowd. By that time, our men were in position. The captain screamed the order to start marching and took off as an example at a double-quick step. A groan went up from the prisoners but they did their best to follow. We went at that pace for perhaps thirty yards until the captain slowed down to a walk and finally stopped altogether to watch the prisoners pass by.

One of our men came up. He saluted and waited for the captain's permission to speak.

"Some of the prisoners demand to stop by the road," he said when Umara nodded to him, "for biological reasons."

"No stopping, it will slow us down," the captain said. The soldier shuffled uneasily, "They have dysentery."

"No stopping," the captain repeated and he shoved the man with his palm. He looked up and down the moving column. Men were squatting along the road every few feet. The captain started for them with a scream of rage. He interrupted a prisoner who had just reached the roadside.

"No stopping," he yelled at him. I translated. The man looked at me wide-eyed.

"I'm dying of these cramps, what can I do?" he asked me.

"The captain orders you not to stop."

He looked over at Umara. "Ask the brass what the hell he thinks a man is made of!" the prisoner said in disgust. The captain didn't bother calling for a translation. He kicked the stricken man in the belly. He folded quietly and lay there.

Two prisoners stepped out of the column and braced the fallen man under the armpits and dragged him with them. They knew his fate if left there.

While we stood there, a tall man worked his way to the side of the road. His face was stark white and he clutched his belly. He made clear gestures to the guard as to his intent. The guard looked briefly over at the captain and blocked the man's path. The pause was more than the prisoner could take. He stained himself with slime and blood then stood shocked at his lack of ability to control himself. Suddenly, he started to weep. The captain approached him brandishing his sword. The man looked like an animal in shock, evidently realizing the threat, but was more concerned with the pain of the blow. He flinched under the expected blow. That pleased the captain. He stopped in front of the man.

"Stopping is not permitted," he said. The prisoner didn't understand him but he had reached the end of his personal rope. He looked at the captain.

"Get the hell out of my way, ape," he said and pushed past him toward the brush. He stopped and loosened his filthy clothes. The captain looked around briefly to be certain he was thoroughly covered.

The Ox and the boy flanked him with arms at ready. The captain walked up behind the tall man and swung the flat of his two-handed sword against the back of the man's head. It knocked him flat. Before he could recover himself the Ox was on him smashing his rifle butt down against his kidneys. He dropped flat and moved around slowly. The Ox stood over him with his bayonet poised for a thrust.

"Stopping is not allowed!" the captain screamed at the fallen man. "Make him move."

And he strode off. I started to follow him and from the corner of my eye saw the beaten American trying to pull himself up on his arms. Even as I turned I caught the sickened look on the boy's face. Then I saw the Ox push the man flat with his foot and drive the bayonet into his back.

When I caught up with the captain, he already had two more culprits lined up. One was on his knees, the second stood near him holding his hand as a child holds a battered but precious toy. They turned to me in relief when they realized I spoke their language. I explained the captain's orders.

"We're sick," the one standing explained, "we can't help it. You'll wind up having to kill every man in camp, we all have the trots." I relayed what he said to the captain. He had to admit there was some truth in what the man said.

"It is not allowed, so they must be punished," he reasoned. "Tell them they must eat their own dirt." I told them what he wanted. They looked at each other in dumb horror and neither moved. The captain assumed that they didn't understand his command and made gestures to clarify his order. The one on his knees began to retch. The standing one looked at him in disbelief, then reached for the captain in speechless fury. The Ox shot him through the body. He crumpled on top of his friend, crushing him to the ground. The other worked himself from under him in tears to find Ox's rifle barrel pressed to his head. He looked around at us realizing that this was his last chance at life. His fingers dropped into the bloody slime, then slowly started toward his dark, tortured, tear-stained face.

"Yedo, pure spirit of Yedo," a voice said behind me. Tamura had come up behind us as the incident had closed. 'Yedo' is the old name for Tokyo and in Japan it is used as the incarnation of chivalry. I returned his nod.

"They want you up ahead," he said. I moved forward with him. One of our men was holding several prisoners at bay with his rifle. He said they were breaking off leaves to suck on as they moved along. It was their only form of moisture. The guard wanted to know if it was allowed.

"The leaves don't belong to you," I told him sharply. "Let them eat the trees themselves, as long as they keep moving."

"Who gave you permission to give orders?" Captain Umara asked.

"I gave it in your name," I snapped without turning, "before this idiot and a few others let themselves be drawn in among the prisoners to dig out a few leaves." He was willing to concede a point where his own safety was concerned. He said nothing and moved off. Tamura looked after him. There was an open sneer on his face, and I was certain that the captain saw it.

The trail began to tighten at this point. The heavy growth pushed down against the path in a thick, almost impenetrable tangle. The guards and prisoners were thrown together too closely for my liking. I said as much to Tamura.

"I don't like this place, either," he agreed. "If there are guerrillas in the area, they will hit us here." He moved up ahead and approached the captain. I noticed the captain was being covered by the boy alone and looked around for the Ox. I located him off the road a bit, beating a young Filipino across the face with a belt wrapped around his fist.

"What do you think you are doing?" I asked him. He turned cold eyes on me.

"What does 'Baboui' mean?" he demanded in a rage. I knew if I told him it meant 'pig' he would kill the youngster and I had a fair idea why the Ox had hauled the boy off the road and why the boy had cursed him.

"It's like their 'Sus Maria,' a sort of prayer," I told him easily. "You better get back to the captain before he finds you missing." I took the boy out of his grasp and shoved him among the moving prisoners.

The captain was standing and drinking water. He told us he had sent Tamura up ahead to scout the area and we would proceed with caution even though he knew the area was secure. He arranged himself with the Ox between him so that no sniper could take him without hitting the Ox first, and the boy on his outer flank for the same reason. I was given the honor of leading the way in case there was a grenade set waiting.

We moved on for perhaps half a mile and suddenly found ourselves in a large clearing. Tamura waited, pressed against the roots of a giant tree, mostly hidden as usual. He pointed up ahead without a word.

There was a small flap tent rigged as a sun shade under which several of the brass lounged, watching for the approach of the prisoners. They were flanked on the sides by heavy Hotchkiss 7.7-mm machine guns of the new 01 type.

Our captain wasted no time running over to his superiors; he evidently assumed if they were there, no harm threatened. He was probably right. They saluted him casually and sent him on his way. They sat there, so that the parched prisoners could watch them drink. From time to time, when they noticed a particularly parched American, one of them would pour some liquid on the ground and they would all laugh. One of the prisoners worked his way up beside me as we moved on.

"You are the one who speaks English, aren't you?" he asked. I nodded that I did. "Is there no way of getting some water, any kind of water?" he asked, then quickly added, "For the sicker men I mean." I shook my head.

"We only have what is in our canteens, there is no other," I told him.

"Where can we get water, finally?" he asked, and I realized the thought of water possessed him to a point where even discussing it was a relief. I turned and asked Tamura. He answered without taking his eyes from the tree tops he was searching. "At O'Donnell probably ... the Bamban River is only three miles from it."

I told this to the man who spoke to me.

"That must be twenty or thirty miles from here," he said desperately. "None of us will make it."

I shrugged.

"Isn't there anything along here that we can use... a creek, a well, a spring... anything?"

I told him I didn't know the area. We walked further and he turned again.

"Is the Bamban water drinkable?" I relayed the question to Tamura who by now was moving along like a hunting cat. He answered off-hand.

"It isn't Sakurayu," his reference was to a drink which is a delicacy among our people. It is made of hot water with salt and cherry blossoms added.

"It's foul," I advised the prisoner. He shook his head gravely.

"There probably isn't one water-purifying pill among the lot of us. The dysentery will kill half the camp," he said.

I moved away from him. As I did so, I could feel a dozen pair of eyes glued to my water bottle. They must have been praying that the talk would lead to a taste of water for one of them.

There was one more commotion ahead. I ran forward. The captain and his guards reached there the same time as I did. Several of the prisoners had come upon a small puddle by the side of the road. The radiator of an auto or something similar had broken and the discolored water had not soaked completely into the ground. Several men had thrown themselves on it and were licking at it wildly.

"It is not allowed!" the captain screamed. "It is a breach of discipline." He had the guards shoot them where they lay. He was stamping around pointing out his handiwork to the passing prisoners when Tamura doubled back to him. There was something happening up ahead. It could be a trap. The captain immediately covered himself with his arrangement of men as shields and gave Tamura permission to move ahead of us. I walked a few feet with him.

"What's wrong?" I asked. He was peering ahead of him.

"Bird calls," he said, "where even in the jungle these birds are quiet when groups of men approach. Someone is up ahead." I fell back to the captain and Tamura worked his way into the brush. The captain was giving orders that in case of attack alternate guards should fire at the attackers and the others should kill as many prisoners as possible. In that way, he reasoned, the attackers would have to realize what harm they were doing to their friends and retire.

We slowed almost to a halt and the prisoners quickly realized something was happening. I think they had less hope for rescue than the pleasure of seeing their captors on edge. We moved along for perhaps five minutes. Then from up ahead there came a flat sound like a shot and a shrill scream. The captain didn't move. After a minute, he pointed to the boy guarding him, myself and two guards and ordered us to investigate.

We worked our way cautiously through the brush until I heard a groan. It was Tamura. He lay face down and when he heard me coming up, he raised a finger and pointed at something hung on a bush. I didn't recognize it for what it was until I sniffed at it. It was a firecracker. In sudden understanding, I stood up and ran for Tamura. But he was dead, the victim of a Filipino booby trap. They used a firecracker on a trip device, and lined the surrounding territory with beds of sharpened bamboo stakes. The sound of a shot would send men diving for cover and they would meet their death on the stakes. Tamura's jungle-fighting reflexes had been too good. He moved before he thought.

I went back and told Captain Umara what had happened. It was possible that the trap was old, but it was equally possible that a guerrilla band was in the vicinity. Once darkness came, it wouldn't take much of a diversion to start the prisoners rioting. At this point, they knew that they had little to lose.

Umara realized this and, after checking his maps, decided we could make the rail depot before dusk if we picked up the pace. His orders were passed down the line and our guards went among the Americans with kicks and bayonets and butts to force them into action. We no sooner got them underway when a captive non-commissioned officer approached Captain Umara.

"The men just can't stand the pace," he pleaded. "Can't you allow us a few minutes rest?"

"That would leave us in a bad tactical position, where your friends are concerned, after dark," the captain answered him. The man listened to my translation.

"We will give some kind of guarantee that we won't try to escape ..." he started to argue but thought better of it. The captain motioned him back to his men. He refused to move.

"The pace will kill some of them!" he shouted. Umara didn't so much as ask for a translation. He waved the guards to push the man back among the prisoners. The man went and started to pass a word which the others nodded to. I moved in closer and caught what he was saying.

"He is advising a slow-down," I warned Umara. At the captain's command two guards broke the prisoners away from the offender. The Ox walked behind the man with his bayonet pressed against his back.

"Move faster," I told him, translating Umara's orders. The prisoner looked at me and kept his slow step. The Ox moved faster pressing the blade into the man's back. For a brief second, it looked certain that the man would break and move faster. Instead, he drew himself erect and stood his ground. The Ox moved toward him slowly. As we watched, the blade entered the man's back. Suddenly, it showed in the front of his chest. He pitched forward, falling free of the blade. Then he slowly started to his feet and regained them. Umara walked over and blew off part of his head with a big lead bullet from his 9-mm revolver.

Several prisoners started forward and the guards cut them down with rifle fire. They put down five or six and immediately the Ox was among the fallen men finishing them with his rifle butt. The others turned stricken faces away from the carnage and moved on; the possible rebellion was broken.

We reached our destination some twenty minutes later. Other Imperial troops loaded the prisoners into box cars and our end of the job was done. Umara walked around patting his belly with both hands like a man well satisfied with a large dinner.

"They will not forget us," he kept saying as the many faces turned for a last look at us as they disappeared into the box cars. "They won't forget us," he repeated and laughed.

I wondered if he remembered his words later when he was part of a regiment of the Fifth Division when it was annihilated by American troops on Saipan.

The 26th Cavalry
in the Philippines

A Classic Delaying Action

by Jeffrey W. Woodhall

THE history of American horse cavalry did not end with the Indian Wars, nor with World War I. In 1941, while the world watched in apprehension as massive armored formations wrestled for control of North Africa, a determined band of horsemen trained and waited for war with Japan. They were the 26th Cavalry Regiment (Philippine Scouts), and they were the last of the type of men who rode with General "Light Horse Harry" Lee in the American Revolution. The 26th Cavalry's story has never been properly told.

In 1920, the American Expeditionary Force Cavalry Board recommended that since "the mounted combat of large bodies of cavalry is probably a thing of the past, cavalry units should be stricken from the Infantry Division, and the number of total (cavalry) units cut." The reorganization went into effect in 1921, and effectively cut the mounted force to less than half its former strength.

Between 1922 and 1932 reorganization resulted in more cuts in units and personnel. The only bright spot for horse cavalry units came in 1922 when the 26th Cavalry was organized in the Philippine Islands.

This unit with two squadrons, each with two cavalry troops, one light machine gun troop, and a headquarters troop, was unique, as it was manned by Filipinos and officered by Americans.

However, the demise of the horse soldier accelerated in 1931 when Chief of Staff, General Douglas MacArthur, directed the Army to adopt mechanization and modernization "as far as is practicable and desirable." This type of pressure led to the establishment of a cadre for a mechanized cavalry regiment at Camp Knox in late 1931 and the mechanization of the 1st Cavalry Regiment at that post in 1933.

In 1938 the War Department directed the mechanization of all remaining cavalry units. The era of the horse soldier was thought to be over, except for the 26th Cavalry—for they had been forgotten. In early 1941, the 26th was beefed up, from 575 to 789 men, and one additional troop was added to each squadron.

However, the regiment was still smaller than other cavalry regiments. About this time, a scout car platoon was assigned to the regimental headquarters and headquarters troop. The 26th had no artillery, but a considerable number of trucks were added.

The regiment lacked anti-tank guns and mortars. In fact, there was no modern equipment or weapons in the entire regiment. Most equipment was World War I issue or older—some dating to the Philippine Insurrection.

The 26th Cavalry might have been short in men and modern weapons, but they were definitely stout in heart. The regiment was known as the best trained Regular unit in the Philippine Islands, if not the whole U.S. Army.

The reasons for the high state of training were many, foremost being that the regiment was a Regular U.S. Army unit with all the tradition and esprit de corps which that implies.

Second, many of the Filipino career non-commissioned officers (NCOs) had over thirty years service, and even though the regiment was fairly new, most of the NCOs had come from the old, island Cavalry Guard units.

Third, even the lowest private in the Scouts held a very enviable position in Philippine society. Their service was fairly prosperous in a very structured pre-war caste system where money and birthright dictated social status. Due to the benefits accorded them, the scouts were proud of their units and intensely loyal to their officers. The scouts actually considered themselves more American than Filipinos. This was not generally true of conscripted Philippine Army units.

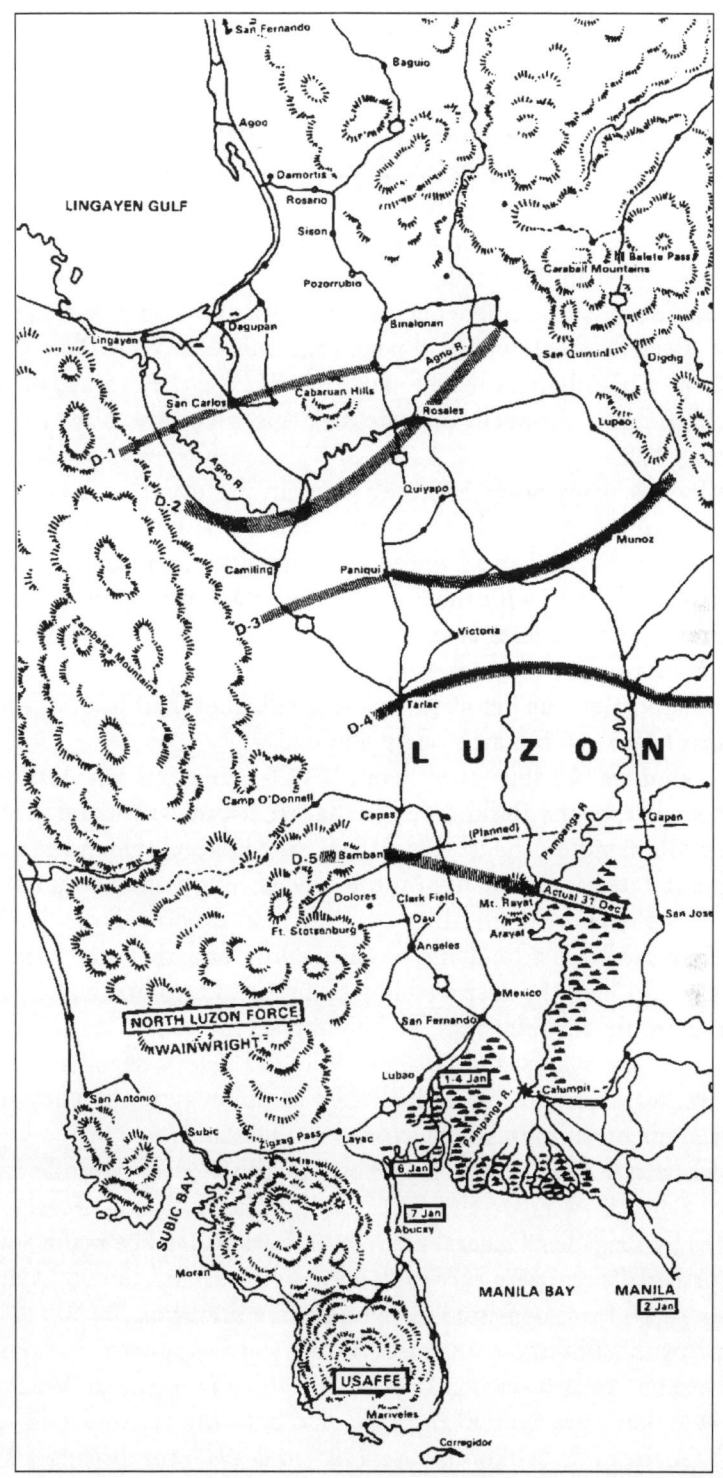

Finally, the 26th Cavalry's officers were the best. Some, like General Jonathan M. Wainwright, Philippine Division commander, and Colonel Clinton A. Pierce, Commander, 26th Cavalry, were old-style cavalrymen who never quite got over the days when cavalry meant horses, not smelly, noisy tanks. Others like Captain T. J. H. Trapnell would prove themselves again and again during the coming days.

The Islands were a lush paradise, and life was good in 1940. But it suddenly ended in the spring of 1941. The threat of war with Japan was imminent, and all dependents were ordered home to the United States. General Wainwright knew that the old War Plan Orange (WPO-3), which he had helped draft in 1922 for the defense of the islands, had been dropped and the strategic plan was now to defeat Germany before Japan.

WPO-3's main point had been that, in the event of invasion, the troops would immediately withdraw onto Bataan and hold there for up to six months and await reinforcements. But Army and Navy planners knew that even with the Pacific Fleet intact, due to the war in Europe it would be at least two years before sufficient troops and equipment could reach the islands' garrison.

So, almost a year before the islands fell, they had been effectively written off—the troops arbitrarily doomed.

To counter the shift away from WPO-3, General MacArthur was transferred from the Philippines to the American Army and placed in overall command on the islands. He instructed his commanders to plan to fight and defeat the enemy on the beaches. No withdrawal onto Bataan was planned. MacArthur believed the firepower of the Navy would be available to aid his beach defense and that the Army Air Corps would "add the decisive blow to any invading enemy."

It is ironic that the massive modern technology MacArthur was planning to use against the Japanese would in reality devolve to a band of brave horsemen whom he had tried to do away with. They would give him his most impressive victories in the islands.

MacArthur created the Northern Luzon Force, commanded by Major General Wainwright, and the Southern Luzon Force, commanded by Brigadier General George M. Parker, Jr. The major units in the northern force were three infantry divisions and the 26th Cavalry. The southern force consisted of two infantry divisions.

All of the Filipino-manned divisions were supported by artillery, but no tank units were stationed in the islands. General MacArthur requested that some be sent immediately, but only two federalized National Guard tank battalions, the 192nd and 194th comprising a Provisional Tank Brigade arrived in the late fall of 1941. They were equipped with the new M3 Stuart tanks armed with one 37 mm gun and two .30 caliber machine guns. However, the crews were untrained. General MacArthur firmly believed that the war with Japan would not start until April or May 1942 and was very optimistic about the readiness of his troops.

What General Wainwright found instead were units unprepared except for the 26th Cavalry. He made rough plans to do the impossible—defend 600 miles of open beach with untrained troops and understrength units.

The one bright spot was the 26th Cavalry that had been training as though they were already at war. They never moved without full packs and wartime ammunition loads. Since the invasion was expected to come after dark, the 26th's night problems were stiff and exacting.

Training was first perfected in the classroom and then moved to the field with platoons and troops competing. Each session was followed by blistering critiques that spared no one, including the regimental commander. Exercises were repeated to correct weaknesses.

Blank ammunition of all calibers helped accustom both men and horses to gunfire. Special attention was paid to conditioning horses and pack mules. Horses were repeatedly loaded on and off trucks to accustom them to this mode of travel.

On the night of 7 December (6 December in Hawaii), General Wainwright had dinner with Colonel Pierce. They talked of the old cavalry days and joked about the movie review of the week in the local paper, a new Errol Flynn film, entitled "Custer's Last Stand." They hoped that history wouldn't repeat itself.

Then he and Colonel Pierce rode their horses over to inspect elements of the 26th Cavalry and its pack train. After leaving Colonel Pierce, General Wainwright returned to his quarters and turned in at 2300. The next day the waiting was over.

When war exploded over the American fleet on the morning of 7 December, the 26th Cavalry was deployed as follows:

- Troop F was at Nichols Field (an Army Air Corps base);
- Troop A was practicing tactics in the field;
- small detachments of Troop B were on outpost duty at Baler and Dingalan Bays on the east coast of Luzon
- and the remainder of the regiment was at Fort Stotsenburg, Pampanga, about sixty miles north of Manila.

When word of the Pearl Harbor attack came, General Wainwright ordered Colonel Pierce to place the regiment on full alert and they worked out details for dispersing the regiment to make it safe from air attacks. The bulk of the regiment was to be moved into a concealed bivouac about three kilometers north of Fort Stotsenburg. Troop F would rejoin the regiment by forced march as soon as possible. In less than three hours, the regiment was moving with all equipment and ammunition—the 26th Cavalry was going to war.

The first day of war was one of mass confusion supplemented with impotent rage when Clark Field, the major Army Air Corps base, was bombed and the bulk of the Army Air Corps in the Philippines was destroyed on the ground. Fort Stotsenburg was attacked at the same time, but with little effect.

Troop F rejoined the regiment on 10 December, and recently promoted Major Trapnell learned from the Regimental S3, Lieutenant Colonel William E. Chandler, that General Wainwright had ordered the 26th Cavalry to act as a mobile reserve for the Northern Force and to remain where they were until further notice. The regiment bivouacked in the Bamban River valley.

On the afternoon of the 10th, General Wainwright ordered Colonel Pierce to move the regiment to a position in the hills northeast of Clark Field to cover potential drop zones to preclude an expected enemy paratroop drop to seize the airfield. Prior to the movement, an urgent message was received that enemy paratroops were landing in the vicinity of Cabiao, about fifty kilometers west of the regiment.

Colonel Pierce asked for a platoon of tanks from the provisional tank brigade and a platoon of self-propelled 75 mm guns from the artillery. He dispatched the 2nd Squadron under their new commander, Major Trapnell, to destroy the enemy paratroops.

The remainder of the regiment, less Troop G which was dispatched to relieve the elements at the Baler and Dingalan Bay area, was to screen northeast of Clark Field from Mabalacat to Wardville.

Early the next morning, the 2nd Squadron reported that no enemy paratroops were found and that the parachutists had been U.S. pilots shot down by Japanese pilots. The screen also had not turned up anything and the regiment was ordered to return to a new bivouac in a woodline along Taconda Hill, three kilometers south of Fort Stotsenburg. Although not as safe as the first bivouac site, being smaller and more open, the regiment would be closer to likely enemy drop zones.

During air attacks approximately forty horses and twenty troopers were wounded and two soldiers were killed. After the bombing, one section of the regimental scout car platoon was dispatched to the infantry forces at Tuguegerao, to enhance communications in the Cagayan Valley.

As a result of constant air attacks, Colonel Pierce ordered officers' calls and meetings to be held at the regimental headquarters building at Fort Stotsenburg, believing that the air attacks there had ceased. This worked well until Major Ketchum, Commander of the 1st Squadron, and his officers had to abandon the headquarters through windows and doors when the building was bombed and strafed. No one was hit, but Colonel Pierce had had enough and received permission from General Wainwright to move the regiment to a more concealed assembly area, south of Clark Field.

Early on 13 December, the regiment began to move and completed it without any losses, due to wide dispersion and the regiment's excellent march discipline. However, at the time, the Japanese Air Force was elsewhere supporting the first, yet undiscovered, landing of troops at Aparri, on the northern tip of Luzon.

When discovered, these landings were believed to consist of only two reinforced infantry companies. General Wainwright believed that the main landings would come in the Lingayen Gulf area and the Aparri landings were "nothing more than a decoy." As a result, he did not oppose them.

Late in the afternoon of 13 December, General Wainwright moved his Northern Force headquarters to Bamban, twenty kilometers north of Fort Stotsenburg. In the early morning hours of the 14th, General Wainwright ordered the 26th Cavalry to move quickly to Bamban to plug any gaps in the lines as the Japanese forces advanced.

This was very important now that hostile landings had also been confirmed in the west at Vigan, located just north of the Lingayen Gulf. If the main landings were still to come in the Lingayen Gulf area, the 26th Cavalry would be the only trained unit that General Wainwright could throw at them. Also, if the landings at Vigan and Aparri were, in reality, the beginnings of the main landing effort, then the 26th Cavalry would be in position to reinforce other Philippine Army units already engaged.

By 15 December it became apparent that the worst was happening. The untrained Filipino troops were no match for the Japanese forces who were rapidly driving south from Vigan toward Lingayen Gulf. General Wainwright now knew that the main landings would take place at Lingayen Gulf, and if the enemy force at Vigan was allowed to come in contact with the forces defending the gulf, his troops would be fighting on two fronts and would be unable to defeat the landing force. Therefore, the 26th Cavalry was ordered to Vigan, and Colonel Pierce was told to either defeat or delay the enemy long enough to allow the main Japanese landing at Lingayen Gulf to be defeated.

During the night of 16 December the 26th Cavalry, now numbering 699 men and 28 officers, began moving toward the town of Rosales, where Colonel Pierce believed he could launch a counterattack against the Vigan force if they broke through the Philippine Army units and continued down the coast toward the gulf. The regiment arrived in Rosales before daybreak on the 18th, where it remained for two days.

On 20 December the regiment was ordered to dismount Troop C and send them north of Bowtac to guard the critical mountain road that would connect the Aparri hostile forces with those in the Vigan area. Troop C turned their horses over to Troops A and B, mounted school buses, and moved north, never to rejoin the regiment until they were in captivity.

The fight against the Vigan force grew critical when the Japanese slipped across a mountain range that was thought impassable, and struck the Filipino force that had been containing them on the right flank. The Filipinos broke, allowing the Japanese to flood into the coastal valley along Lingayen Gulf and to capture the town of San Fernando, in La Union province on the gulf. General Wainwright, disturbed that his line could be broken so easily, ordered Colonel Pierce to counterattack north immediately since the regiment was only about a two-hour march south of the enemy lines. The 26th Cavalry, while underway and under air attacks, received further orders attaching it to the 11th Infantry Division, Philippine Army (PA), and calling for it to halt at Pozorrubio and await further orders.

The 26th Cavalry waited on the orders all through the night of 21 December. Only the animals were fed and watered that night. Troopers later reported that that night's lonely vigil was the longest they could remember. At 0300 hours the order was given to move "with all possible speed" to Rosario to help the 71st Infantry (PA), which had been ordered to secure the Manila north road to preclude further southward movement of the Vigan force.

But before the regiment could move, it received reports that the Japanese had landed troops at Banang, just southeast of San Fernando, and at Agoo, southwest of Banang, cutting off the 71st Infantry with repeated attacks from the flanks and rear of the unit dividing it in two.

The situation was rapidly deteriorating even though the bulk of the Japanese invasion force was still aboard ship.

General Wainwright realized the only hope was to keep the enemy from advancing farther south and cutting off the remainder of his troops still defending the beach area. General Wainwright also knew that the Japanese were heading for Manila and it was necessary for him to hold up the enemy's southern advance. The 71st Infantry must be left to fight its own battle.

General Wainwright ordered Colonel Pierce to hold the enemy advance at a line along the Damortis–Rosario road. The scout car platoon was detached and sent to Damortis to gather intelligence for General Wainwright's headquarters, since the enemy that had landed at Agoo was flooding onto the gulf plain and threatening Damortis.

The weary days and nights of marching and countermarching appeared to be at an end and the 26th Cavalry moved to their positions north of the road and prepared to fight and die to hold the invading force. General Wainwright believed that the 26th Cavalry was his last hope. They had to give him enough time to remove the remainder of his beach defense force before it was encircled. In fact, he remarked to his chief of staff that, "The 26th [cavalry troopers] are the only ones sure to stop them [the Japanese] from being in Manila in a few hours."

Colonel Pierce knew his regiment would fight, even though they suffered a severe lack of food and sleep. They were under strength, having detached troops C and G, the scout car platoon, and eighty-five key NCOs and officers for staff and command duties in other Philippine Army units. They had no artillery, and Colonel Pierce wondered how long they could last. General Wainwright received five tanks of a battalion he had requested for the 26th Cavalry. However, due to a lack of fuel and their late arrival, the tanks added nothing to the battle of Damortis.

The biggest problem facing the 26th Cavalry in holding the Rosario–Damortis line was the road itself. It was a hard-surfaced road winding through the foothills between the two towns and its curves hindered observation and fields of fire. To the north were the mountains of north Luzon, and to the south was heavily wooded, rolling terrain. Additionally, no fewer than five separate trails, all originating from the Japanese-held Agoo region, entered the road at various points and could allow the enemy to bypass defending units almost at will. Colonel Pierce decided that the key to defending the line was to move the regiment to Damortis, and delay back to Rosario, rather than to defend the easily breachable line between the two towns. This way, the

26th could keep the enemy forces to their front and prevent them expanding south and west toward Rosario without first defeating the regiment.

It was a dangerous gamble since the enemy might be able to slip forces behind the regiment by infiltrating toward Rosario on the trails from Agoo. Colonel Pierce did not forget those trails, and broke Troop F into three strong patrols, each reinforced with a machine gun section. They were ordered to advance northward along each of the three largest trails until they made enemy contact. Then they were to delay back toward the road, falling back under extreme pressure. Smaller patrols were picketed along the two smaller Agoo trails. The remainder of the regiment started for Damortis.

Colonel Pierce arrived on high ground overlooking Damortis around 0900 and immediately linked up with the scout car platoon. The platoon leader informed Colonel Pierce that he was in contact with strong Japanese forces about one kilometer north of Damortis, and that at least thirty enemy ships were in the gulf unloading troops and equipment, with about forty-five other ships standing by.

Colonel Pierce could mark his regiment's advance from Rosario by watching the Japanese dive bombers and fighters attacking the road below him. By 1300 the regiment began closing on Damortis, but losses to air attacks had been heavy.

Colonel Pierce ordered the 1st Squadron (–), to take up defense positions about 600-800 meters north and 500 meters east of Damortis. The 2nd Squadron (–) would establish a second line along the road about three to five kilometers east of Damortis. The machine gun troop (–) was supporting the flanks of the regiment and protecting the regimental command post on a hill about halfway between the squadrons.

The defensive positions were almost totally lacking in overhead cover and were occupied under a hail of bombs and bullets, but the discipline of the regiment held and no troopers broke under the heavy, continuous attacks. By 1230 the positions were occupied and the thin line of cavalrymen was about to do battle with the entire Japanese invasion force.

They did not have long to wait. Shortly after 1300 hours the enemy struck the 1st Squadron with infantry, tanks, artillery, dive bombers, and naval gunfire. It soon became apparent that the 1st Squadron could not hold on very long, even though they were extracting a terrible toll from the Japanese attackers.

Finally, around 1440, Major Ketchum requested permission to withdraw to the second defensive line, which the 2nd Squadron had been preparing. Before the withdrawal could be executed, the machine gun platoon, which had been attached to the 1st Squadron and guarding the regimental left flank, was overrun by enemy tanks. Major Ketchum ordered the withdrawal to continue, but threw a desperate mounted counterattack at the tanks hoping to save some of the machine gun platoon.

A composite platoon from Troop A attacked the enemy tanks with hand grenades and pistols while riding among and past the vehicles. The surprise cavalry charge allowed some members of the machine gun platoon to rejoin the regiment and the remainder of the 1st Squadron to withdraw at a full gallop past the regimental command post toward the regimental lines. The cost had been high for Troop A for it had lost about half of the counterattacking force, but the enemy tanks halted in confusion. It is believed that one enemy tank was destroyed.

Colonel Pierce found it hard to hold his position and was reinforced by a company from the 12th Infantry (PA), a company from the 71st Infantry (PA), and five tanks of the 2nd Platoon, Company C, 192nd Tank Battalion. These tanks started up the road toward Damortis to support the regiment, but would arrive too late to help. Meanwhile the regimental command post was fighting as the rear guard against the Japanese who had again begun to advance. Fortunately, Troop A's attack had made the enemy hesitant about entering the draw through which the 1st Squadron had escaped, for they feared another attack on their armor while in the confined area.

Troop A by this time, around 1500, had successfully slipped east and was headed cross-country to rejoin the regiment, leaving only the command post and the machine gun section to guard the right flank. Colonel Pierce started moving the remainder of his force back toward the second position, and by 1530 the regiment was in place along their second position, halfway between Damortis and Rosario. The five tanks arrived and moved past the regiment's defensive position, heading back along the road toward Damortis. Somehow, they ended up a little north of Damortis, headed toward Agoo, when the lead tank was destroyed by enemy tank fire. The other four tanks, each struck by light anti-tank fire several times, quickly retreated back toward Rosario. No enemy tanks were reported destroyed.

The battle of Damortis ended by 1900 when the Japanese took control of the town and the surrounding area. The battle had not been a victory for the 26th Cavalry, but they had held the enemy for about three hours, and the road to Manila was still denied the Japanese. Although the regiment had suffered severely during their baptism of fire, morale was high and they dug in to await the enemy's new advance.

By 1700 hours on 22 December, the regiment had completely closed on its second defensive line, which was now about five kilometers west of Rosario, with Troop E astride the road and Troop A farther to the right. The machine gun troop was closer to Rosario and regrouped with the regimental command post.

Around 1730 hours, the four surviving tanks returned to Rosario and their crews informed Colonel Pierce that they had been ordered by the provisional tank brigade commander to operate forward of the 26th Cavalry to provide early warning until 2000 hours, or until the regiment's re-organization was completed. No mention was made that the tankers were to also cover the withdrawal of the 26th Cavalry from Rosario to a new defensive line, which appeared to be the basis of the newest orders from the commander of the 71st Infantry Division (PA), to whom the 26th Cavalry was now attached.

Contact with Japanese forces along the 26th Cavalry's front had been lost, but Troop F was resisting increasing enemy pressure along all five of the Agoo–Rosario trails. Colonel Pierce told his squadron commander to quietly prepare to withdraw, for he knew that with Troop F slowly being pushed back by superior numbers and massive firepower, their current position could not be held.

At 1900 the 71st Infantry Division ordered the 26th Cavalry to march to Agat and guard the right flank of the Division along the Bued River. The four remaining tanks would be the rear guard for the 26th Cavalry. Colonel Pierce was ordered to the division commander for a briefing and would link up with the regiment at Agat. Troop A was to deploy on the road at 1930 in columns of twos and proceed at a slow walk while Troop E moved in behind them.

Meanwhile, the depleted tank platoon started moving through the regiment, headed toward Rosario. Lieutenant Colonel Lee C. Vance, regimental executive officer, stopped the tankers and informed them of their new orders to rear guard the 26th Cavalry. The tank platoon leader said he could not disregard his original orders to depart at 2000 hours and that he did not belong to the 71st Division or the 26th Cavalry but, rather, to the Provisional Tank Brigade. Colonel Vance asked him if he had been in contact with the enemy and was told that they had not seen anything, and that the enemy must still be around Damortis. Closely pursued by the motorcycle-borne regimental S3, Lieutenant Colonel Chandler, who was intent on getting the tank support straightened out, the four tanks rumbled toward Rosario.

What really happened in the next few minutes may never be sorted out. Some say that a lieutenant from Troop E yelled something about a fifth tank and opened fire on the vehicle as it rounded the corner, moving toward the horseman. Others say it was Captain Wheeler, the troop commander, and yet still others say that all hell just broke loose when enemy tanks suddenly opened fire without warning from point-blank range. If nothing else was apparent, there is no doubt that the Japanese tanks had been right behind the American tanks as they moved out, and now were right in the middle of the regiment in the pitch darkness.

Individuals attacked the tanks with small arms and hand grenades, but the majority of the regiment was utterly confused. Attempts to get the regiment off the road were thwarted by barbed wire on the left and steep embankments on the right. Near panic broke out as some troopers tried to calm their terrorized mounts in the darkness, lit only by muzzle flashes. The horses were crashing into each other, sometimes unseating riders or running headlong into the enemy tanks. Colonel Vance ordered a retreat to Rosario, and the troopers raced down the road in disarray.

Some troopers were seen on top of the enemy tanks, either grappling with other shadowy figures or firing small arms into the open hatches. It seems that Japanese crewmen did not button up, so the open hatches provided the only way for the horsemen to disable a tank. (Later, the troopers would perfect a maneuver to attack a tank with four horse-mounted troops each attacking from a different direction. At least one might make it to the tank and attempt to disable it with grenades. This maneuver became a Bataan legend and is often told to illustrate the bravery of the 26th Cavalry.)

Troopers died trying to hold the enemy armor with little more than their bare hands while others were unhorsed and trampled by terrified mounts running completely amok. More died from the constant streams of enemy tank fire.

There was barbed wire on both sides of the road so they could not deploy. Captain Wheeler heard Major Trapnell calling his outfit and found him at a bridge. Major Trapnell wanted to defend the bridge but he and Captain Wheeler seemed to be the only ones left.

At that moment Lieutenant Michelson of the Veterinary Corps came up with the veterinarian truck. The three officers then pushed the truck, which had now stalled, onto the bridge, poured gasoline on it and the bridge, and set it afire. For this action, the three officers were later awarded the Distinguished Service Cross.

The regiment had hoped to regroup in Rosario but upon arriving there they found Troop F fighting Japanese in the town square and the regiment continued through town toward the Bued River. Order was quickly restored, mostly as a result of Lieutenant Colonel Chandler, who, while returning to the regiment, was knocked off his motorcycle by a riderless horse, which he wrestled under control and mounted. Lieutenant Colonel Chandler began riding up and down the column, calming the troops. Troop F continued as rear guard until Rosario was cleared.

The day's fighting had been hard for Troop F, since they were only about platoon strength when they broke contact. General Wainwright was very surprised when Colonel Pierce told him that the 26th Cavalry only had 175 effectives upon reaching the Bued River. The next couple of days saw the 26th Cavalry's strength grow, as stragglers and groups of men cut off earlier slowly made their way back to the regiment.

It is estimated that on 22 December the actual losses were 150 killed or wounded. But General Wainwright had been able to extract his other forces and was ready again to oppose the Japanese advance with what was thought to be a unified line.

During the night of the 22nd and the early morning hours of 23 December, the regiment was able to stop for a few hours along the Bued River line. General Wainwright instructed Colonel Pierce to hold the river crossing at Agat, and keep the old road to Baguio open to allow any cutoff troops to rejoin friendly lines. Some intact units of the 71st Infantry Division did come through during the night, but would not join the defensive effort and continued to the rear.

The depleted 26th covered the withdrawal of the 71st Division until around 0900 on 23 December. Then they blew up the bridge right under the noses of the Japanese and withdrew to Pozorrubio to reorganize.

General Wainwright was determined to give the 26th Cavalry some rest and ordered them out of the line and moved them about twelve kilometers farther south to a position near Binalonan, the headquarters of the 71st Division. Movement began after dusk, and was completed by 0100 on December 24th. The march had been a nightmare; the troops had been without food or sleep since 21 December, and were utterly exhausted. Even though the regiment was behind friendly lines, Lieutenant Colonel Chandler ordered outposts to be established north and west—just in case.

Meanwhile, General Wainwright was planning a counterattack to cut off the southernmost Japanese units and had requested that his old Philippine division be attached to him. When the request was made to General MacArthur, General Wainwright was surprised to learn that not only was the answer no, but that the old WPO-3, the retreat onto Bataan, was in effect and to be executed immediately.

The news was hard for General Wainwright to accept. He knew that the retreat onto Bataan probably meant their death. Also, he had hoped to attack at least once more since he believed that the enemy was disorganized and could be defeated. Years later, a senior Japanese commander bore out that belief when he said, "We feared more than anything else more counterattack from the exhausted Philippine-American troops, since it might have driven us into the sea because of our confused state."

General Wainwright realized that it would do little good to force the issue with General MacArthur since the order had already gone out, and units were moving toward Bataan. General Wainwright told his aide that, since the next day was Christmas Eve, he would visit the 26th Cavalry and the 71st Division in the morning and personally deliver their orders. This morale-building trip would almost cost the general his life.

The fortunes of war again turned against the 26th Cavalry. At approximately 0500, Colonel Pierce and his staff were awakened by outpost messengers reporting that enemy tanks and infantry were attempting to overrun their positions. A bivouac defense was established and by 0530 heavy fighting was raging. The 26th Cavalry was fighting with a stubbornness never before encountered by the Japanese troops and the invaders were being slowly pushed back by the horsemen.

Colonel Pierce kept looking for help from the 71st Division and wondered how such a large enemy unit could have bypassed this force. His questions were answered when the enemy had been forced northwest of the town of Binalonan, and Colonel Pierce entered it to find it completely empty—the 71st Division was gone!

Around 1130, a very angry General Wainwright arrived in Binalonan, after almost being killed or captured by a splinter group of Japanese infantry and tanks, which had worked behind the 26th Cavalry and cut one of the two roads into the town. There was supposed to have been a whole division there, and what did he find? Nothing. Major Trapnell and some others who were supposed to have been out on the line were filling soda bottles with gasoline to use on enemy tanks.

General Wainwright asked where Colonel Pierce was, and a trooper pointed in the direction of the sound of heavy firing. He found Colonel Pierce at the regimental command post a scant 400 meters from the enemy lines and under mortar, tank, and small arms fire. The mere presence of General Wainwright and the absolute calmness of Colonel Pierce inspired the troopers.

By 1300 the fighting had slackened, and General Wainwright ordered the 26th Cavalry to delay to the Agno River where he believed the 71st Division had gone. Colonel Pierce moved all of his wounded south by 1400 and began to plan the delay. By this time, General Wainwright had departed unescorted in his Packard sedan.

The fighting continued until about 1530, when the 26th Cavalry withdrew by trotting five minutes and walking five minutes—all the way back to the Agno River and the village of Tayug. The last men out of the battle area were Colonel Pierce and Colonel Vance, on foot, and leading their horses. The losses of key personnel during this battle were heavy with Lieutenants Vanderlester, Bowers, and Mark killed.

Lieutenant Mark was killed when he single-handedly attacked a tank which was cutting his platoon to pieces. The tank withdrew after killing him. The most serious loss was Major Ketchum who had gone to the right flank of his squadron during the heaviest period of fighting and was never seen again.

All of the regimental records, journals, guidons, and standards were lost when a scout car in which they had been carried was destroyed.

Despite the losses, the 26th Cavalry accomplished a masterful job and, except for the Japanese troops who had bypassed and almost bagged General Wainwright, they had stopped the Japanese advance cold. This allowed the first defense/delay line, D-1, on the Agno River to be established. General Wainwright, in his after-action report, stated:

I was personally present during a portion of this fight and cannot speak in too glowing terms of the gallantry and intrepidity displayed by Colonel Pierce and all officers and men of the 26th Cavalry on this occasion. This devoted little band of horsemen, weakened by detachments and by heavy casualties sustained at Damortis on the 22nd of December, held up the advance guard and caused the deployment of the enemy's main column. It effected a delay of nine hours and maintained the best traditions of the American cavalry. The 26th Cavalry clearly lived up to its code name of MIGHTY that day. I speak of this from the point of view of an eyewitness.

The general withdrawal onto Bataan would actually begin on Christmas Day once the 26th Cavalry was in place. Then the 71st Division would withdraw to Umingan while the regiment held the river crossing at Tayug. It was a memorable day, since the troopers were fed for the first time in three days. Colonel Pierce informed General Wainwright that since Damortis, his losses were approximately one-third of his total force.

Around 1200 on Christmas Day, the Japanese attacked the regimental scouts along the northern bank of the Agno, and by the early evening had forced the troopers back to the river itself. The 2nd Squadron had already established a defense on the other bank and allowed the scouts to pass through before blowing the bridge. The regiment knew the river banks were too muddy for enemy tanks to cross, so they continued to harass the enemy as they tried to repair the bridge. By the time the Japanese had repaired the bridge enough to allow some troops to cross, they found that the 26th Cavalry had vanished.

They had, just minutes before, pulled out at a trot. The maneuver was best summed up by Lieutenant Colonel Chandler who said, "It was a beautiful exhibition of careful planning, timing, and execution by disciplined troops, permitting the last moment of delay to be extracted from the operation."

Since the main defending units had now reached the D-3 line, Colonel Pierce found that there was no point in remaining forward of that line, and started moving toward Umingan, and safety. On the way, the cavalrymen played havoc with the Japanese advance by destroying eight bridges between Tayug and San Quintin. Two troopers were lost. The Japanese admitted, later, that their attempt to cut off the defending forces before they could move onto the Bataan Peninsula was a complete failure, due mostly to the delaying tactics of the 26th Cavalry. One Japanese officer said it was like fighting "spirits and devils."

In fact, the delay had been so successful that General Wainwright ordered the 26th Cavalry to move to Santa Rosa to become the Northern Luzon Force reserve. When the regiment arrived at Umingan at 0600 hours on 26 December, Colonel Pierce learned of the new orders.

He realized that Santa Rosa was just too far for tired men on horseback to reach without marching day and night and the current physical state of the men and horses would make it impossible.

He put the unit in laager and went to visit General Wainwright, who was gone, but his chief of staff approved a change of location. Their new bivouac site would be the town of Mexico, well behind phase line D-5. Since the horses and men were in such bad shape, the regiment was told to take its time reaching the new rest position.

Colonel Pierce also received the good news that Troop G would rejoin the regiment at Mexico, and the scout car section would rejoin the unit before it reached Mexico.

Except for Troop C, which was still in the northern mountains, the regiment would be back together for the first time since before the war. The regiment left Umingan at 1900 hours on 26 December, and did not reach Mexico until 0130 hours on the 29th.

Colonel Pierce told Colonel Vance as they watched the troops close on their new bivouac that, with just a little rest, the regiment would be ready again. Fate would intervene again as the Japanese made determined attacks against the D-5 line that ran along the Bamban River. Fearing an early breakthrough, General Wainwright ordered the 26th Cavalry north to Porac, 26 kilometers behind D-5.

Colonel Pierce immediately sent Lieutenant Colonel Chandler to plead with General Wainwright's headquarters for a few days delay. A 24-hour delay was approved and the regiment left Mexico at 1900 hours on 30 December. They marched over 60 kilometers and reached Porac by midnight. The regimental re-organization was as follows:

Troops E and F were combined into one troop, and along with Troops A and G, were horse-mounted and under the command of Major Trapnell. Troop B and the machine gun troop were mounted in trucks, buses, and even some British Bren carriers (armored track vehicles) that had been found. This composite troop was commanded by Captain Joe Barker, Jr.

On 1 January 1942, the Japanese attacked D-5 and, by the end of the day, the door to Bataan was held open by only two badly battered Philippine Army divisions—the 11th on the left and the 21st on the right. The 26th Cavalry was determined to hold the center.

Fortunately for the 26th, the attacks on D-5 slowed and then stopped as the Japanese realized that the city of Manila, only twenty-four kilometers away, was wide open. The Japanese commander raced to the city for he believed that when Manila fell, Bataan would fall in only a few days. Instead, it took four more months.

The blow fell on 4 January when fresh attacks broke the line of the 21st Division which, in turn, forced back the 11th Division. By now, the gateway to Bataan was only twenty kilometers wide and closing fast. The 26th Cavalry passed troops through both divisions and covered their withdrawal to Danpe, executing a delay until reaching Danpe around midnight. Early on the morning of 5 January, Colonel Pierce told General Wainwright that the withdrawal would have to be accomplished soon, for he did not know how much longer the gate could be held open. General Wainwright ordered the final withdrawal around 1100 on the 5th.

The 11th and 21st Divisions quickly fell back on, and began crossing, the Layac Junction bridge. The 26th suffered heavily all day under air-directed artillery fire, losing about ten men and twenty-five horses, but they held.

Finally, at 2330, the 21st Division finished crossing, and the 26th Cavalry began crossing the bridge. As they reached the other side, the weary troopers were met by General Wainwright, who thanked them for their efforts. At 0100 the rear guard, with Colonel Pierce crossed, and then the few remaining tanks of the 192nd Tank Battalion (who had been overwatching the scouts) rumbled across—the last Americans to do so.

General Wainwright then asked Colonel Pierce if all the troops were across the bridge. After a barely audible "yes" was heard, General Wainwright gave the signal and the bridge was blown up, sealing the Bataan Peninsula. The door had been slammed in the faces of the enemy but for the 26th Cavalry it was the beginning of the end.

After the withdrawal on 5 January, the regiment moved to a concealed bivouac on the left flank of the 31st Infantry, a regular U.S. Army unit, which was on the left of the Layac Line, around Kulis. The regiment arrived at 0330 on 6 January. Late in the day due to enemy air activity and artillery bombardment the regiment moved about two kilometers farther west. Due to threat of infiltration by special Japanese shock troops, the 26th Cavalry was fired upon by nervous soldiers from the 31st Infantry when they tried to regain contact with their flank. Attempts to make contact were stopped until daybreak.

At 0230 the regiment received an encoded radio message that could not be decoded. The code key list had changed at midnight, and no one had informed the 26th Cavalry! Patrols soon reported that it appeared as if the 31st Infantry had abandoned their positions and withdrawn.

They had indeed withdrawn. This was the message that the 26th Cavalry could not decipher. Colonel Pierce knew the Japanese had probably already started moving forward and might have bypassed them by this time. He immediately ordered the scout car section out by the only route possible—down the road through the position that the 31st Infantry had held.

At 0430 Colonel Pierce was informed that the scout car section had been ambushed, and three out of the four cars were destroyed. Now it was confirmed that the only way out was cross-country over very mountainous terrain. The trip was agonizing for the regiment, for the troopers had neither food nor water for themselves nor their animals.

General Wainwright feared the worst when he learned that the 26th Cavalry had been cut off. While some of his staff assumed that the regiment had been destroyed, he refused to believe that Clint Pierce would not bring the troopers through.

And bring them through Colonel Pierce did, reappearing at Bagac around midnight on 10 January.

The last mounted action of the U.S. Cavalry took place in the village of Moran on the west coast of Bataan on 16 January 1942. The composite Troop E-F was sent on the 15th to the vicinity of Moran to relieve Troop G which had been there since 11 January. Early on the 16th, the Japanese attacked and seized the village of Moran, and not even repeated counterattacks could dislodge them.

There were about 300 Japanese infantry in and around Moran. Captain Wheeler, Troop E-F commander, knew his troopers would have to close quickly with the enemy to get out of their machine gun-killing zone as fast as possible. Since speed was important, a mounted attack was the only way. The one suitable place to initiate the attack was from the point where the road entered the southern edge of the village and the 26th charged in four-man waves.

"First, there was the sound of pounding horses running very fast; then four horsemen abreast with drawn pistols came into view," said an observer. "They were already disappearing when another wave came in sight, followed by another and another—until the whole troop had thundered by. The Japanese, thoroughly surprised, had not fired at the first wave or two, but then fire came from all directions. Groups of four horsemen, yelling and firing their pistols, turned off the road and charged the enemy. Japanese were running everywhere trying to get away from the horses. Most of the cavalrymen dismounted and fought on foot right in the midst of the enemy."

It was a very hard fought battle. Captain Wheeler later described it: "Moran was a hail of bullets that never stopped. There were so many in the air that if you had put out a sheet of cloth in five minutes it would have been riddled. We were, however, outshooting them, as we could any day... we fought all day... the scouts were loyal to the nth degree and fought like devils."

The 26th Cavalry, in its last mounted action, was successful in driving the Japanese out of Moran and inflicting heavy casualties on them.

Late on 16 January 1942, the regiment was ordered to dismount and the horses sent to Mariveles. The regiment joined sailors, Marines, airmen, and other soldiers as line infantry. The end was near, and the defenders knew it. Their feelings were best summed up by the favorite verse of the times:

We are the battling bastards of Bataan,
No Mamma, no pappa, no Uncle Sam;
No aunts, no uncles, no cousins, no nieces;
No pills, no planes, no artillery pieces;
And no one gives a damn.

While the men of Bataan continued to fight and die, starvation further weakened the defenders. Finally, the end came for the Cavalry when General Wainwright, on 15 March, ordered the last horses slaughtered for food and 250 horses and forty-eight baggage mules met their end.

Less than six months later, on 9 April 1942, Bataan surrendered. The survivors of the regiment would now face almost four years of imprisonment but first they would face the inhuman torture of the Bataan Death March.

No records of the regiment exist; however, it is believed that total losses were as follows: twenty out of twenty-eight American officers were killed or missing in action; about eighty percent of the enlisted men were killed or missing in action; and all animals and equipment were lost.

The campaign fought by the 26th Cavalry was a classical use of horse cavalry: long-range reconnaissance, delaying operations, and violent hit-and-run attacks. Coupled with well-trained and disciplined troopers, these tactics cost the Japanese invaders heavily. Most historians believe that the delay tactics of the 26th Cavalry were directly responsible for the upset of the Japanese timetable and the removal of their Commander-in-Chief, General Homma.

The saga of the 26th Cavalry is more than the story of a single campaign, or even of a single unit, but, rather, tells the end of a whole way of warfare. The American cavalrymen, with less than 200 years existence, never had the lengthy traditions of European cavalry, and it can be argued that the American horsemen were never really pure cavalry at all, but rather only mounted riflemen. But the glory of American cavalrymen was always found in their horsemanship, pistol marksmanship, and their extraordinary courage in pressing home the attack.

The epitaph of the 26th Cavalry was written in 1946, in a letter from General Wainwright to Brigadier General Pierce (he was promoted during the final days of Bataan) which stated:

> From December 22, 1941, until about January 16, 1942, this devoted little band of horsemen were in action almost daily, always gave a good account of themselves, and suffered heavy casualties. During these trying days, it was the most reliable unit under my command and so remained during the defense of Bataan where after being dismounted, it carried on its fine tradition of combat excellence, first on the west coast and then on the east coast, especially during the last bitter days before capitulation. My great respect and deep thanks go to the old horse regiment and its few survivors, and to the glorified dead of that band of horsemen goes the salute of a nation for a task well done.

So now the history of the American horse cavalry is complete. Now the horseman's hall of heroes has new names: Wainwright, Pierce, Vance, Chandler, and Trapnell and they are enshrined alongside the likes of Stuart and Patton. It is so important for us to never forget the gallant 26th Cavalry—for they deserve better as America's last horsemen.

SOURCES

Information for this article was obtained from interviews with members of Defenders of Bataan and Corregidor; articles by Captain Whitehead and Colonel Chandler; from a biography of General Wainwright that included his after action reports; after action reports of unit commanders, and from the official history of World War II.

Interrogation of
Vice Admiral Takeo Kurita, IJN

Battle of the Philippine Sea
and Battle for Leyte Gulf

Interrogation NAV No. 9 / USSBS No. 47

Tokyo, 16-17 October 1945

Interrogation of: Vice Admiral Takeo Kurita, who was Commander-in-Chief Second Fleet during the battles of June and October 1944.

Interrogated by: Rear Admiral R. A. Ofstie, USN; Lieutenant Commander J. A. Field, Jr., USNR.

Allied Officers Present: Brigadier General Grandison Gardiner, U.S. Army; Captain T. J. Hedding, USN; Commander T. H. Moorer, USN.

SUMMARY

When U.S. forces landed in the Marianas in June 1944, the Japanese Fleet offered battle for the first time since the Guadalcanal campaign. In the Battle of the Philippine Sea, the Japanese suffered the loss of three carriers sunk and one seriously damaged, plus the virtual annihilation of the air groups of three carrier divisions.

In October 1944, the landing of U.S. forces on Leyte caused the Japanese to commit their entire remaining Navy to a desperate three-pronged attack on our forces in the hope of repelling the landings and, by holding the Philippines, of being able to continue the war. Admiral Kurita commanded the Center Force of battleships and cruisers which, under heavy attack, succeeded in penetrating the Philippines, engaged our escort carriers, and reached almost to the entrance to Leyte Gulf only to withdraw at the moment when success seemed within his grasp.

Admiral Kurita briefly discusses the planning for these operations and his part in the Battle of the Philippine Sea. The role of the Japanese Center Force in the Battle for Leyte Gulf is analyzed in considerable detail, with the reasons for the failure of the Japanese plan and his own reasons for withdrawing without entering the Gulf. He also offers miscellaneous comments on various features of the Pacific War.

TRANSCRIPT

(Admiral Ofstie) Admiral Kurita, before the Battle of the Philippine Sea in June 1944, where was your fleet based?

The Second Fleet had been basing at Lingga, but had recently moved to Tawitawi so as to be closer to expected operations.

When you left Tawitawi, about the 10th of June, did you have full knowledge of the plan for that operation?

I received instructions concerning the plan and orders for action from Admiral Ozawa.

What was the plan of the operation?

Through San Bernardino Strait, to refuel about 130 degrees east and attack the enemy about 136 degrees or 137 degrees east and retire to refuel a little north of the original position. The fleet under Admiral Ozawa proceeded towards Guimaras Strait, upon receipt of the intelligence that the American force had made an attack on the Marianas Islands; the operation at that time was to change base in order to be nearer to any succeeding action. On the way to Guimaras Strait, orders were received to proceed to attack operation on the American task force. The fleet fueled in Guimaras Strait and proceeded through the Sulu Sea. They proceeded out of Tawitawi on the 12th.

What was the principal difference in the attack plan if the American force had gone to Palau instead of to the Marianas Islands?

If the American task force had not gone to the Marianas but further south, the plan was for the fleet to abandon the Sulu route for a southerly one around Mindanao.

On 19 June what was your flagship?

The flagship was the cruiser *Atago*.

Where were you personally relative to *Taiho* and *Shokaku* on 19 June?

I do not know; communication was not maintained successfully and I learned of the damage the following day.

When did you first hear the report of the result of the air attack on the American fleet on the 19th, and what was the substance of that report?

I got only unreliable reports from the returning fliers.

When did you get the report, and what was contained in it?

We received running reports of all planes damaged from radio reports from our own fighters at the scene.

Were the losses reported such that the plans were changed that night, and if so what were the changes?

Because the damage report consisted of only the planes of the Second Fleet, I did not have knowledge of losses in the Main Body; the main plan, however, was not changed because of the losses of which I had knowledge, which were confined to the Second Fleet. The 3rd Air Squadron, assigned to my force, consisted of the *Zuiho* and *Chitose*, which were carriers converted from tankers, and the *Chiyoda* which was the submarine tender *Taigei* before conversion.

Of the three carriers that you had in your command, what were the total number of planes that went on the attack and how many came back—approximately?

The most of the wave that we sent out were fighters. Those which went to cover came back, but the attacking fighters did not. Something like one hundred were in the total that took off. The attacking fighters came under American attack, apparently some twenty miles before reaching the target, and more than half were destroyed at that time.

On the next day did you continue to have control of these three carriers?

Yes.

How did you operate those planes on the 20th?

I had only three or four torpedo planes, no body of fighters, and used six or seven for scouting.

Did you lose any more planes on the 20th of June?

We made no offensive operations on the following day, but when taking aboard the scouting planes, we received bombing attacks from the American task force which damaged some of them.

On the 20th during that bombing attack, were any of your ships damaged—that is, in the Second Fleet?

The *Zuiho* and battleship *Haruna* were slightly damaged. The *Haruna* apparently slight damage at first. The shaft brackets were loosened but it was not known that it was so serious until they did 27 knots.

The *Zuiho*, what damage to her?

Just a hole in the after end of the flight deck.

Do you know what damage was done to the tankers and their escorts?

One tanker was sunk, no damage to the tanker's escort.

Where did the fleet retire after this operation?

To Okinawa to fuel, and then to the Inland Sea for training of pilots; the Second Fleet returned to the Singapore area.

When the Second Fleet left the Inland Sea, begin there and please tell us what your movements were.

All ships of the Second Fleet and the 10th Squadron of destroyers from the Third Fleet left Kure the 12th of July.

Describe the movements of the Second Fleet from then on.

They departed through Bungo Suido to Okinawa and then to Lingga. Some ships brought troop reinforcements to Okinawa and Manila and all rendezvoused at Lingga.

What was the purpose of going to Lingga?

For training. The shortage of fuel in the home area required training operations in Lingga.

How long did you stay at Lingga?

Until October 1944.

During this period between June and October, what new plans did you receive for operations against the American fleet or against American operations?

Planning was done according to whether the next American operation was directed against the Philippines, or secondarily Okinawa, or possibly Formosa, and finally the home islands.

How much did you yourself enter into the planning; that is, did you receive a plan from the Commander-in-Chief, Combined Fleet, or did you do some planning at Lingga?

Orders and directions from Admiral Toyoda only.

(Lieutenant Commander Field) These new plans you speak of, were they known as the Sho plans?

Sho-Go, that is correct.

Did you see or have a conference with Admiral Ozawa between the time you left the Inland Sea and your departure from Lingga?

Staff of Ozawa came to Lingga for a conference in the middle of August, but I had no meeting.

Was the command organization originally the same as for "A" Operation (defense of Marianas)?

The command originally was not the same as in the "A" Operation; Admiral Ozawa had command of the carrier force only and then I had command, independent command, of the remaining force.

Admiral Nishimura was responsible to you, and you in turn were directly responsible to Admiral Toyoda, is that correct? Who was responsible for the coordination of the movement of the three forces with each other, and with the land-based aircraft?

That is correct [see Annex A]. The only coordination command rested with Toyoda, otherwise coordination was by communication among the units concerned and that was by radio message.

What was the coordination with Army land-based planes?

I do not know under what command such coordination was executed, whether under the Army or the Navy.

What training was emphasized at Lingga?

The first point is that if you seized the Philippines it would cut off fuel supply to the Empire and that all supply of fuel being severed, the war in all areas south of the Empire must end. The Philippines were vital to the continuation of the war. The training was therefore so conducted as to prevent landing operations—coast defense landing parties and then in radar and anti-aircraft defense, and especially night action.

From the 12ᵗʰ to 14ᵗʰ of October, our task force was heavily attacked off Formosa by your aircraft. Did you receive reports of the damage done to our forces and if so, did the report influence the operation plans?

We got the report, but don't think that the intelligence affected future plans too seriously.

When was the Second Fleet alerted for the operation?

I am not sure, but I think that the alert was received on the 15ᵗʰ.

Do you remember what information led to this alert?

Your mine sweeping activity. Based upon the intelligence report of your mine sweeping activity in the vicinity of Leyte, I received orders from Commander-in-Chief Combined Fleet to shift base of operations nearer to the Philippine Islands. Although Brunei was not specified in the orders, it was the best, and had been so considered in the planning.

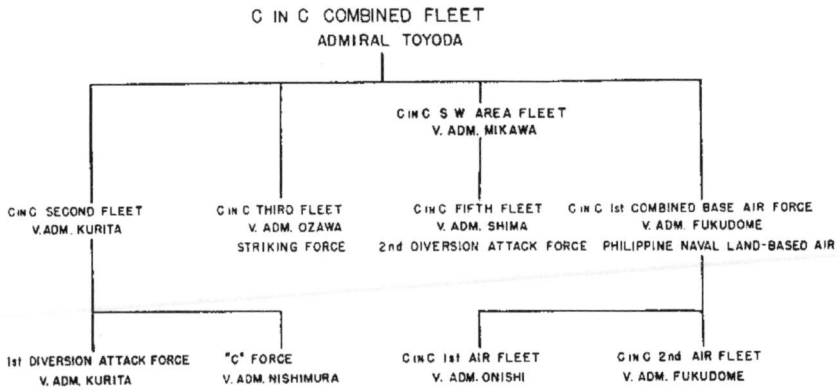

COMMAND ORGANIZATION
BATTLE FOR LEYTE GULF
INTERROGATION OF VICE ADMIRAL KURITA
ANNEX (A)

USSBS No. 47
NAV. No. 9

When did the Second Fleet leave Lingga for Brunei, and was Admiral Nishimura's force in company?

I do not remember the date; we departed Lingga together and from Brunei separately.

Were refueling facilities available anywhere other than at Brunei, in the Philippine area?

There was no shore facilities at Brunei, but there were tankers there and at Coron Bay.

Were these tankers awaiting you at Brunei and Coron, or did they travel in company?

There was one tanker waiting at Coron and two tankers came from Singapore to the Sulu Sea.

Who did you believe commanded our invasion forces?

We had believed that General MacArthur would come from the south to here [*indicating Philippines on chart*].

Did you know who commanded our task forces?

No, I did not know.

What was the mission of your force?

It was to attack and destroy the landing forces at Leyte at daybreak of the 25th of October.

Does that apply to Admiral Nishimura's force also?

The same orders applied to Admiral Nishimura's force also.

Were they intended to be simultaneous attacks by both forces—attacks at the same moment?

We planned for a two hour interval between, the two hours because of the great movement of ships in confined waters. Admiral Nishimura was to proceed first and then my force.

How were both forces to approach?

Admiral Nishimura was to approach through Surigao Strait from the south and my force through the San Bernardino Strait from the north.

What was the mission of Admiral Ozawa's force?

He was to divert your task force and bring it under attack from the north.

When you left Brunei to launch your attack, what information did you have of our force inside of Leyte Gulf?

I thought you had about two hundred transports, about seven battleships and appropriate accompanying cruisers and destroyers.

Was that estimate modified in any way from further information received on the 24th?
Because of the bad weather, we did not receive any further intelligence. I requested them to send seaplanes from San Jose (Mindoro) to scout, but because of the weather they found nothing.

Did you have no information from land-based planes in the Philippines?
Nothing whatsoever.

What losses were expected inside of the Gulf from our battleships?
We expected more than half of our ships to be lost.

Was it expected that Admiral Nishimura, by his early arrival at Leyte, would draw our force to the south and facilitate the entrance of the San Bernardino force?
No; in fact it was thought that knowledge of the larger body coming from the north might draw the American ships out from the Gulf and thus leave Nishimura free to enter.

On the morning of the 24th, our planes sighted Admiral Nishimura's force off Negros and your force off Mindoro; at about what speed were you proceeding at this time?
About 22 knots.

What was the originally planned time of entry into the Gulf?
Admiral Nishimura's force about five—the Second Fleet about six in the morning.

Did you plan to steam at 22 knots all day?
Twenty-two or 24 knots. The point was that the tankers could not supply the ships enough fuel for long distance voyages at high speed and they had to save their fuel for the trip back to Brunei.

Where were you embarked on leaving Brunei?
In *Atago*.

SUBMARINE ATTACK ON SECOND FLEET
23 OCTOBER, 1944

FROM A SKETCH BY V. ADM. KURITA

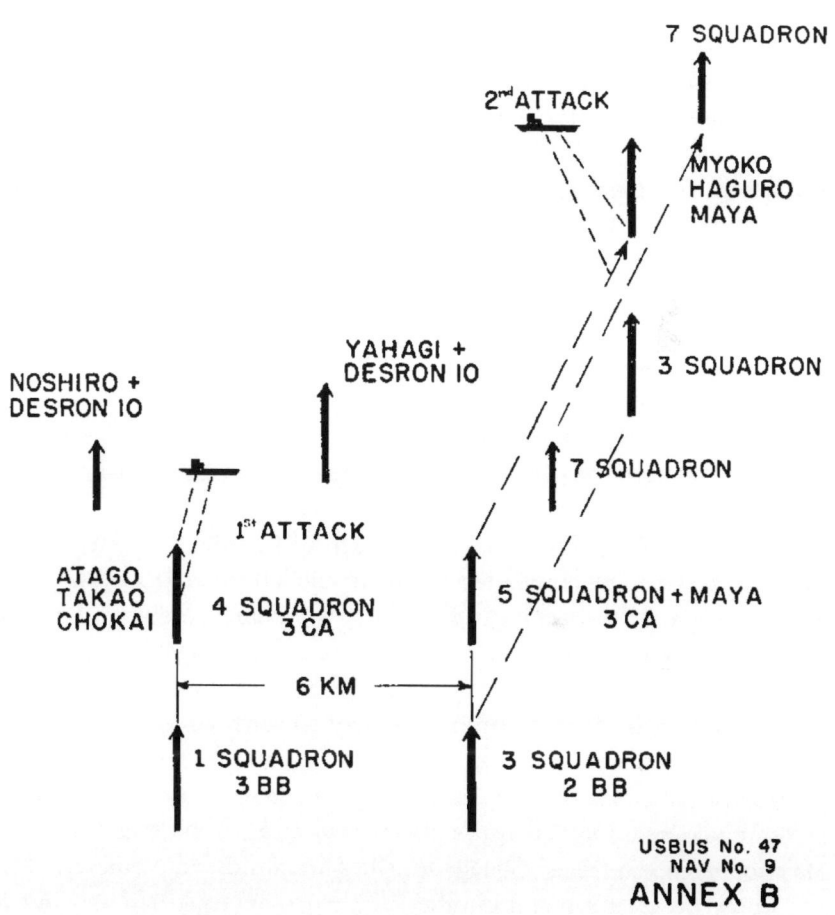

7 SQUADRON

2ⁿᵈATTACK

MYOKO
HAGURO
MAYA

YAHAGI +
DESRON 10

3 SQUADRON

NOSHIRO +
DESRON 10

7 SQUADRON

1ˢᵗ ATTACK

ATAGO
TAKAO
CHOKAI

4 SQUADRON
3 CA

5 SQUADRON + MAYA
3 CA

6 KM

1 SQUADRON
3 BB

3 SQUADRON
2 BB

USBUS No. 47
NAV No. 9
ANNEX B

Was *Atago* attacked by our submarines?

    Yes.

Had you had any warning of the attack?

    We knew that submarines were there and there were three possible
routes planned. First the most southerly route which would bring our

forces under land-based plane attacks from Morotai; second, the most northerly route which would take too long; and third, the route adopted which was known to contain patrol submarines; but considering the time and other factors, it was decided to proceed on the middle route.

Did the fact that you were forced to change flagships inconvenience the rest of this operation?

It did not interfere with the plan; in fact, it rather improved control. The shift to the *Yamato* improved the command possible because she was designed as a flagship and communications were therefore better and the anti-aircraft defense was also better.

What was the total loss and damage sustained because of our submarines on the 23rd?

Atago and *Maya* were sunk; *Takao*'s engine damaged and she was stopped and could not navigate.

Did *Takao* return safely to port?

Returned to Brunei and then to Singapore.

Will you sketch the disposition of your ships at the time of the submarine attack?

[*See Annex B*] At 0643 when the attack was made, the fleet was zig-zagging and had just completed a turn to the left when both *Atago* and *Takao* were hit. The second in column was *Takao*; there were two hits in her stern which interfered with navigation. The right-hand column turned to starboard because of the submarine attack on the left-hand column; the right-hand column gave way to starboard but within ten minutes had resumed course when the second attack opened. A second submarine attack on the right-hand column occurred immediately after resuming course, interval between the two attacks about ten minutes. *Maya* belonged to the 4th Squadron; she sank almost immediately; I do not know the location and number of hits. *Atago* took half an hour to sink.

On the 24th when you were passing through the Central Philippines did you expect air attacks?

Yes.

Were there plans to have protective fighters overhead?

I requested that they send fighters from land base, but they did not send any.

Was fighter cover provided for in the operation plan or was it merely requested at that moment?

Both. The plan was, first the planes from land bases were to attack the American task force and then to shift south to act as cover for our force; but the size of the American task force made it necessary for all land-based plane activity to center on that part, namely the American task force, leaving the Second Fleet without the expected cover.

And that was in the operation plan?

Yes, also provision for the Carrier Division 3 to accompany the fleet; but that plan was not carried out because the American task force arrived earlier than expected. Carrier Division 3 plus *Zuikaku* was included in the plan. The plan was for Carrier Division 3 plus the *Zuikaku* to join the Second Fleet at Lingga and accompany it on the succeeding operation; but the early arrival of the American task force prevented the junction.

When had Carrier Division 3 been expected to reach Lingga?

It was expected to leave Japanese waters on 15 October. That delay was due to the training of the flight personnel. The training of new personnel for Carrier Division 3 was because all skilled flight personnel had been lost in the June engagement.

When you requested fighters from Luzon, to whom did you address the request?

To Admiral Onishi, who was in command of the First Air Fleet in the Philippines.

Were there any Army aircraft in the Philippines that could be requested?

No.

Do you mean that there were none in the Philippines, or that no arrangements had been made to obtain their help?

No request was made of the Army; I do not know whether there were any Army planes there or not. When called upon for planes, the Navy would send planes if they had them; if not, the Navy would request them locally from the Army. That was my opinion.

What warning of our air attack on the morning of the 24th did you have?

First received intelligence that your planes had been over Manila; then from own radar.

At what distance did your radar warn you?

About 100 or 120 km.

How many attacks did you receive on the 24th?

It differed according to the ship, but I think that my own ship received six large attacks with forty to fifty planes in each attack.

What damage was incurred by the ships of your force?

The *Myoko* received damage to two shafts and returned to Singapore, and towards the evening the *Musashi* sank. All other battleships received one or two hits, but were able to continue to fight. No battleships torpedoed, nor cruisers. They were in ring formation and because American attack was directed at major units, the cruisers and destroyers suffered less.

Did any cruiser receive bomb hits but still continue with the operation?

With the exception of *Myoko*, the cruisers were not damaged.

In the course of the afternoon under the attack, did you reverse course and retire for a time?

About four I reversed course to the westward and because your bombing attack ceased, I again resumed the advance.

Did you report the damage received to Admiral Toyoda?

Yes.

Was your change of course to the westward your own decision or on instruction from Admiral Toyoda?

I informed Admiral Toyoda that I was retiring temporarily to the westward to avoid attacks and would return to the action later, and then Admiral Toyoda sent a response with an order to continue the operation.

During the day had you received any report from Admiral Nishimura that he was under attack?

About ten o'clock in the morning I got, not a detailed report, but a short message from Admiral Nishimura that his part of the operation was not going successfully.

Do you know if Admiral Nishimura's force was damaged by that air attack?
Yes, I assumed that it was serious damage.

As a result of the air attack on the Second Fleet, did you order Admiral Nishimura to delay his advance?
No change in the plans.

On the afternoon of the 24th, where did you believe our task force was located?
Northeast of San Bernardino Strait about 80-100 miles.

What speed was maintained during the night?
Twenty knots.

How did you navigate through the narrow channel at 20 knots?
We navigated in single column through the narrow places and as it was very clear, I could determine the position visually.

What was the condition of the battleships that had been damaged? What type of damage had been received?
The *Nagato* had received some damage to her communication system, but all guns were able to shoot; nothing important on other ships.

Any damage to fire control?
No.

What time did you sortie from San Bernardino Strait?
At midnight. The plan was to come through San Bernardino Strait at 6 p.m., but the delay was six hours. We were at the exit at midnight.

Did you expect to have to fight your way out of the Straits?
Yes.

Did you have any further information in the course of the night on the position of our task force?
No.

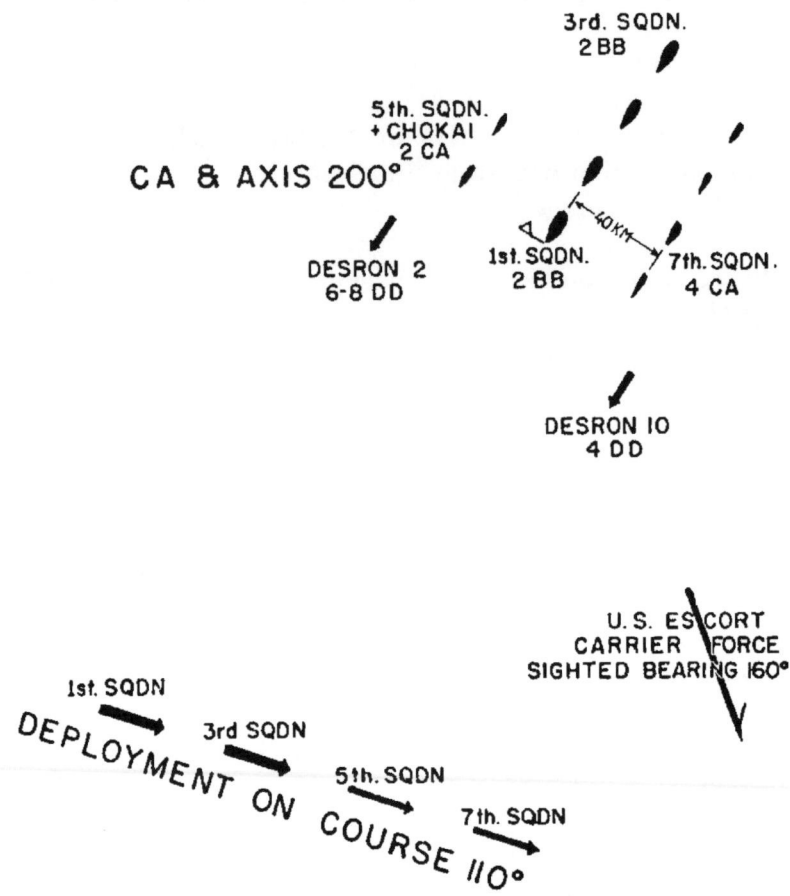

DISPOSITION OF SECOND FLEET ON CONTACT WITH U.S.FORCES – 0650 25 OCTOBER, 1944
FROM A SKETCH BY V.ADM. KURITA

3rd. SQDN.
2 BB

5th. SQDN.
+ CHOKAI
2 CA

CA & AXIS 200°

DESRON 2
6-8 DD

1st. SQDN.
2 BB

←40KM→

7th. SQDN.
4 CA

DESRON 10
4 DD

U.S. ESCORT
CARRIER FORCE
SIGHTED BEARING 160°

1st. SQDN

DEPLOYMENT ON COURSE 110°

3rd SQDN

5th. SQDN

7th. SQDN

USSBS No. 47
NAV No. 9
ANNEX C

When you came out at midnight were your ships at General Quarters?

Yes, all of them were ready to fight.

What conclusion did you draw when you found no force there?

Since there was no force there, there was no conclusion and I continued the operation.

What was your first contact with American forces?
First contacts were with the planes. They were fighters, I think. I did not see them, but there was one or two fighters, and then I saw the masts and I then was able to see the shape of the aircraft carriers to the southeast.

Was the first contact with aircraft carriers made visually or by radar?
The first was by eyes.

[Interrogation adjourned 1645; resumed 17 October, 0930.]

Admiral Kurita, would you sketch the disposition of your force on the morning of the 25th as you came down the coast of Samar?
[*See Annex C*] The engagement off Samar opened about 0700, not at 0650 as suggested yesterday. On the right flank was the 5th Squadron plus *Haguro*, *Myoko* having been disabled the previous day; in the center the 1st Squadron, less *Musashi* which had been sunk, and the 3rd Squadron; on the left flank the 7th Squadron; on the starboard bow Destroyer Squadron 2 and on the port bow Destroyer Squadron 10. About four kilometers interval between columns.

How many destroyers were in this right-hand group, roughly?
We had had to assign several destroyers to take back the ships that had been damaged on the 23rd and 24th. Therefore, we were greatly reduced in the number of destroyers we had with us. There were six or eight on the right and four on the other.

You said yesterday that you thought we had six or seven battleships inside the Gulf along with our transports. Did you believe there were any battleships with the task force in this region (northeast of San Bernardino Strait)?
I didn't think there were many. I thought there might be one with the carriers.

In the course of the 24th or during the night before the battle opened here, did you have any reports from Admiral Ozawa as to the events in the north?

No reports except that Admiral Ozawa's planes had attacked and some had landed in the water and the able ones were landing in Luzon.

Up to the time of beginning the action here, had you had any report from Admiral Nishimura subsequent to the first one in the morning which said that operations were not going too well? I remember you said that on the 24ᵗʰ you heard from Admiral Nishimura that he had been attacked from the air. Did you have any later information from Admiral Nishimura before seven o'clock?

I don't know exactly where he was when he sent the first message but he was somewhere around in there. [Indicating south of Negros.] I think I had a report in this area, that is due south of Leyte, that he had been brought under attack by torpedo boats.

And that was the only report before the battle began here?

That was followed by one more report to estimate the time of arrival at the target.

In the course of the night, did you receive any messages from Admiral Toyoda giving further information or additional instructions?

I don't remember for certain but I think the last message I got from Admiral Toyoda was the order to proceed with the action which I mentioned yesterday. I certainly remember no other messages.

Late on the night of the 24ᵗʰ when your force was passing through this area by Masbate Island, were you aware that you were being followed by our aircraft?

I did not know it.

Had you considered the possibility that our forces might have mined San Bernardino Strait?

There were certain Japanese fields but I did not consider your having mined any of the area.

Just before seven o'clock in the morning, you sighted the masts of carriers. What happened then?

It was just at the time when we were changing formation so that these two cruiser divisions came back. We were preparing to change formation but had not changed formation when the masts of your ships were sighted.

Changing formation for entry into the Gulf?

No, going to change formation into the ring formation. On a course of 200 degrees masts were sighted to the southeast. All ships altered course to 110 degrees. The wind was in the northeast. I altered course to 110 degrees in order to come up-wind of your formation. The resultant formation was with squadrons in column. The first sighting was at a range of about 35,000 meters. The intention was to reduce the range, keeping to windward of the American forces. At the time of the sighting, though I do not know the precise course of the American forces, I think it was an opposing and meeting course but it soon changed to right-turnabout. I thought it was a right-turnabout because the flight decks being full of planes, all planes were visible at the time of the turn.

I opened fire from the *Yamato*. I am uncertain of the range but I think it was between 32,000 and 33,000 meters. At the same time American cruisers and destroyers commenced laying a smoke screen.

What did you do then as our ships turned, reversed course and proceeded to the southwest? What was your speed?

The speed of my ships varied at that time. They were all on full speed. The *Haruna* could do no better than 25 knots at the outside, the *Nagato* no better than 24 knots. Also, because your planes were coming over in groups of three, for more adequate defense the ships were separating and scattering.

What speed was the *Yamato* making ?

The *Yamato* was doing full speed at 26 knots. On the 24th the *Yamato* had three bombs on the deck, forward. She was heavy by the bow, having taken water forward as a result of the bombing.

Then all ships were going at their individual top speeds, not at a uniform speed?

That is correct.

Well then, as our ships reversed course and headed southwest—?

As your ships altered course, I continued individual full speed on course 110 degrees until I got up-wind and then bore down on your ships.

Did you believe that our carriers immediately changed course like that [indicating] or that they went in a larger circle. Or, in other

words, could you draw what the track of our carriers appeared to be?

I believed this course: that you were coming into the wind to send off planes and then retiring and coming into the wind again and retiring. Coming into the wind only to send off the planes but in general it was a zig-zagging wide curve. The Japanese course gradually curved as it approached position up-wind.

When did our air attacks begin that morning?

The attacks were in small formations. As the battle opened, small formations of your planes attacked my ships and about half past eight, thinking that there would be a concerted attack, I altered my plans, partly because the small formations had ceased to come for awhile. In preparation for a concerted attack by American bombers, I ordered the closing of the formation. I thought that the American formation was retiring rapidly to the southeast and at about 0830 the small formation attacks ceased. I therefore thought that there would be later on—perhaps an hour later—a large formation attack. Therefore, I ordered the formation to close.

Did you, at that time, break off the battle with these carriers?

The 10th Destroyer Squadron having finished its torpedo attack upon your formation, thinking that this engagement was over and that we would come under attack from your northern carrier force, I ordered the formation closed. It was about ten minutes past nine o'clock. I then intended to enter Leyte Gulf, and passed through the damaged or sinking ships of your formation, aircraft carriers and cruisers of your formation. I came under air attack just as I had given the order to the destroyers to pick up survivors in the water.

Now in the course of this first battle with the carriers, what damage had you inflicted on our forces and what damage had your force received from any cause?

Because of the smoke, I could see very little but we felt certain on the *Yamato* that one of your carriers, which had a bridge, was listing seriously and we therefore concluded that we had hit it, and one cruiser was down by the head. That is all I saw. Perhaps one more of your cruisers and perhaps two or three of your destroyers. I am not certain of my memory on this. The 10th Destroyer Squadron having launched its torpedo attack in the smoke, reported to me that three or four of your carriers were seriously damaged or sinking.

By the torpedo attack?

The destroyers and cruisers from gunfire and the aircraft carriers, after the first one that I mentioned, from torpedo attack.

What damage had your force received?

One torpedo in the *Kumano*, which reduce the speed to about 16 knots.

Aerial torpedo?

Destroyer torpedo. After the fast torpedoes had passed and missed, a slow speed one got it near the stern. Now the *Suzuya* received a hit or near miss or misses which caused damage near the bridge to such an extent that later, after the battle was over, her own torpedoes exploded.

Fire?

Yes. The fire extended to the torpedo tube chamber and there exploded.

That was from aircraft bombing?

Yes, it was aircraft bombing.

What was the result of that?

It sank, after the battle. The *Chokai* and the *Chikuma* couldn't maneuver. I couldn't tell whether it was because the engines had given out or because they had been under attack but they were unmaneuverable. They were sunk by our own destroyers after they had removed their personnel, by torpedoes from destroyers. I do not know whether the engines had simply been over-taxed or from bombing or gunfire. From gunfire or any other cause, there was no further damage to my force.

You know of no damage specifically from gunfire?

No damage except that I later received a report that the *Yamato* had received one 15-cm shell that had damaged a motor.

What kind of a motor?

Above the engine room, starboard side. It was a dud.

What type of aircraft carriers were the American carriers present? Were they the *Essex* or *Enterprise* class? Did you recognize them?

I don't remember. Starboard bridge structure was all I could tell. There wasn't enough visibility nor adequate reports from the scouting planes.

Was the use of smoke by the U.S. forces a serious trouble to you?

It was very serious trouble for us. It was exceedingly well used tactically.

Did you fire by visual control or by radar control in aiming the guns?

Both. Commenced visually when we could see anything. Thereafter we tried to work it with radar.

Did you assign specific targets to your ships or merely tell them to fire on all ships they could see?

Because I concluded that it would not be possible to make a formation attack, I left it to each individual ship to fight on its own.

From the *Yamato* or from reports from other ships, did you feel that the gunfire was hitting? Was it effective?

In the beginning the gunfire was effective; toward the end it was very bad.

Do you know why?

We were making a stern chase on your ships which were zig-zagging and that made it difficult to get the range. That is what I think was the cause. Also, the major units were separating further all the time because of your destroyer torpedo attacks. The second or third salvo of the *Yamato* was followed by a very great explosion from the middle of the smoke. I do not know what ship.

Did your ships fire continuously as long as they had a target?

I saw only that one high explosion. So long as they had a target they all kept on shooting.

What speed were the American carriers making?

I didn't know.

Was it difficult to close the range? Was it fast enough so that you had trouble closing?

At first the range closed quickly. At first, even after we had altered course, the range narrowed rapidly. After that your ships were making good time away and my ships were becoming more and more separated and we didn't consider that the range was closing.

Did you expect to have protective air cover that morning from land-based planes?
I did not think so. I did not expect it.

Did you expect assistance from land-based planes on the attacks on our ships?
No, I did not. I thought that I would have no assistance or cover from land-based planes because most of the Japanese land-based planes were in Luzon, assigned for action that might occur in the north. The southern sector was my own responsibility.

Did you have any information later that day, in the middle of the day, of attacks by Japanese planes on our forces in this area here where the battle was and inside the Gulf?
No, no information of such attacks.

Could you describe the attacks made on your ships by torpedo, by our cruisers and destroyers?
The torpedo attacks were launched from inside the smoke screen; the paths of the torpedoes were almost parallel and very obvious. The speed of the torpedoes was so slow that it was possible to avoid them by turning away from them, which however resulted in the separation of the formation.

Did you see any of the ships at the time they were launching torpedoes?
I could see that the ships were there occasionally but did not see them launch any torpedoes.

During this action you mentioned being attacked several times by small groups of torpedo planes and bombers. Did you maneuver to avoid all those attacks?
Yes. We received no torpedo attack I know about. Each vessel turned course and avoided that bombing. Each ship undertook evasive action in attempting to avoid the bombing action but I know of no torpedo attacks.

How far off course did a ship usually turn?

When there were few bombers, as much as 45 degrees.

Were these maneuvers done by the individual ships and not on signal from you?

That is right, individual ships maneuvered on their own.

And that led to further scattering of the formation?

It led to gradual separation, breaking up the formation.

Did these attacks by scattered groups continue up until 0830 when they stopped entirely?

I am not certain of the time the attacks ceased; it was about 0830.

Did they stop suddenly or did they just taper off—less frequent, less strong?

It diminished gradually.

When you first sighted our disposition, why did you maneuver around to get to windward rather than closing directly upon it?

To prevent launching and retaking of your planes, I intended to intercept to windward as much as possible.

Did you consider sending part of your force to do that and to continue towards the Gulf with the rest?

No. I did not consider that. The idea was that I would make a concerted action of the fleet.

After this attack, however, you still intended to enter the Gulf?

I held to that intention until I received the second bombing attack.

At what time was that?

I can't remember.

How long after you broke off the action with the carriers was this second bombing attack?

At about ten o'clock our ships had made a formation, at which time they received the first bombing attack. The first attack came when I had hoisted the signal for ring formation after they had assembled.

Was this a heavy attack?

The attack was big but the damage was small.

What type of damage, specifically?

The extent of damage was not such as to interfere with ability of the ships. I did not receive details of damage at that time. Now the sort of information I did receive when damage was great was breaking of oil tanks, gasoline, rudder control and that sort of thing; but I did not receive any of that on the first attack.

Were you still on a course west or southwest towards the Gulf when this attack was delivered?

I was on a course for Leyte Bay. The conclusion from our gunfire and anti-aircraft fire during the day had led me to believe in my uselessness, my ineffectual position, if I proceeded into Leyte Bay where I would come under even heavier aircraft attack. I therefore concluded to go north and join Admiral Ozawa for coordinated action against your northern task forces.

About what time did you make this decision and start north?

I think about ten or eleven o'clock. From that time on I steamed north.

You think, then, that it was about two hours after you broke off the attack on our carriers there that you finally turned north? Is that correct?

About two hours; anyway less than three hours. I am not sure about the exact hour.

You said you expected very heavy air attacks inside the Gulf. From what source?

From land-based planes, on Leyte.

You believed at that time that we had planes operating from Leyte?

I was convinced that your aircraft planes had gone to Leyte after the attacks upon my fleet. I therefore expected that they would bring us under heavy attack if we entered the bay. I did not know whether there were normally land-based planes situated there but I knew there were fields there and there might be.

Did you have knowledge of any other American aircraft carriers in this neighborhood, that is, except those with whom you had had a battle already?

I thought I had seen a mast or masts to the east, which was the only guess I had that there might be other carriers in the vicinity. I knew of nothing to the south. We were listening in on your communications at that time, at the opening of the original battle. We intercepted a message which said, "We are under attack by Japanese ships, hasten with aid," and for two hours, we heard the message that it was useless. From the assistance that had been called, we heard the reply that it would take two hours to render aid.

What type of aid did you think was referred to?

I didn't know where any other aid was but understood from the message that it was air aid.

Was it this aid promised in two hours which you expected to hit you inside the Gulf—was that part of the reason you did not enter the Gulf?

Yes, that is one reason. It had gotten very late too; that is, the schedule was very much delayed because of the engagement.

As far as fuel and ammunition went, were you in satisfactory condition to enter the Gulf?

There was no consideration for fuel. There was no consideration for how to get home. We had enough ammunition.

You had enough to take on these battleships you expected inside?

Yes.

In the course of that morning's engagement, had you received any information from either Admiral Nishimura or Admiral Ozawa?

No information.

Then at the time you turned north you did not know what had happened in Surigao Strait the night before?

No. I had no wireless information or intelligence of any sort. I therefore sent up two planes from the *Yamato*, one to go over the Surigao Strait area, the other to scout to the north. Neither brought any information.

Did the planes return?

They landed ashore and never came back to the ship. Not a word. There was a message from the one that went to the north saying that he had seen nothing. There was no message from the one that went through the Surigao Strait area.

Did you have any information as to Admiral Ozawa's operations in the north from anyone else?

Sometime during the day—I do not remember when—I received word from Admiral Ozawa. The message did not come from Ozawa but I received intelligence by wireless—I do not know the source—that Admiral Ozawa had become engaged and damaged and was intending a night torpedo attack upon your formation; that he was going to change his flagship but he did not name the ship. The extent of damage that Ozawa's fleet had sustained was not known to me.

Do you remember if you received this information before the decision, I concluded it was best to go north, or afterwards?

After I changed the course to north.

So that the reason for changing course to the north was the threat of a heavy air attack if you entered the Gulf, is that correct?

It wasn't a question of destruction, that was neither here nor there. It was a question of what good I could do in the bay. I concluded that under the heavy attack from ship and shore-based planes, I could not be effective. Therefore, on my own decision, I concluded it was best to go north and join Admiral Ozawa.

Was this alternative plan provided for in the original plans, or was it a decision of the moment only?

The decision was a momentary one. I sent a report to Admiral Ozawa that I had turned north and would be able to coordinate my attack with the night destroyer torpedo attack which I learned Admiral Ozawa was going to make, which I had learned from other sources.
You are sure that Admiral Ozawa did intend to make such an attack?

I did not get that from Admiral Ozawa. I got the news of it that such an attack was intended. I had the distinct impression that Admiral Ozawa was going to launch that night attack and I myself, coming north, was determined to help and if I didn't find anything up in here, I would withdraw through San Bernardino Strait.

Did you not feel on this northern trip that you would be brought under heavy attack there from our task force in that region?

I concluded to do it, no matter what came from the north.

Well, I wanted to get the distinction between an air attack here and an air attack there. Why did you prefer this one?

It is the same under attack in either case; but I would be no good here while I might by coordination assist up there in the north.

Do you mean that you felt it more profitable to attack our task force than to attack our transport invasion shipping in the Gulf?

In the narrow confines of Leyte Gulf I couldn't use the advantage that ships have of maneuvering, whereas I would be a more useful force under the same attack with time advantage of maneuver in the open sea.

Yes, but was there a choice of targets involved?

By the time the question arose, your landing had been confirmed and I therefore considered it as not so important as it would have been before.

[Admiral Ofstie] Admiral Kurita, when you came through San Bernardino, why did you attack the carriers and delay your movement rather than going on down the coast of Samar directly to Leyte Gulf?

I thought that the course I actually took was the best course for Leyte and I encountered your force in the way. That is, closer to shore was not the best course for Leyte.

[Lieutenant Commander Field] What speed did you take when you started north?

Twenty knots when we saw no enemy planes—24 knots whenever we saw enemy planes.

Did you receive other air attacks while moving north?

I think it is about eleven times that I was under attack from the air on the way north.

On what scale were the attacks?

Forty or fifty plane attacks, both bombing and torpedo.

Did these attacks inflict serious damage?

It was at that time that the bulges got perforated and all the major ships were trailing oil. The ability of the ships wasn't seriously interfered with but they left a long conspicuous trail of oil in the water. There was no vital damage to any ship. They could maintain speed and they were able for battle all the way through it.

What course did you take going north? Did you sweep around here? Could you draw the course on the chart?

I do not remember the precise course.

Well, approximately. Were you headed for Admiral Ozawa or were you headed for San Bernardino?

My intention was not primarily to join Admiral Ozawa but to go north and seek out the enemy. If I failed to find the enemy, having reached here [indicating about 13 degrees 20 minutes north] my intention was to go north and seek out the enemy but to be able to retire through San Bernardino Strait at dark.

You did not then plan to coordinate with Admiral Ozawa in a night battle?

I considered my mission to go north and seek out your carrier task force and bring it under engagement with the assumption that Admiral Ozawa to the north would thereby be assisted by it.

But it was not to join forces with Admiral Ozawa. Secondarily or overall, I wanted to be at San Bernardino at sunset to get through and as far to the west as possible during the night.

If you planned to be there by dark, surely you could not get very far north?

No, I didn't know how far. I thought perhaps Admiral Ozawa's action might lead them to be in my path if we went through quickly that afternoon.

Did you have any information as to their location?

I had no information.

Did you expect American forces in this area to come south in answer to the calls for help which you mentioned earlier?

Yes, that is right. I also thought that the engagement with Admiral Ozawa might produce them in my path.

When you turned north at eleven or twelve o'clock, was the governing consideration to reach here by dark or to attack our forces? Which was the more important?

The point was the immediate objective to hit the enemy. I won't say which was more important; because if I did not get into the Straits by night, the next day was hopeless for me because I could be brought under attack by land planes and by this force. When I got about this area [indicating about 12 degrees 30 minutes north], I found Japanese airplane flying over this area so I thought that the American forces might be located about this area and I tried to seek out the American forces but couldn't find them.

If you found American forces, you then would have stayed to fight and not bothered about being here by dark, is that correct?

Yes. If I could attack American forces about this area, I would abandon that decision to get to the Straits by dark.

While traveling north did you receive any instruction from Admiral Toyoda?

No instructions.

No intelligence from Admiral Nishimura?

No instructions. I did receive, during that northward course, information as to what had happened to Nishimura; that it was not good; but no instructions from Toyoda.

Is it correct then to say that the decision to proceed north here and the decision to proceed west here [indicating] were both dictated by fear of air attack; in the first case, air attack inside the narrow gulf, in the second case, air attack the next day? Is that correct?

Going north with the hope of encountering the enemy and keeping touch, but with the intention of making this by sunset if I did not encounter the enemy, in order to withdraw clear back to my base because I was low on fuel.

Was the decision to pass through San Bernardino Strait by dark due to shortage of fuel for further operations or due to fear of air attack while in this area [indicating Sibuyan Sea] the next day? Which was the governing consideration?

It was primarily fuel. Furthermore, if and when brought under air attack on the following day in the passage through the islands, I would have to use extra fuel in dodging and maneuvering. Therefore, the fuel was very important consideration; the basic one.

Did you have any knowledge of a plan to use Kamikaze attacks by land-based aircraft in the Leyte area on that day?

I had no connection with Kamikaze; neither had I heard anything about the Kamikaze method; but I now believe that after I had left my base, the Kamikaze first came under planning. As I understood it, my operation was without regard to land-based planes and that developments separate from my activities governed the beginning of the Kamikaze sort of operation. The Kamikaze method was used because the fleet was attacking here with few planes. So to aid this operation, they planned for Kamikaze. Fundamentally, because the fleet action was not a success.

At the time you were fighting off Samar you had no knowledge of Kamikaze?

I did not know anything of that. It was developed from the shore-based plane units, the Kamikaze, as an assistance to a situation which as far as the fleet was concerned, had not been a success.

Did you receive any communication from Admiral Toyoda during the late afternoon, while passing through here?

No communication from Toyoda.

[Interrogation adjourned 1200; upon reconvening at 1330, Admiral Kurita was joined by Captain Ohmae.]

Captain Ohmae, this morning we discussed the battle down here on the 25th, and when we stopped for lunch, we had just gotten the Admiral back to San Bernardino Straits. Were you in this action?

Yes, I was on the flagship of Admiral Ozawa's forces. There was no coordination intended on the afternoon of the 25th.

Admiral, on the next day, on the 26th, did you receive more air attacks while retiring through the Sibuyan Sea?

From about eight o'clock on, received three attacks.

Where were you at that time, near Tablas?

Southeast of Mindoro. B-24s were the third attack; the first two attacks were search planes, carrier planes.

What damage was done in each attack?

In the first attack, one torpedo hit on the *Noshiro*. The *Noshiro* was stopped dead in the water from the first attack, torpedo, and was therefore bombed and sunk in the second attack.

Was there any other damage in the first attack?

Something happened to the stern of one of the destroyers, but I don't know what. That is the entire damage from all three attacks.

In the first attack, the *Noshiro* had a torpedo hit which stopped her, and that is all that happened in the first attack?

That is correct.

In the second attack, the *Noshiro* was hit by bombs and sunk, and that is all that happened in the second attack?

Yes.

The third attack was by B-24s; no hits at all?

They were using very large bombs and there were no hits.

Was it a heavy attack, many planes, the third one?

Twenty-four planes.

Were there any damaging near misses?

There were some very near misses but not to do any appreciable damage to the ships.

Where did your force then retire, to what port?

The destroyers fueled north at Coron; the other ships without fueling went on around to Brunei where the destroyers joined them later. The tankers and destroyers came under air attack later on and some of the destroyers were sunk in the area of Coron and one tanker, having received one hit, fled away to the northwest. One tanker was sunk in Balabac Passage and the other escaped in Paitan Bay. The first was sunk by submarine torpedo; the other was damaged by one submarine torpedo.

These were the tankers that had followed your force and were in the Sulu Sea during the action, is that correct?

Yes. When the fleet went up, the order was issued to return to Brunei. When passing the Balabac Passage, each was torpedoed by submarine.

Would you tell us very briefly what were the subsequent movements of your fleet? Where did you go? What did you do?
Fueling, loading ammunition, and repairing in Brunei. The orders for that came from headquarters; also that would be hospitalized.

Did the fleet stay at Brunei or did it go to Singapore?
Most of the ships returned to the Inland Sea.

Reaching there about what time?
About the end of November, arriving in the Inland Sea.

Now, in general, covering this whole operation, do you feel that your communications were satisfactory?
I thought that the communications were not entirely adequate partly because, when I switched my flag from the *Atago* to the *Yamato*, communications personnel were divided between two destroyers, one of which had to accompany the *Takao* back to Brunei, and for that reason I consider that the communications were not adequate.

Did you receive as much information about our forces throughout this operation as you expected?
From the first, I did not think I was getting enough.

To what do you attribute that failure of information?
I thought it was not a matter of communications but of scouting.

Had there been any planned arrangements for you to receive information gathered by land-based planes in the Philippines?
There had been a plan, but no specific orders providing for it at that time.

Now did you receive any?
I received information from the land-based planes, but I don't remember in detail which communication received or when.

Was it of importance or value to you?

Yes, it was very important. All the information received about the location of your carrier forces came from land-based stations.

Was it precise, or did you at that time think it precise?
I thought it was. That was on the 24th.

Do you remember where our carrier forces were reported?
The information that I had from land-based planes on the 24th indicated that American carriers were east of Luzon and about 18 degrees north.

You spoke of using your battleship scout planes to provide you with information. Was that your intention from the beginning of the operation, or was it a last resort due to failure of other methods?
The commanding officer of this detachment [*indicating San Jose, Mindoro*] made a plan to search this area but I didn't know the plan precisely; but anyway I received no information about the American fleet, only that force east of Luzon.

So you used the planes from the *Yamato*. But did you expect to have to use battleship planes?
Because they were observation planes, I did not send them out on scouting until at this point when I turned. I sent out in three directions at that time. I had about twelve planes for search purposes which I might have used out here going north except that they had been damaged in previous action from air bombing and gunfire. I had also sent them off in order to avoid own gun blast.

Did the original plan for this operation contemplate that you would use your own scout planes that way or was information to be gained from land-based planes?
The plan was to receive information from the Air Forces and if I wanted to search on my own, I would send my own airplanes.

Did you send your own to search or just for spotting gunfire?
All scouting was sent from land but for a suspicious place I would send my own planes for limited scouting.

From what you said this morning we gathered that you received no early report from Admiral Ozawa or Admiral Nishimura about

their actions. Did you expect more ample reports? Did you expect full, prompt reports?

[*Captain Ohmae*] This northern fleet sent three or four reports to Tokyo and to the 2nd Fleet but for some reason they were not received, at Tokyo or by the 2nd Fleet on the 24th. I think that these important reports were the reason for the unsuccessful operation. Four messages were sent on the 24th from the Japanese 3rd Fleet to Tokyo and to the 2nd Fleet. They were not received and I think the lack of success of the entire operation depended upon that failure of communication.

Admiral Kurita, in relation to Admiral Nishimura's force, apparently you received no good reports from them. Do you know why?

I don't know. The 2nd Fleet did not receive that.

Did you receive any information from Admiral Nishimura?

As I said this morning he was under air attack. He sent three messages; one that he was under air attack, that he was under torpedo boat attack, and one saying that he will be delayed in getting into Leyte Gulf. Perhaps I received some other messages thereafter but I don't remember.

Do you remember when you heard the results of the battle in the Strait? When did you receive news of what happened in the battle there?

About eleven o'clock. I did not receive any direct report but got word which made me think that it had been a failure, about eleven o'clock of the following day.

And from whom did that message come and what was the substance?

I think it was from a destroyer with Admiral Nishimura.

Did it give specific details of the action, of damage suffered and damage inflicted?

It was very serious; that there were very serious fires, but no details. They were very short messages. It seems that the source had not actually seen the action or the results.

Did this report of the action of Admiral Nishimura have any influence on your decision not to enter the Gulf?

I did know, when I made that decision at eleven o'clock on the following day, that the Nishimura action was a failure.

Was that a reason contributing to your decision?

I did not know where the Nishimura fleet had met disaster, whether it was in Leyte Bay, in the passage, or where. Therefore, it did not influence my decision.

How often in the course of the engagement did you send reports to Admiral Toyoda? That is, did you send a regular series at stated times or only when something important happened? About how many reports did you send?

Not at a fixed time. For example, when we were brought under observation, air attack or gunfire I instantly reported to the Combined Fleet. When in sight of enemy forces I used radio but when not located by enemy forces, I did not use radio.

Why did not Admiral Nishimura make further reports when he was in this action in the south?

Thinking about it afterwards, I cannot say why he didn't. I don't think that Admiral Nishimura knew the extent of damage to his fleet because the sea is very narrow. The area was confined so he didn't send any message, I supposed.

Admiral Nishimura was under your direction; should he have reported what was happening?

I think that Admiral Nishimura could not observe the condition because of the confined waters in which he was maneuvering. I don't know why he did not report more, other than that guess now.

Captain Ohmae, did you have a special communication channel between the three admirals and Admiral Toyoda, a special channel for important messages, a special frequency?

Yes, I think there was a high command channel.

Admiral, do you remember about how long it took to send a message to Admiral Toyoda and to receive a reply?

About thirty minutes. Sometimes long and sometimes very short, but when I passed here [*indicating 250000 sortie from San Bernardino Strait*] he returned the answer in a minimum of about thirty minutes.

That message was in code naturally, wasn't it?

Yes.

If thirty minutes was the minimum, what was the longest delay? Was thirty minutes exceptionally good?

It was very good.

What did you usually expect?

The messages were sometimes long in the number of words but anyway I didn't expect to receive answers so quickly. The exact time I don't remember. In my opinion it takes usually about three hours for an urgent message to get a reply.

Admiral, in your opinion, was the general plan for this operation, the Japanese plan, the best that could have been made at that time with the forces available?

I think that was the best plan which we could apply but not the best theoretical plan. According to your question, I think it was the best plan under the conditions.

You said this morning that in this operation you were prepared to accept fifty per cent losses in ships. What did you expect to gain in exchange for that fifty per cent?

About the intention in my mind was, for that price, to succeed in damaging one-half of all your ships in Leyte Bay.

Did you expect to stop the landings before they could be completed or to destroy the supply of shipping and thus isolate the troops ashore, or to destroy our fighting ships?

Only to delay the landing for two or three days. It was to achieve a temporary delay of landing progress.

How were you going to exploit this delay?

It was then a limited objective, to delay that particular landing for two or three days. We could do nothing about succeeding landings, not having enough strength.

Your purpose was to attack the landing ships and the transports and cargo ships rather than the fighting ships?

Both.

Any choice?

Combatant ships; if both were present I would engage the battleships.

What particular thing or event do you believe caused this operation to fail? What was the main cause of the failure of the operation?

The lack of planes, either for search or for attack, overall.

Was that lack known in advance when you set out on the operation, or did you then believe you had sufficient planes?

It was understood from the beginning, before the plan was put into operation, that we did not have enough.

What chance of success did you believe there was in beginning the operation?

I thought that it would be useful only if the land-based troops had a piece of luck.

[*Captain Ohmae*] When this whole plan was in Tokyo at that time, we thought that there wasn't such a good chance but if we did nothing, the whole Philippines would be seized. So we had to do something and we did our best. It was the last chance we had, although not a very good one.

Admiral, you said you had knowledge that there were not enough planes in advance. From whom did you receive that information? Was it in the operation plan or did you receive a message from Admiral Toyoda, or what was the source of that knowledge?

I knew it from my own knowledge that there weren't enough for such a operation. I did not receive any word from headquarters to that effect.

What do you think was the cause of that lack of planes?

Considering it after the war, I think perhaps it was failure of production, transportation, and lack of pilots.

Did you have an opinion at that time which was different?

Nothing except to try to do my best with the supplies that we could get.

[Admiral Ofstie] What was the principal agent for the loss of Japanese air power?

Sudden attacks from your carrier task forces everywhere prevented or injured our air operations; and second, submarine attacks on our transportation system [of aeroplanes and fuels], including the transportation of supplies to manufacturing plants.

Referring to the Battle of the Coral Sea in May 1942, do you have an opinion as to what effect that had on subsequent Japanese strategy or strength?

I have not given it specific study but I think it had no great effect.

The same thing with respect to the Battle of Midway?

The Battle of Midway had effect precisely to the extent of the loss of new carriers. That was the effect on future operations.

The same question referring to the long period down in the South Pacific, the Rabaul–Guadalcanal area; the naval losses there for a period of six months perhaps.

Because of the attrition and loss of planes and destroyers having effect upon escorting supply ships, all operations therefore suffered.

What was the relative effect, in order of their importance, of the loss of naval vessels, loss of naval air strength, and the loss of merchant shipping?

Loss of air strength was the worst. There is a great gap between that and the next. It is by far the most important. It depends upon the circumstances, without saying which is the more important, the loss of merchant shipping or naval vessels.

Admiral Kurita, do you believe that you were kept well informed of the American strength and the losses as the war went along?

I received a great deal of official information about American losses but I myself reduced that to about a half.

In your opinion, was the information you received any more accurate from either the Japanese Army or the Japanese Navy?

At the beginning of the war I thought that naval intelligence about your losses was the better but as the war continued I thought the two services were about equal in the inaccuracy of information, particularly from air, in that there was repetition on the same item. Therefore, I added up the reports and divided them by two for total damage.

Did you have specific information on the loss in 1942 of the *Lexington*, *Wasp*, *Hornet* and the *Yorktown* at that time?

I did not have precise information. I saw the burning and sinking of one of them and thought it might be the *Hornet*, off Guadalcanal, Santa Cruz, at night.

Were you able to put any people on board the *Hornet*? Did you board the *Hornet* or did you fire any torpedoes into it?

Two American destroyers were shooting at the *Hornet*. I was on the *Kongo* at the time. My own ship did nothing. I don't know whether somebody put a torpedo in her or not.

About how long after the destroyers finished shooting did she sink?

I don't know how long afterwards. It was still at night that she sank. I heard the noise, the sound of her destroyers firing, as I thought, into the *Hornet*, and we approached indirectly and they fled. That was my impression.

What is your personal opinion of the basic planning of the Japanese Naval General Staff?

I didn't know very much about it but I thought that there wasn't a sure touch, a sure treatment of plan making. The planning lacked a sureness of touch.

At what stage in the war did you feel that the balance had swung over against you?

Guadalcanal.

What was the actual bore of the *Yamato* guns?

I never knew, it was very secret, about 45 centimeters I think. Neither did I know the maximum speed of the *Yamato*. But in formation she was going 26 knots.

Interrogation of Vice Admiral Kzutaka Shirachi, IJN

Occupation of the Philippines and Dutch East Indies

Interrogation NAV No. 7/USSBS No. 33

Tokyo, 15 October 1945

Interrogation of: Vice Admiral Kzutaka Shirachi, IJN, retired, was Chief of Staff of the Second Fleet from December 1941 to March 1943, operating in the Southwest Pacific.

Interrogated by: Commander T. H. Moorer, USN.

Allied Officers Present: Brigadier General Grandison Gardner, U.S. Army; Lieutenant Commander J. A. Field, Jr., USNR.

SUMMARY

The Second Fleet (Vice Admiral Kondo) was assigned the mission of supporting the invasion of the Philippines, Netherlands East Indies and British Malaya. The fleet rendezvoused in the Inland Sea about the middle of November 1941. About 23 November the fleet sortied from the Inland Sea and proceeded south towards Formosa. There a dispatch was received establishing "D" day and the move on the Philippines was initiated.

During the approach to the Philippines, no attack was expected and none received. Probable attack by B-17s was expected within the 600 mile circle. To reduce the weight of these attacks, land-based planes from Formosa were assigned the mission of destroying American air power on the ground. This they succeeded in doing and consequently no major unit of the fleet was damaged in the Philippines operation.

The Second Fleet was divided into various task forces as the move southward into the East Indies progressed. Although the Battle of the Java Sea was a victory for the Japanese, Admiral Shiraichi considered that the Japanese used poor tactics and were unnecessarily delayed by the battle.

The entire campaign went exactly according to plan except for a few small delays caused by submarine attacks and fuel oil shortage. Total losses suffered by the Japanese were less than expected.

TRANSCRIPT

Were you actively engaged in the general planning, prior to the outbreak of the war, for the campaign of the Philippines and East Indies?

As the Second Fleet was under the Grand Fleet all the plans were made by the Grand Fleet. I merely carried out orders according to the plans provided. I did not take part in the overall planning.

Were you familiar with the general plans for the entire Pacific operations? Were you aware of the Pearl Harbor strike?

I had complete instructions sent from headquarters.

Will you give me a brief summary of the various forces into which the Japanese Fleet was divided?

The Grand Fleet was divided into five fleets as follows:

1st Fleet—battleships;
2nd Fleet—battleships, heavy cruisers, light cruisers, destroyers;
3rd Fleet—carriers;
4th Fleet—light cruisers, destroyers;
6th Fleet—submarines.

Forces were reassigned as necessary to various fleets.

What were the five rendezvous points of the various forces prior to commencement of hostilities?

Fleet One and Two assembled in the Inland Sea. The other two rendezvous were kept secret but I believe that the Third Fleet rendezvoused at Hokkaido. The Fourth Fleet consisted of small ships in the Guam-Wake area. I am not sure about the Sixth Fleet.

When did the Second Fleet assemble in the Inland Sea preparatory to leaving Japan?

The approximate date of the rendezvous was about a month before the start of the war, and I think the fleet left the Inland Sea about two weeks before the start of the war.

Where was the Second Fleet when the orders were received establishing "D" Day?

Right after we left Bako, Pescadores, we received the orders establishing "D" Day.

Do you know who thought of the attack on Pearl Harbor and who worked out the plans?

I haven't the slightest idea who devised the plan.

Do you know if any thought was given to the possibility of the Japanese moving into the Dutch East Indies without attacking Pearl Harbor at all?

I did not know that the war was going to break out at all and did not know the actual plans. I thought that the differences would be settled by negotiations and that there must have been a way out for Japan rather than to go into war.

Were you surprised at the outbreak of the war?

I thought war should have been avoided, but once the war started I did my utmost to carry out the orders I received. I was not surprised at the start of war. I realized that the situation had deteriorated.

Were Army and Navy planes engaged in the Philippines and Dutch East Indies campaign?

Yes.

In general was the Japanese Navy pilot considered superior to the Army pilot?

Yes, the Navy pilots are better.

Describe the movements of the fleet from Bako down to the Philippines. What reaction was expected from the U.S. Fleet?

I didn't think the American fleet would attack the Second Fleet. Strong opposition from American planes based in Nichols Field was expected.

After receiving news of the success of Pearl Harbor, was the plan for the occupation of the Philippines changed?

There was no change in the plan.

During the Philippine operation, did you expect the U.S. Fleet to be reinforced?

Yes, I expected reinforcements from the States but I thought it would take about one month for reinforcements to come to the Philippines.

At what time during the approach to the Philippines did you expect the attack by aircraft?

The fleet was alerted when 600 miles away. Attack by B-17 was expected but I didn't think it would be severe.

During the approach did you have air coverage from Formosa?

I didn't expect any direct reinforcement from the Japanese land-based air, but expected indirect coverage. That is, destruction of B-17s on the ground before they could take off.

Did the planes which attacked Nichols Field take off from Formosa?

They all came from Formosa.

Army or Navy planes?

Both. I knew nothing of the air operations but knew that the fleet was going to get a certain amount of air force assistance which was used.

On 10 December there were about 200,000 tons of Allied shipping at Manila Harbor. Why was this 200,000 tons of vital shipping allowed to escape?

Reasons were:

- The duty of the airplanes was to attack American planes.
- Poor intelligence regarding the fact that the shipping was there.
- The attack was not in the plans, this is the first news that I have of such shipping. The general plan was to knock out only those offensive weapons which might be used against the Japanese.

In what ship were you?

Atago (heavy cruiser).

Did the American seaplanes attack the Japanese Fleet?
The main body of the fleet was not attacked by air.

Was the Second Fleet attacked by B-17s?
As far as I know there was no attack by B-17s.

Was any damage at all suffered by the Second Fleet?
The destroyers were damaged by airplanes as they went so close to the shore to transport troops. Big ships didn't go near the shore. One light cruiser was damaged however.

And the heavy cruiser and battleships weren't damaged?
No.

Why did not the movement from the Philippines south proceed at a faster pace?
Mostly due to the fuel supply. The shortage of fuel made the movement very slow. The supply fleet had to go around Formosa in order to deliver the fuel.

Do you feel that the occupation of the Philippines and Dutch East Indies went exactly according to plan as far as time was concerned?
There was a delay about one week but no more, otherwise it went according to plan.

Was the loss of ships and personnel more or less than expected?
Less than expected.

Do you know what type of airplanes attacked the *Repulse* and *Prince of Wales*?
Navy planes, land-based.

Did the destruction of these two battleships change the plans for the occupation of Singapore?
Did not change the plans but the effect on Japanese morale was very great.

Did you expect the British to replace those ships?
No.

Where were the planes that attacked the *Prince of Wales* based?
Saigon.

At what time during the overall campaign did the carriers take part? When did they join the fleet?
I don't remember the actual date when the carrier aircraft participated, but it was not until the fleet was actually in the Sulu Sea area.

What places did the carrier airplanes attack?
The planes from the task force attacked Trincomalee, Darwin, and others that I can not recall.

Did the Dutch react as expected during the invasion of the Philippines and Netherlands East Indies?
I thought the combination of the American and Dutch forces would furnish stronger resistance.

Did the action at Makassar Straits delay the Japanese advance?
Yes, but do not know how long.

Do you consider that the American and Dutch submarines delayed the campaign in anyway?
To a great extent. One time I received a report that the planes saw twelve to thirteen submarines but the fact was that they were whales. It took two or three days to make sure, which caused a certain amount of delay.

Did you expect that additional aircraft would be flown into Java from Australia?
Yes.

Did the Japanese know that the American heavy cruiser *Houston* was damaged and only had two-thirds of their 8-inch guns in operation?
No.

Did you know that the other American cruiser *Boise* ran aground and had to be sent from the area?
No.

After the Japanese had occupied Bali there was a night action with the Dutch and American ships. Two Allied destroyers were sunk and two cruisers damaged. Do you know what damage was sustained by the Japanese?

Four Japanese destroyers took part and the damage was one destroyer sunk and one damaged. No Japanese cruisers were involved.

Did the Commander of the Second Fleet know that the Langley was coming from Australia to Java with aircraft reinforcements?

No.

How was it discovered?

By search planes.

What is your estimate of the damage suffered by the combined Dutch, American and British Fleet in the battle of Java Sea?

I was not on the scene. I heard the result of the battle and thought that the battle should not have lasted so long. Japanese strategy was unskillful.

What damage was suffered by the Japanese Fleet?

Several ships damaged but no ships sunk.

Do you know how the British ships *Encounter*, *Exeter* and the American destroyer *Pope* were sunk while en route to Soemba Straits?

I know of it, but don't know whether it was by land-based planes or submarines. I think that they were sunk by submarines before they got to the Straits.

After the occupation of the Dutch East Indies was completed, many of the merchant vessels retired to Freemantle. There were several thousand tons of shipping without fuel. Why didn't the Japanese send a striking force to attack those ships?

It was thought that there might be women and children on the ships so we were afraid of attacking the ships, and also our plans took care of immobilizing your offensive weapons only.

Did you realize that the entire western coast of Australia was defenseless?

Yes.

Was any consideration given to the possibility of invading the western coast of Australia?

There weren't enough forces available to make an invasion without over expansion of limited forces.

Were Army troops used at Java?

Yes.

Were there any lessons learned in this entire campaign which caused the Japanese to change their plans for future operations?

Nothing changed the overall plan.

After the occupation of the East Indies did you move into the Solomons and New Guinea?

After the campaign I returned to Japan with the Second Fleet. The entire fleet was sent into dry dock in April, just prior to General Doolittle's attack.

Hunted by Japs for Years, American Flier is Rescued

by Al Dopking

First published 1 November 1944

WITH the 7th Division, Leyte, P.I.—A slender, blue-eyed American who escaped at Bataan's fall was rescued from Leyte mountains Monday, ending three years of secret missions in the Philippines with the Japanese constantly hounding him.

Second Lieutenant Joseph Francis St. John, twenty-four, Philadelphia, related the story from the bamboo hut where he was given his second pair of shoes in three years. He was brought through American lines by First Lieutenant Claude Hornbacher, Sebewaing, Michigan, whose patrol reached him by crossing the bay south of Abuyog.

Rescued also was red-haired Ensign Edwin J. Eattie, twenty-one, Columbiaville, Michigan, naval pilot who crashed in a dogfight during the invasion and took refuge with St. John.

(The dispatch failed to reveal any details of the "secret missions.")

St. John came down from the mountains with a burning hatred for the Japanese and a great admiration for the Filipinos who helped him hide. A B-17 gunner of the 14th Bombardment Squadron when he was bombed out 7 December 1941, St. John reached Bataan Christmas eve and later with nine hundred other airmen went to Malabang Airfield on Mindanao where "we waited for planes that never came."

When the surrender came, St. John and eleven other Americans fled to the hills and finally reached Leyte 8 May 1942, in a frail native launch, passing through the straits in the darkness. There, Col. Cornell, the island commander, told them they must leave before 5 p.m., 10 May, to avoid surrender. They left two hours before the deadline in an outrigger boat for Australia but they were shipwrecked off Cauit Point, Mindanao, 17 May, in a storm. It was St. John's birthday.

Then began his guerrilla life. He subsisted on fried monkey meat and tropical fruit. He once wasted from 155 pounds to one hundred before he was cured of malaria with "ditto," tree bark brews concocted for him by a native. His escapes were many. Once two hundred Nips charged his hide-out, shooting everything at him without success.

Printed in Great Britain
by Amazon.co.uk, Ltd.,
Marston Gate.